MANAGERIAL FREEDOM

AND

JOB SECURITY

# MANAGERIAL FREEDOM AND JOB SECURITY

By Morris Stone

62759

*HD 6483*
*.S87M*

18 17

HARPER & ROW, PUBLISHERS

NEW YORK, EVANSTON, AND LONDON

# CONTENTS

# PREFACE

In discussing the apparent conflict between management's right to "direct the work forces" and the right of employees to job security, it was my plan to show how professional arbitrators have resolved grievances, not how I would have solved them had I been the arbitrator.

The awards discussed in this volume were composed for the parties immediately concerned, not necessarily for publication. This fact imposes caution on those who would draw inferences from the written record. One arbitrator will find it possible to set forth in detail all the background facts, and show the reasoning process by which he reached his decision. Another arbitrator in another case, sensing that the parties will get along better if he omits some of the contentious history from his discussion, will leave a great deal unsaid. Obviously, both serve the parties equally well, although the former's award is more likely to be published. Furthermore, even written opinions that seem complete may be lacking in some detail or fact the arbitrator thought it expedient to omit. For this reason, it is hazardous to assume from the available record that one can tell precisely how an arbitrator might rule in apparently similar cases.

As none of the arbitrators cited herein was consulted in advance, each has, in a sense, become an unwitting collaborator with me in this work. Every effort has been made to represent their views as accurately as their written awards and opinions permit. If any errors have appeared, I am responsible, and I tender apologies in advance.

One collaborator was anything but unwitting. Estelle R. Tracy has worked closely with me for more than four years, preparing digests of awards for publication in the American Arbitration Association's *Summary of Labor Arbitration Awards*. My impatience to get on with the job often needed Mrs. Tracy's restraining hand. It may not always have seemed so, but I was, and am, grateful to her for not yielding on any point of disagreement until every ambiguity was clarified. Two other AAA staff members also deserve mention. Ruth E. Lyons and Catherine F. Salisbury added more than secretarial skills in converting difficult copy into a workable manuscript.

Finally, I express my gratitude to the hundreds of management and labor representatives who consented to the publication of their awards. That the successful party should have permitted such publication is perhaps not surprising. But every case also has a disappointed party. That the latter, too, permitted errors and shortcomings to be revealed tells a great deal about the maturity of modern collective bargaining. I can only hope that this volume will bring to the parties who contributed to it the better understanding intended for the labor-management community at large.

M.S.

*September 1963*

MANAGERIAL FREEDOM

AND

JOB SECURITY

# 1

# INTRODUCTION

Before the collective bargaining era, the employer was sovereign in his own establishment. Except for a few unobtrusive restrictions imposed by law, management was free to determine wages and other working conditions, to direct the work forces, and to decide how materials and machinery would be used in accomplishing the purposes of the business.

Insofar as control of property was concerned, managerial freedom undoubtedly was, and still is, based upon legal rights. But the power to dictate the terms upon which jobs would be offered never had the same status. Authority over employees was derived not from legal rights which the employer had, and the employee had not, but from economic strength. In the eyes of the law, if not in reality, the worker had an equal right to withhold his efforts unless he was paid his price, to refuse assignments he objected to, and to regard any bargain made with his employer as terminable at will. In short, employer and employee had the same legal right to impose their will. That the ability to dictate terms came to be thought of among management representatives as a natural right, fortified in law, was a consequence only of the employer's superior bargaining position.[1]

1. Those who believe that the "right to direct work forces," in the absence of contractual restriction, is a *legal* right, are invited to test their theory in areas of employment where, because of a labor shortage, the customary bargaining roles are reversed. For instance, what *legal* rights does an employer have with respect to a domestic servant who refuses to wash windows, or who will not work at all unless she is permitted to use the family car on personal errands? Is it not clear that, as far as law is concerned, both are on absolutely equal

The economic sovereignty of management over wages and working conditions was challenged by the Congress of the United States on July 5, 1935. The National Labor Relations Act (Wagner Act) declared it to be national policy to encourage the organization of unions,[2] and this had the intended effect of stimulating the rapid growth of labor organizations. By the end of 1960, a remarkable transformation in labor-management relations had taken place. The Bureau of Labor Statistics was able to report that some 18 million wage earners were enrolled in unions.[3] No longer were their wages and other working conditions subject either to unilateral determination by employers or to individual bargaining. The conditions under which jobs would be offered and performed were now determined jointly by management and union representatives. Although these 18 million constituted only a third of the non-agricultural work force in the United States, they were so heavily concentrated in basic industry and in larger establishments that their agreements tended to affect the standards of all.

### Enlarging the Scope of the Partnership

Nor did collective bargaining long remain limited to wages and clearly related working conditions. Pressing for a greater role in the new partnership, unions sought to bargain over welfare plans, pensions, merit increases, job transfers, and even such matters as the right

---

footing? The distinction between rights fixed in law and authority derived from economic strength may have been academic when employers generally dealt with an abundant supply of unorganized workers. But the distinction has become vital in interpreting and applying modern collective bargaining agreements.

2. Section 1 of the National Labor Relations Act (49 Stat. 499) stated: "The inequality of bargaining power between employees who do not possess full freedom of association or actual liberty of contract, and employers who are organized in the corporate or other forms of ownership association substantially burdens and affects the flow of commerce . . . Experience has proved that protection by law of the right of employees to organize and bargain collectively safeguards commerce from injury, impairment or interruption, and promotes the flow of commerce . . . by restoring equality of bargaining power between employers and employees."

3. "Membership of American Trade Unions, 1960," *Monthly Labor Review*, U.S. Dept. of Labor, Bureau of Labor Statistics, December 1961.

of management to relocate plants or discontinue the business altogether. Efforts by labor to penetrate areas management regarded as
traditionally its own were, of course, resisted. But the National Labor
Relations Board, both under the Wagner Act and the Taft-Hartley
Act, which followed in 1947,[4] generally gave liberal construction to
the statutory phrase "wages and other terms and conditions of employment." Health and accident insurance, Christmas bonuses, holi-
days, vacations, profit-sharing plans, stock purchases, sick leave,
severance pay, and other employee benefits that were once thought to
be voluntary gratuities were declared to be "emoluments of value,"
entitled to the same recognition as wages. Although a party might
decline to negotiate on such matters, he could not carry his refusal to
the point of impasse without violating the law's requirement of good-
faith bargaining. On the other hand, subjects more remote from wages
and working conditions were declared to be "permissive"; an employer
could remain adamant in his refusal to negotiate over the location of
plants, for instance, but should the union prevail upon him to include
a clause on that subject in the contract, it would be as enforceable as
any other provision. Thus the degree of union penetration beyond the
"mandatory" subjects was determined by judgment of what was proper
and by the power to enforce that judgment.

At the theoretical level, labor and management have never been
able to draw a line between subjects proper to collective bargaining
and areas of exclusive managerial control. The most notable attempt
to do so took place at a labor-management conference convened by
President Harry Truman in 1945.[5] After weeks of fruitless discussion
labor and management representatives remained in total disagreement.
"Labor members of the Committee on Management's Right to Manage have been unable to agree on any listing of specific management
functions," the management members complained in a separate report.
"Management members of the committee conclude, therefore, that the
Labor members are convinced that the field of collective bargaining
will, in all probability, continue to expand into the field of management."

For its own part, the management spokesmen drew up a list of

4. 61 Stat. 136.
5. *The President's National Labor-Management Conference, Nov. 5–30,
1945,* U.S. Dept. of Labor, Division of Labor Standards, Bull. No. 77, 1946.

what they said were "clearly the functions of management." Included in the list were

the determination of job content (this refers to establishing the duties required in the performance of any given job and not to wages); the determination of the size of the work force; the allocation and assignment of work to workers; determination of policies affecting the selection of employees; establishment of quality standards and judgment of workmanship required; and the maintenance of discipline and control and use of the plant property; the scheduling of operations and the number of shifts; the determination of safety, health, and property protection measures, where legal responsibility of the employer is involved.

It did not go unnoticed that on this list were subjects which, even at that time, were commonly negotiated!

The refusal of the unions to identify subjects that could be excluded from bargaining was not based upon an intention to intervene at an early date in such matters as management's accounting procedures, the size of inventories, or marketing practices. It was simply that they saw no advantage in excluding anything from the sphere of operations without knowing how issues might develop. "It would be extremely unwise to build a fence around the rights and responsibilities of management on the one hand and the unions on the other," they wrote. "The experience of many years shows that with the growth of mutual understanding the responsibilities of one of the parties today may well become the joint responsibility of both parties tomorrow."[6]

## The "Ambiguous Silence" of the Agreement

The union contract is like no other. If buyer and seller cannot agree on fundamental matters, for instance, each is privileged to go his separate way. But labor and management can never escape one another; both are under obligations imposed by law, by self-interest, and by the very nature of their relationship to bargain until they *do* reach agreement. Moreover, the negotiators must usually complete their work within a reasonably short time, and the results must be acceptable to a large number of individuals who will live under it and execute its terms. The impossibility of reaching a compromise on matters that separate the parties so profoundly that they dare not even discuss them

6. *Ibid.*

during negotiations lest they delay a settlement, and the practical impossibility of *not* concluding an agreement, is one of the dilemmas of modern labor relations. It explains why, as Harry Shulman wrote,[7] the union contract has become a "compilation of diverse provisions," some dealing with "objective criteria [which are] almost automatically applicable," others containing "more or less specific standards which require reason and judgment in their application," and still others doing "little more than leaving problems to future consideration with an expression of hope and good faith."

A number of theories of union contract interpretation have evolved to cover the gaps in the agreements and to explain what Archibald Cox has called "the more or less ambiguous silence" of the contracts.[8] One view, which has come to be called the residual rights theory, holds that the employer has all the rights he would have had in the absence of collective bargaining, except those specifically bargained away.[9] If this doctrine were universally accepted and applied, there would seem to be little need for the usual language in contracts stating that the right "to manage the plant and direct the work forces" resides with the employer. Even where the management rights clause contains the proviso, "except insofar as the contract specifically restricts that right," this language would seem to be superfluous. That management representatives insist so strongly on clauses to fortify the plausible sounding residual rights theory suggests, at the very least, some uneasiness with it.

One management representative acknowledged the apparent incon-

7. Harry Shulman, "Reason, Contract and Law in Labor Relations," *Harvard Law Review*, April 1955.

8. Archibald Cox, "The Legal Nature of Collective Bargaining," *Michigan Law Review*, November 1958.

9. ". . . Except as management has agreed to restrict the exercise of its usual functions, it retains the same rights which it possessed before engaging in collective bargaining. This view is the only one that gives full recognition to the realities of the collective bargaining relationship. In general, the process of collective bargaining involves an attempt by a labor union to persuade an employer to accept limitations upon the exercise of certain of his previously unrestricted managerial rights. To the extent that the union is unsuccessful in persuading an employer to agree to a particular demand, management's rights remain unlimited. It should equally follow that management possesses comparable freedom with respect to rights which the union has not even sought to limit." (James C. Phelps, *Management Rights and the Arbitration Process,* Bureau of National Affairs, 1956).

sistency between a theory which would have the silence of the contract speak exclusively for management and a clause which explicitly reserved to management matters about which the contract would otherwise be silent. However, he defended the management rights clause for its moral and educational value and as a form of insurance. "I have noticed," wrote James C. Phelps, "that even arbitrators who may subscribe to the principle that management continues to possess the residue of rights that have not been bargained away take great comfort in being able to cite or quote explicit language which states what would otherwise be implied. Secondly, collective bargaining agreements are working documents to which frequent reference is made in the shop. The people who interpret them at the shop level may not be acquainted with how contracts are construed, and some of them may take strong exceptions to the common law concept of management rights."[10]

### Residual Rights vs. Implied Limitations

The theoretical answer to the employer's residual rights doctrine is the principle of implied limitations, most often asserted by unions. This view holds that the silence of the contract may be more apparent than real; a number of provisions—usually seniority, job classifications, and wages, but sometimes even the recognition clause—commit the employer to maintaining the *status quo*. To hold otherwise, unions argue, would be to deny employees "the bundle of things,"[11] or the benefits of the contract that was negotiated for them. The parties had agreed that certain rates would be paid for jobs that consisted of specified duties, that employees would have the right to those jobs except under stipulated conditions, and that the longer they remained on those jobs, the greater would certain other monetary and non-monetary benefits be. It is an "unspoken assumption" of the agreement, the argument goes, that management will not do anything that would render the rewards of the contract illusory.[12]

10. *Ibid.*

11. Stephen C. Vladeck, "Comment on Arbitration of Subcontracting Disputes," *Industrial and Labor Relations Review,* January 1963.

12. Arbitrator Sidney Wolff, in *Celanese Corporation of America* (Textile Workers Union of America, Local 1874, CIO), 14 LA 31, wrote: "It is an obligation of a party to a contract not to enter upon a course of conduct, the

Although residual rights and implied limitations seem to be opposite concepts, they have much in common. On occasion, labor and management are found to adopt each other's traditional views. As a practical matter, the union expects management to decide production schedules, for instance; and it does not matter a great deal (except, perhaps, as suggested above by Mr. Phelps) whether this is an explicit management right under the contract, or a residual right omitted from it. A grievance might, of course, be filed protesting an alleged violation of seniority rights during a layoff, but the outcome would not affect the employer's authority to discontinue a certain line of products, let us say, if that were the circumstance that made the layoff of some employees necessary.

Similarly, few employers who adhere to the residual rights doctrine would argue that even in the absence of the usual discharge-only-for-cause provision, they had the right to dismiss long-service employees for no just reason. Clearly, the man's seniority rights would impose an "implied" limitation. And when an employer shows that some action he took in directing the work forces was privileged because it was based upon good-faith economic reasons, is he not acknowledging that the action would not have been justified if *bad faith* were the motive? And would this not be so even if the contract made no reference to either good faith or bad faith? Not surprisingly, the doctrine of implied limitations is sometimes called the "convenant of good faith."

### Union Penetration Through Arbitration

Operating in an environment where change is a rule of life, wrote Neil W. Chamberlain, management is the "instigator" of change. "Unions, on the other hand, very frequently are cast in the role of

---

effect of which is to avoid that contract and to render it null and void. This is well settled in contract law, and how much more applicable is it to a labor contract intended to maintain a proper, stable, working relationship between a company, its employees and the union. Implicit in this Collective Bargaining Agreement is the requirement that neither party, by unilateral act, direct or indirect, do anything the effect of which is to nullify its provisions . . . [The] Company does not have the right, under its existing Agreement, by unilateral action and without joint bargaining, to diminish the scope of the bargaining unit by transferring jobs, which, under the recognition clause belong to members of the Union, to others outside the unit."

forestallers of change. They are seeking to preserve positions involving security for their members."[13] But if the initiative in work decisions is management's, the initiative in filing grievances and pressing them to arbitration is labor's. This has proven to be no small advantage, for arbitration is more than a means of obtaining impartial interpretation of a contract clause; as an avenue of appeal against managerial decisions, the arbitration clause is also a vehicle for enlarging labor's role in the labor-management partnership.

The jurisdiction of the arbitrator, therefore, has been a critical issue in labor-management relations. The employer who is compelled to defend some action he thought was beyond the reach of the collective bargaining agreement seldom feels completely vindicated merely with a ruling that he had the right to take that action *under the contract*. Nothing short of a decision that the subject matter was none of the union's business, and that no defense was called for, would satisfy him. Until recent years, management fared better with disputes over arbitrability in court than in arbitration, although it was in the latter forum that determinations were most often made. Courts were often criticized for holding grievances non-arbitrable solely because the judges thought they lacked merit.[14] Arbitrators, on the other hand, were sometimes criticized for accepting jurisdiction of non-arbitrable disputes merely because the grievances were, in any event, deniable on the merits.[15]

In June 1960, however, the United States Supreme Court decision in the *Warrior & Gulf Navigation Company*[16] case had the effect of bringing federal courts more closely into line with the thinking of pro-

13. Neil W. Chamberlain, "Union Challenge to Management Control," *Industrial and Labor Relations Review,* January 1963.

14. Objections to alleged interference by courts with the right of unions to arbitrate generally focused on "the Cutler-Hammer doctrine," derived from *International Association of Machinists* v. *Cutler-Hammer, Inc.,* 271 App. Div. 917, 67 N.Y.S. 2d 317, aff'd, 297 N.Y. 519, 74 N.E. 2d 464 (1947). It was held in that case that where the meaning of the contract clause in a proposed arbitration is "beyond dispute, there cannot be anything to arbitrate." Under this doctrine, courts had denied motions to compel arbitration where it seemed to the judges that the union's claim lacked substance. The *Cutler-Hammer* doctrine was reversed, as far as federal courts are concerned, by the U.S. Supreme Court's decision in the *Warrior & Gulf* case (see note 16).

15. See, "Do We Need a New Look at Arbitrability?", *Arbitration Journal,* 1960.

16. *United Steelworkers* v. *Warrior & Gulf Navigation Co.,* 363 U.S. 574 (1960).

fessional arbitrators. This followed shortly after a landmark decision on arbitrability by G. Allan Dash, Jr. As the Supreme Court decision referred approvingly to Mr. Dash's award, and as lower court decisions in *Warrior & Gulf,* which the Supreme Court reversed, were cited by management in briefs submitted to Mr. Dash, a description of the arbitration case and the court action, in that order, may demonstrate the identity of views that now prevail in the two forums.

## *The* Celanese *Arbitrability Decision*

On December 23, 1958, the *Celanese Corporation of America* (United Mine Workers of America, District 50)[17] accepted a bid from the Carrier Corporation for installing sheet metal ducts between two buildings to permit recovery of chemicals. Carrier was to fabricate the ducts for this capital improvement in its own shops, and have its own employees install them.

About a week later, eight employees in the Celanese tin shop filed grievances in which they stated that they had in the past done work such as that given to the Carrier Corporation, that they were capable of doing it again, and that they wanted to be paid for all earnings lost by the subcontracting project. Management argued the matter on its merits all through the grievance procedure. When the matter was finally referred by the union to the American Arbitration Association, the company stated that as the contract contained no "express limitation" on the right of the employer to contract out, the grievance was not arbitrable. Management was content, however, to let an arbitrator rule on whether he had jurisdiction to resolve the disputes on the merits. That arbitrator was Mr. Dash.

Three separate but related questions were presented by the threshold issue of arbitrability:

1. Did the company waive its right to assert non-arbitrability by having debated the issue of subcontracting on its merits during grievance procedure?

2. Did the silence of the contract on subcontracting leave this matter within management's exclusive control and beyond the jurisdiction of the arbitrator's review powers? Or, as the union asserted, did oral promises by management during grievance meetings and negotiations

17. *Celanese Corporation of America* (United Mine Workers of America, District 50, United Construction Workers, Local 153), 10 AAA 21.

in the past to favor bargaining unit employees remove the subcontracting from the area of exclusive, unregulated control by management?

3. What effect, if any, should court decisions in similar cases have on the decision in this case?

## An Arbitrator's View of His Jurisdiction

The first question was easiest to answer. Where the contract required the parties to attempt in good faith to adjust all grievances under methods provided for in the agreement, Mr. Dash said, the company did no more than fulfil its obligations when it discussed the merits and raised no procedural or technical questions.

What the parties have done here is to agree to consider "all grievances" regardless of their content and to process them through the several steps of the grievance procedure. At none of these steps prior to arbitration is there any barrier to considering any and all aspects of the merits of the grievances. . . . There is no need, and there would be no point, for the company to raise the issue of arbitrability during the several steps of the grievance procedure at which the company is obligated to consider the merits of the grievance.

In answer to management's contention that the silence of the contract on subcontracting not only leaves its rights to do so unimpaired, but places the issue beyond the arbitrator's jurisdiction, Mr. Dash said that the history of the parties' dealings on this matter was directly relevant. In prior years, subcontracting grievance discussions and contract negotiations (where the union had sought unsuccessfully to obtain restrictions on contracting out) had resulted in oral assurances of some kind that inside employees would be favored. Mr. Dash was not ready at this point to analyze the nature of those promises in detail. That would come later, after the jurisdictional question was resolved in favor of arbitrability. For deciding the threshold question, he said, there was a basis at least for an assumption that the history of bargaining had resulted in some limitations on management, so that it no longer had "the unqualified right to contract-out any and all work it unilaterally decides."

The Union should have the opportunity to demonstrate just what limitations on the Company's right of contracting-out have existed under its several successive Agreements with the Company. Those limitations may be extremely narrow; but they may also be quite extensive. Whatever they may be, the Union has the right under the Agreement, as I interpret it, to prove their existence and to then show, if it can, that the Company's action of contracting-out the specific tin smith work in this case disregarded those limitations and violated agreement provisions as interpreted and applied in the past by the parties themselves. The conclusion that I have reached, then, is that the union has the right under the agreement to have the grievance in this case decided upon its merits.

Finally, Mr. Dash addressed himself to the matter of court decisions in which it was held that similar grievances were not arbitrable. The leading case cited to him was *Warrior & Gulf,* which later came to the Supreme Court but which, at that stage, had been decided in favor of management by the District Court and the Court of Appeals for the Fifth Circuit. There was no question in Mr. Dash's mind that the *Warrior & Gulf* case was, as the employer asserted, similar to the one before him in all the important elements. But he ruled that he was not obliged to follow precedents he disagreed with.

"I look at this case as an arbitrator," he wrote. "[The parties] use my services rather than those of a court because they have mutually decided they must 'live together' in at least a semi-permanent relationship and do not intend merely to exist as litigants seeking to secure a final advantage over each other at the point of termination of their relationship." Moreover, he added, the court in a leading case cited by the employer had made its decision on the arbitrability of a subcontracting issue "only after a hearing on the merits of the claim advanced by the union." If he were to accept that ruling as a binding precedent in this case, Mr. Dash reasoned, he would be depriving the union of its right to be heard on many findings of fact which had influenced the court. "I cannot, with clear conscience, apply the same ultimate ruling here without giving the union a reasonable opportunity to go as far into the merits of the case as did the union in the case ruled on by the court."

## The Weight of Precedent

Ironically, when Mr. Dash declined to follow the precedents set in federal courts, he contributed to the setting of a precedent for the courts to follow. Justice William O. Douglas, in reversing the Fifth

Circuit, found occasion in his *Warrior & Gulf* opinion to refer approvingly to Mr. Dash's arbitrability award.

But if Mr. Dash chose not to be influenced by the courts, he did find the prevailing view of his fellow arbitrators persuasive. In preparing his decision, Mr. Dash studied sixty-four awards by other arbitrators in cases that, whatever their other differences, all involved subcontracting by employers who were subject to union contracts that did not specifically bar such action. "In not a single published arbitration decision that I have been able to discover," he reported, "has the arbitrator ruled this issue to be non-arbitrable under comparable circumstances." The majority of arbitrators "have construed the language of the agreements before them as a whole and have attempted, with confinement of their attention to the specific case, to make certain that the company's action of contracting-out particular work at a specific time has not had the effect of violating other recorded agreement provisions as interpreted and applied by the parties themselves through their past practices."[18]

18. This decision was followed, some months later, by several other Celanese Corporation cases involving virtually identical grievances. Again, management disputed arbitrability, and again, the union relied upon the oral assurances given in the past. With Mr. Dash's decision in the public record, at least two of the arbitrators did little more than follow suit. Carl R. Schedler, in *Celanese Corporation of America* (United Mine Workers of America, District 50), 21 AAA 9; and Ronald W. Haughton, in *Celanese Corporation of America* (United Mine Workers of America, District 50), 20 AAA 4, chose not to indulge in a full discussion of the threshold issue. They identified themselves with the views expressed by Mr. Dash, and proceeded to the merits. Mark L. Kahn, in *Celanese Corporation of America* (United Mine Workers of America, District 50), 19 AAA 4, analyzed the arbitrability problem more fully, and came to the prevailing conclusion that management was confusing lack of merit with non-arbitrability. "If the action of the company that gave rise to this proceeding was within its rights and did not violate either the agreement or any binding joint understanding, the grievance should be denied, not because it is not arbitrable, but because it lacks merit," he wrote.

For cases, involving other companies, in which it was held that the silence of contracts on subcontracting does not render grievances over subcontracting non-arbitrable, see: *Allied Paper Corporation* (United Papermakers and Paperworkers, AFL–CIO), 8 AAA 18, where Leonard A. Keller held that a controversy over the right of management to purchase skids formerly manufactured within the plant involved "the implied covenant of good faith and fair dealing" inherent in the collective bargaining agreement; and *American Enka Corporation* (United Textile Workers of America, AFL–CIO), 34 AAA 14, where Clar-

## *The* Warrior & Gulf *Case*

While the *Celanese* grievance was developing toward its arbitration hearing, a very similar set of problems was developing toward eventual decision by the U.S. Supreme Court.

Briefly, the essential facts were these. For a number of years, the United Steelworkers of America had sought from the Warrior & Gulf Navigation Company an agreement that work would no longer be sub-contracted to other firms. Management insisted upon continuing the letting of some outside contracts for work that might have been performed by bargaining unit members, and the agreement ultimately reached contained no restrictions; it was completely silent with respect to subcontracting. At the same time, the contract contained an arbitration clause that excluded from the arbitrator's jurisdiction matters that were "strictly a function of management." Eventually the company laid off some employees for lack of work. Admittedly, the layoff resulted at least in part from the fact that an outside firm was performing work that might have been done within the unit. A grievance was filed, the union asserting that the layoff constituted a lockout, in violation of the no-strike, no-lockout provision of the contract. When arbitration was sought, the company insisted that the issue was not arbitrable. This started the dispute on its long course through federal courts.

The District Court and the Court of Appeals agreed with management that the contract did not give an arbitrator authority to review the company's business judgment on subcontracting questions, but the U.S. Supreme Court reversed both lower courts. The substance of the final ruling was that the courts have authority to determine whether a dispute is arbitrable—that is, whether it is within the classes of grievances the parties agreed would be subject to arbitration. But because of the special nature of collective bargaining agreements and because

---

ence M. Updegraff wrote: "It must be taken to be fully established that labor agreements must be read in the light of the antecedent past practices of the parties in relation to the conduct of the parties after the agreement was made, since their 'mutual interpretation' as manifested by this conduct is ordinarily considered a reliable guide as to the meaning of the agreement in any part where it appears to be ambiguous or inadequate."

of the arbitrator's greater expertness in such matters, doubts over arbitrability should be resolved in favor of coverage.

### *"Grist for the Mills of Arbitrators"*

The phrase "strictly a function of management," Justice Douglas wrote in that landmark decision, "must be interpreted as referring only to that over which the contract gives management complete control and unfettered discretion." Subcontracting disputes, he added, are the subject of many grievances and are "grist for the mills of arbitrators." Consequently, if the parties had intended to exclude such controversies from arbitration, especially in view of the "absolute no-strike clause," he said they would have done so explicitly. Justice Douglas concluded:

In the absence of any express provision excluding a particular grievance from arbitration, we think only the most forceful evidence of a purpose to exclude the claim from arbitration can prevail, particularly where, as here, the exclusion clause is vague and the arbitration clause quite broad. Since any attempt by a court to infer such a purpose necessarily comprehends the merits, the court should view with suspicion an attempt to persuade it to become entangled in the construction of the substantive provisions of a labor agreement, even through the back door of interpreting the arbitration clause, when the alternative is to utilize the services of an arbitrator.

Understandably, management representatives were dismayed by the *Warrior & Gulf* decision. That it put an end to the *Cutler-Hammer* doctrine,[19] by which courts refused to direct arbitration of grievances that judges thought "frivolous," was only part of the reason for their disappointment. Equally important was their fear that arbitrators would become a more important factor than ever in labor relations, and that Justice Douglas's dicta would encourage them, to a greater degree than before, to hold matters arbitrable merely on the claimant's assertion, however frivolous, that a question of contract interpretation was involved. The evidence since June 1960 is not yet conclusive, for the impact of that ruling is still being revealed. Some arbitrators have indeed held matters to be within their jurisdiction only because of the *Warrior & Gulf* decision. But it appears that those arbitrators who

19. See note 14, p. 8.

always took seriously their obligations to interpret the arbitration clause as carefully as they construed other provisions continue to do so.[20]

Of special interest in this connection was an award by Benjamin Aaron, professor of law and director of the Institute of Industrial Relations, University of California at Los Angeles, and a past president of the National Academy of Arbitrators.[21] Relying upon three Steelworkers cases, of which *Warrior & Gulf* was one, the union had sought arbitration of a wage issue, although the contract did not specifically provide for arbitration of wages. In reply to the union's argument that the U.S. Supreme Court would have held the matter arbitrable, Mr. Aaron wrote:

Those cases all dealt . . . with the power of federal courts, rather than with the discretion of arbitrators. Construing those cases in a way most favorable to the union here involved would lead at most to the conclusion that if the parties had litigated this issue in federal court instead of submitting it to private arbitration, the court would have ruled that the issue was arbitrable; or that, conversely, if the arbitration decision in this case were in favor of arbitrability the court would decline to vacate it on review. Neither of those contingencies has occurred. The parties elected to resolve this dispute through arbitration, and the decision rests upon the judgment of a majority of the three arbitrators selected to hear the case. In exercising that judgment we should not, in my opinion, be influenced by any calculation of what a court might do if confronted by the same problem. The dominant theme of the Supreme Court decision referred to above is that courts typically lack the specialized knowledge, experience, and insight to deal wisely with these problems. Whether either this assumption, or the corresponding one that arbitrators typically possess such expertise, is correct is, to put it mildly, a question on which there is considerable disagreement. In any case, the doctrine enunciated in the Supreme Court decisions places added responsibility upon arbitrators generally. The temptation to uphold claims of arbitrability solely on the

20. It is not without significance that when the *Warrior & Gulf* case eventually went to arbitration, (36 LA 695, CCH Lab. Arb. Reports, 61–2, par. 8401), J. Fred Holly ruled on the merits, but only after making his own decision that the grievance was arbitrable. Presumably, he could have interpreted the phrase "strictly a function of management" differently than did Justice Douglas. In that event, the grievance would have been dismissed for lack of arbitrability.

21. *Hughes Tool Company, Aircraft Division* (Electronic and Space Technicians, Local 1553, AFL–CIO), 26 AAA 1. See also note 24, pp. 17–18.

ground that a court would do so in like circumstances must be resisted; for to yield would be to abdicate the assumed independence of judgment based on specialized knowledge and experience upon which the Supreme Court doctrine is predicated.

## The Perennial Issue of Arbitrability

Neither the Supreme Court, nor even the most persuasive arbitral award, can put an end to disputes over arbitrability once and for all. Under the *Warrior & Gulf* doctrine, the arbitrator plays no role only if it can be said with assurance that the parties have definitely excluded the disputed matter from his jurisdiction. This can, of course, be done by careful drafting of arbitration clauses, and many negotiators are able to do so. But circumstances that result in the "ambiguous silence" of the collective bargaining agreement generally also result in arbitration clauses that only imperfectly express the will of the parties. It is understandable that a party who has obtained, from a court or an arbitrator, an interpretation of the arbitration clause favorable to himself should seek no change in language. But the adverse party, presumably desiring a modified arbitration clause, also frequently permits the same language to be carried over from one contract to the next without change. The reason is that the arbitration clause is a bargainable issue, like everything else in the contract. It is perhaps an oversimplification to say, as the Supreme Court did, that arbitration is the *quid pro quo* for the no-strike clause. It is more realistic to say that everything in the agreement is a *quid pro quo* for every other consideration. The union may have agreed to a no-strike clause not in exchange for the arbitration clause but, let us say, for a more generous incentive plan. And the union may have agreed to a limited arbitration clause, restricting the arbitrator's jurisdiction only to discipline and discharge cases, as a *quid pro quo* of the employer's agreement not to subcontract.[22] The party who wants to eliminate ambiguities in the arbitration clause in a manner more favorable to himself may therefore be expected to grant some concession in return.

22. For a no-strike clause which seems to have been the *quid pro quo* for the employer's agreement not to subcontract five types of work, when a layoff would be the consequence, see *Southwestern Bell Telephone Company* (Communications Workers of America, AFL–CIO), 44 AAA 16, quoted in Chapter 3, note 3.

This is one reason why suggestions that arbitration clauses be eliminated or restricted are put forward by labor and management spokesmen in after-dinner speeches more often than at the bargaining table.

Furthermore, even the best contract drafting is no absolute guarantee that disputes over arbitrability will not arise. "Every grievance in a sense involves a claim that management has violated some provision of the agreement," wrote Justice Douglas.[23] And it would be an unimaginative union leader indeed who could not phrase a grievance to create sufficient appearance of arbitrability for at least a prima facie hearing. True, the arbitrator might dismiss the grievance for lack of arbitrability on discovering that the dispute was frivolously asserted to involve a matter covered by the arbitration clause.[24] But an airing of

23. See note 16, p. 8.

24. When an arbitrator finds a grievance frivolously based and, for that reason, not arbitrable, he is, in a sense, applying the *Cutler-Hammer* doctrine. (See footnote 14, p. 8.) But he is doing so on the basis of the knowledge and expertness which the U. S. Supreme Court said in the *Warrior & Gulf* case was characteristic of him and not of judges. For a case in which an arbitrator said he had no jurisdiction to examine the "pure merits" of a grievance for which the union could not make a prima facie showing, see *Berkshire Hathaway Company* (Textile Workers Union of America, AFL–CIO), 41 AAA 1. James J. Healy was the arbitrator. The union in this case had asked for a wage differential to be given to workers in a classification when certain tasks were performed. Although the contract contained a broad arbitration clause, referring to "any dispute . . . of any nature or character," Mr. Healy dismissed the grievance not because it lacked merit, but because *it lacked the quality of arbitrability.* He conceded that there was "probably" an adequate basis for finding the dispute arbitrable under the *Warrior & Gulf* doctrine. But he interpreted the Supreme Court's ruling to mean that the union had established a *"prima facie* case" for the right to be heard on the merits, and that it still remained for the arbitrator to determine whether he can proceed "to the *pure* merits" of the claim. In view of the "explicit contract terms," he said, the grievance had to be denied "without prejudice to the position of either party concerning the correctness or incorrectness of the present rate." This decision was based upon the following facts: (1) the agreement specified a single rate for the classification concerned in the grievance; (2) the union did not exercise its option to seek reconsideration of the rate during two wage reopening periods; (3) "nothing new or unusual" had occurred with respect to the job since the last reopening of the agreement; and (4) the arbitrator was barred by the contract from changing its terms. In summary, Mr. Healy concluded, "the union has chosen the wrong arena for seeking redress of its claim," and this leaves the arbitrator "without power . . . to move to a close study of the merits." If the union continues to believe a differential ought to be established,

the issue in an arbitration hearing room may have been all the claimant wanted in the first place. Similarly, because arbitration does involve a risk, the arbitrator having the right to make the wrong decision as well as the correct one, it is not to be expected that employers will completely forego the defense of non-arbitrability, however futile or frivolous, when this strategy seems to minimize the danger of an adverse decision.

### The Limitations of the Data

In the chapters that follow will be found many statements by arbitrators for and against the reserved rights theory and the doctrine of implied limitations, and many "principles of contract interpretation" will be cited to explain the meaning of gaps in the collective bargaining agreement. My object, however, will not be to show adherence to one theory or another. Indeed, it is doubtful whether, given the limitations of the arbitrator's office, theoretical generalizations can be fairly drawn from the dicta of particular cases.

Mr. Dash pointed out that in nineteen of the sixty-four cases he studied before writing his *Celanese* award the arbitrators "expressed the reserved rights theory in some form." But then, having put them-

---

he advised, "it should pursue its claim in negotiations of the terms of the new agreement."

For other cases in which the distinction is made between a prima facie case, or "some reasonable basis" for the grievance, and what Mr. Healy called "the pure merits," see: Charles A. Rogers's award in *Marine Products Company* (International Association of Machinists, AFL–CIO), 8 AAA 16; A. B. Cummins' award in *Pyramid Rubber Company* (United Rubber, Cork, Linoleum and Plastic Workers, AFL–CIO), 9 AAA 6; James V. Altieri's award in *E. R. Squibb Company* (Oil, Chemical and Atomic Workers, AFL–CIO), 30 AAA 4; S. S. Kates' award in *Babcock and Wilcox Company* (International Brotherhood of Boilermakers, AFL–CIO), 17 AAA 15; G. Allan Dash, Jr.'s award in *Wayne Pump Company, Division of Symington Wayne Corporation* (United Automobile Workers, AFL–CIO), 22 AAA 14; and Leonard Oppenheim's award in *Southwestern Bell Telephone Company* (Communications Workers of America, AFL–CIO), 44 AAA 16. In not all of these decisions was the grievance held non-arbitrable. In some, the arbitrators found that a prima facie case, or sufficient substance, *had* been established by the claimant. But even in the latter cases, the implication was clear that if no question of contract interpretation had been shown to exist, the grievances would be dismissed for lack of jurisdiction, not necessarily for lack of merit.

selves on record in favor of that doctrine, they proceeded to decide the cases on other grounds. In fact, their discussion of the issues before them seemed to indicate simultaneous adherence to the implied limitations theory.[25] Similarly, among the cases discussed in the following chapters will be found many in which management rights clauses were cited in support of work-load or job changes. But can it be inferred that those arbitrators would have held differently in the absence of management prerogative clauses? Certainly it seems likely that at least in some cases the strategy suggested by Mr. Phelps is effective: the presence of a management rights clause merely helps an arbitrator justify an award he would have come to in any event.

To say that the arbitrator forms an impression of the rights and equities of the parties and then selects the rule of contract interpretation or the theory of collective bargaining that supports his conclusion is not to speak ill of the profession. "There is no single rule of interpretation, or approach to interpretation, and no group of rules which, taken together, always will lead to a single 'correct' understanding and meaning," wrote Sylvester Garrett, chairman of the Board of Arbitration, United States Steel Corporation and the United Steelworkers of America, AFL–CIO.[26] Arbitrators, he said, exercise a "creative and intuitive" function, and in this respect they are no different from judges. He went on to quote one "knowledgeable judge" who explained that the vital motivating impulse for a judicial decision is a "hunch" as to what is right or wrong for a particular case.[27] The "astute judge" then "enlists his every faculty and belabors his laggard mind, not only to justify that intuition to himself, but to make it pass muster with his critics."

And so, what we will seek in the several hundred labor-management arbitration cases reported herein will not be a set of absolute principles, but a series of criteria that, in a general way, arbitrators look to in reaching their decisions. As the cases to be discussed in the following chapters were all heard under the rules of the American Arbitration Association, certain assumptions about them are possible. The

25. G. Allan Dash, Jr., "The Arbitration of Subcontracting Disputes," *Industrial and Labor Relations Review*, January 1963.

26. Sylvester Garrett, "Are Lawyers Necessarily an Evil in Grievance Arbitration?," *UCLA Law Review,* 1961, pp. 535–554.

27. Joseph C. Hutcheson, Jr., "The Judgment Intuitive: The Function of the 'Hunch' in Judicial Decision," 14 *Cornell Law Quarterly* 274, 285 (1929).

most important is that the arbitrators will not have resolved the disputes solely on the basis of their own unfettered insight into industrial relations, or their conception of what would satisfy abstract principles of justice, but rather on the basis of their understanding of the agreement of the parties. The collective bargaining contract (and the practices of the parties which shed light on their own understanding of its meaning) constitute the framework within which arbitrators make their decisions.[28]

28. Three cases may be cited to illustrate the arbitrator's limited authority to apply his own concepts of pure justice. These cases also reveal something of the realities of collective bargaining. During the negotiation of a new contract at *Anheuser-Busch, Incorporated* (International Union of Operating Engineers, AFL–CIO), 4 AAA 3, management representatives responded to a union demand for a wage increase by pointing out that it offered regular Sunday overtime, while its competitors did not. The wage increase demand was subsequently dropped. Shortly after the new contract went into effect, Sunday overtime was discontinued. The union called upon Arbitrator James C. Hill to restore Sunday overtime or to rescind the contract which had allegedly been induced by fraud and "bad faith." Mr. Hill said the evidence was "quite persuasive" that the company negotiators had indeed "consciously withheld knowledge of the probability, if not the certainty, that Sunday work would be eliminated in the future." But he could not accede to either of the two requested remedies because the contract did not require Sunday overtime, and because the arbitrator, a creature of the agreement, was barred by that document from changing it in any way. Moreover, he said, he had no way of knowing "what would have happened if the reduction of Sunday work had been accomplished or was known to both parties."

Another case of this kind, but one in which the union was the offender, was that of the *Barboursville Clay Manufacturing Company* (United Glass and Ceramic Workers, AFL–CIO), 16 AAA 24. While negotiating a piece rate for a loading job which was then in the experimental stage, the union's representative had stoutly denied that the job could be done in the way prescribed by management. His view prevailed, and on the strength of his argument, a rate increase was agreed upon to compensate for the alleged extra effort required. Immediately after the contract was signed, however, the loaders began doing the job exactly as management had said they could. The result was excessively high earnings. The company revoked the wage increase, which brought the matter to Arbitrator A. B. Cummins. Although the union president conceded that he had elected not to admit that the company's proposed method was practical, Mr. Cummins would not permit the company to rescind the contractual increase. The parties had been bargaining at "arm's length," he observed. If the company chose to accept the union's word, instead of undertaking studies of the job to obtain exact information, it was not for the arbitrator to mitigate

Arbitration practices in the United States are of many kinds. Some parties prefer a form of arbitration which borders on mediation; they select an arbitrator who is expected to perform that kind of service, and they endow him with broad authority. Other parties prefer arbitrators to be limited to "interpretation and application" of the agreement, and they often specifically forbid him to modify their contract in any way. There is reason to believe that a correlation exists between preference for the latter kind of arbitration and for proceedings administered by the AAA. That is why the emphasis of this volume, which deals largely with AAA cases, will be to show how management's technological radicalism and labor's security-conscious conservatism bring the two partners into conflict, and to reveal how those conflicts are resolved within the scope of the arbitrator's authority under typical collective bargaining agreements.

---

the loss that resulted. Mr. Cummins added—and this may have been a contributing factor in his decision—that the company was not without a remedy in the situation. He pointed out that the contract establishes procedures for correcting loose rates. The contract "lays down a clear procedure for negotiating a proposed change, and, failing that, utilizing the grievance procedure." He added that invoking this procedure would lead to an "amicable solution."

In the third case, *Merrill-Stevens Dry Dock & Repair Company* (Industrial Union of Marine and Shipbuilding Workers, AFL–CIO), 16 AAA 8, apparently neither party had bargained in bad faith. But somehow, according to the employer, an oversight had occurred when rates were set. The result was that for ten years, sand washers were paid the same rates as the more highly skilled sand blasters. Paul W. Hardy declined to permit the employer to correct that "error" unilaterally by reducing the sand washers to the laborers' rate that once prevailed. He wrote: "Precedent . . . has . . . established an understanding on the part of employees that insofar as rate of pay is concerned, Sand Blasting or Washing are synonymous. Job content may be different but that issue is not before this Arbitrator for decision. . . . Lacking a rate for Sand Washing in the contract, the Company, I believe, is duty bound to negotiate a new rate if one is desired by the terms and conditions of [the contract], for there it is clearly set forth that it is their obligation to collectively bargain as to rates of pay during the life of the contract. Assumption by the Company that they are now going to unilaterally reduce the wages previously paid for Sand Washing to the laboring rate of pay cannot be condoned . . ."

For another case in which bad faith in bargaining was alleged, see *The Specialty Paper Company* (International Brotherhood of Bookbinders, AFL–CIO), 13 AAA 21, discussed in Chapter 7.

# 2

## SUBCONTRACTING: THE IMPLICA-
## TIONS OF SILENCE

"The only thing I can say to you people is that we are not going to contract work to intentionally injure any of our employees. . . . [But] the work which is rightfully yours is the work you can do cheaper than somebody else."
—From a statement by a management representative during union contract talks.

"This is important to us . . . When there are . . . people walking the streets and out of a job and they are beating you over the head and say that somebody is doing their job, you feel pretty bad about it."
—From a statement by a union representative during the same negotiations.

Few manufacturing plants in the United States are so thoroughly integrated that they need not rely upon other companies for the manufacture of parts, the installation of equipment, or the performance of some service. If the work contracted to an outside firm is of a kind that cannot, under any circumstances, be done by bargaining unit members, very few problems are presented. A union representing unskilled women employees, for instance, will seldom complain when an employer contracts with a machine tool company for the installation of new equipment. But there are many instances where an argument can be made that the bargaining unit employees could have done the

22

work, even if less efficiently. And, as we shall see, many cases arise over the subcontracting of inventory parts or the performance of other work that, admittedly, unit members had been given in the past. Not surprisingly, disputes over management's rights to contract out are always hard-fought, and especially so during periods of job insecurity.[1]

It is perhaps because the differences between labor and management on subcontracting matters are too profound for easy resolution that more than 75 per cent of major contracts contain no direct reference

1. The term "subcontracting" is generally taken to denote an arrangement made by one company for work to be performed by employees of another company, on or off the first company's premises. Although disputes are frequent as to whether a particular subcontract was proper, controversies seldom arise as to the meaning of the term itself. However, one exception may be cited. At *Alco Products* (United Steelworkers of America, AFL–CIO), 6 AAA 5, the contract required the employer to discuss subcontracting plans with the union before putting them into effect. Management did not believe this rule applied to the transfer of work to another plant of the same company. Sidney Sugerman upheld the union: "The word and concept of 'subcontracting' in ordinary dictionary usage and in legal relationships are generally of the strict connotation argued here by the Company. However, in collective bargaining relations and labor-management practices in negotiations, grievances, and arbitrations that narrow sense of topical reference and definition does not necessarily or customarily govern the parties' practical, contract-making intentions. So encrusted upon the word 'subcontracting' have grown the other, very different concepts of contracting out any work or services to others even as prime contractors and of transferring work even to other bargaining units of the same employer, that it has tended to take on the general meaning in the context of labor relations, unless otherwise specially limited, of any removal of otherwise available work belonging and normally assigned to a defined bargaining unit and, within the discretionary control of the employer, the delegation, transfer, or arrangement of it to be done for the employer by outsiders or any others than those deprived of it in the bargaining unit." This interpretation was also supported by the fact that the employer had tried unsuccessfully to amend the contract to read "outside contractors."

For a case involving the right of a company to move machinery to another of its plants two hundred miles away, but one in which the question of subcontracting as such was not raised, see *Weyerhauser Company* (United Papermakers and Paperworkers, AFL–CIO), 29 AAA 14. The Milk Carton Division of this company operated a plant at Three Rivers, Michigan, where it manufactured unfolded components for its half-gallon milk containers. All through 1959 this was a money-losing operation. Finally, in January 1960, management decided to move two of its principal machines to another plant two-hundred miles away, where wage rates were lower, where productivity was 29 per cent

to the subject.[2] Inevitably, when grievances arise, the employer argues that silence signifies unrestricted power, and the union replies with the doctrine of implied limitations.[3]

As we saw in the previous chapter, the silence of a contract on a particular matter does not necessarily leave the arbitrator without jurisdiction to consider the merits of a dispute. There may have been

---

higher, and where employees were represented by a union which the union in the instant case said was "less aggressive." The union argued that, although the contract was silent on removal of equipment, it did contain a "manning table" which expressed an expectation that jobs would continue. It was within the company's rights to let the two machines remain idle if profitable operation was impossible, the union said, but not to move them out of its jurisdiction. The company answered that the manning table does no more than describe the "job situation" when the machines are running, and insisted there were "overpowering economic considerations" making it essential to manufacture the cartons elsewhere. John F. Sembower found the company's economic arguments plausible. The higher productivity in the plant to which the machines were moved resulted not only from lower wages, but from the structural advantages of a more modern one-story building, more efficient layout of equipment, and "perhaps also the character of supervision and work scheduling." In fact, Mr. Sembower observed, comparative wages were not a primary consideration in the move. The employer had shown that one of his plants in California had cleared a profit during 1959, although it paid the rates which prevailed in Three Rivers. He wrote: "The deep apprehension and even anguish of employees at seeing the machines on which they may work being taken from their plant and community is a distressing thing. History tells of many pathetic instances when employees have done all within their power to deter the departure from the community in which they live happily . . . of the equipment which in this machine age is symbolic of their means of livelihood at the time. Some such situations have heartrending aspects, and it must be observed also that often they are of the gravest concern to those who operate production facilities, the employers and manufacturers, as well. But if they ignore economic realities, such businesses cannot long exist. The bona fide economics are therefore the crux of the matter, in the absence of any specific agreement to the contrary."

2. *Subcontracting Clauses in Major Collective Bargaining Agreements*, U.S. Dept. of Labor, Bull. No. 1304, August 1961.

3. Whether a contract is, in fact, silent on the question of subcontracting can itself be a disputed question. At the *Continental Can Company* (United Papermakers and Paperworkers, AFL–CIO), 23 AAA 14, for instance, the contract barred employees "excluded from the bargaining unit" from doing work customarily performed by unit employees. Clearly, employees of another company were not within Continental Can's unit. But did the negotiators of the agreement intend the quoted language to apply to subcontracting? If the answer

understandings that the parties, for one reason or another, preferred not to reduce to writing. And past practice, if it was consistent enough over a long period of time to have created an expectation that certain standards would be maintained, may be regarded as part of those conditions of employment that are not subject to change at will by the employer. And finally, inferences can be drawn from the recognition, wage, and seniority provisions of the contract that establish at

---

was in the affirmative, the contract was not silent on contracting out; if negative, this was another typically silent contract. The issue in dispute was whether the company had the right to permit an outside company's employees to move a load of lumber into the plant at a time when its own equipment was inadequate because of a heavy snowstorm. Dudley E. Whiting ruled that the clause relied upon by the union had "no possible application to outside contractors and the subject of contracting-out is not mentioned in the agreement." The grievance was denied, despite the fact that a supervisor had erred in not notifying the union steward of the intended subcontracting. In view of the emergency and the fact that the supervisor was new with the company, the error was forgivable.

For another case with the same characteristics, see *Gamewell Company* (United Automobile Workers, AFL–CIO), 46 AAA 7, arbitrated by James J. Healy. The union had sought for many years to obtain a contractual restriction on subcontracting, but had never succeeded, and no grievances were filed on this matter until after the Supreme Court's *Warrior & Gulf* decision. The dispute in the instant case involved two types of work: the erection of office partitions and the manufacture of parts for inventory. The first question before Mr. Healy was whether the contract *was* silent on subcontracting, for the union had relied upon a clause barring "employees outside the bargaining unit" from bargaining unit work. This question was answered in management's favor. The reference to "employees," Mr. Healy said, "cannot be interpreted as applying to employees of other companies to whom the work is subcontracted." This construction flowed not only from the language of the contract as a whole, but from the fact that when the clause relied upon by the union was discussed during negotiations five years earlier, union representatives gave assurances that it was not intended to interfere with managerial rights to contract work out. Having found the contract silent on subcontracting, Mr. Healy went on to say that, particularly in view of the "strong and forceful" management rights clause, it would take more than the recognition clause, upon which the union also relied, to prohibit "the usual right to subcontract work." As a word of caution to the parties, however, Mr. Healy added that his remarks should not be construed as giving the company unlimited rights to subcontract work. "Obviously, any overt abuse of this right, such as subcontracting to undermine the union or to subvert its essential contract obligations, would not be tolerated."

least a prima facie case for the union's assertion that the contract has been violated.

## The Chief Criteria

But if the union's reliance on oral assurances and implications usually prevails in disputes over arbitrability, the situation is otherwise when arbitrators rule on what James J. Healy called the pure merits. Summarizing his conclusions from the sixty-four awards he studied, G. Allan Dash, Jr., said that to be upheld management needed only to show that the subcontracting decision, under a "silent" contract, met one or more of the following criteria:

1. [It] must not have been intended to, nor actually, deprive a substantial number of bargaining unit employees of work in classifications covered by the agreement.

2. [It] must be in conformance with past practices not previously objected to by the union, or must not be instituted by the company as a new practice.

3. [It] must be in good faith or not an effort to subvert the expressed terms of the agreement.

4. [It] must not be an attempt to evade substantial provisions of the agreement, nullify the agreement, or violate the "spirit, intent, or purposes" of the agreement.

5. [It] must be dictated by the requirements of the business for efficiency, economy or expeditious performance.

6. [It] must not be unreasonable, arbitrary, discriminatory, nor intended to harm, prejudice, or undermine the union.[4]

4. G. Allan Dash, Jr., "Arbitration of Subcontracting Disputes," *Industrial and Labor Relations Review*, January 1963. Virtually all the criteria Mr. Dash spoke of were present at the *Hinde and Dauch Division of the West Virginia Pulp and Paper Company* (International Brotherhood of Sulphite and Paper Mill Workers, AFL–CIO), 20 AAA 15. It was not a violation of the recognition clause, wrote John A. Hogan, when the employer subcontracted janitorial services under these circumstances: (1) The work contracted out was done with equipment not possessed by the employer; (2) the outside contractor did certain additional cleaning work, not previously performed by bargaining unit employees; and (3) cleaning was accomplished in fewer man-hours, resulting in considerable saving of money. "Management's action on these facts was within its right to run its business efficiently and did not constitute violation of the contract," he said. *"The evidence does not show that the exercise by manage-*

## The Leading Case

Applying these criteria to the *Celanese* case,[5] the arbitrability aspect of which was discussed in Chapter 1, Mr. Dash dismissed the grievance of the eight tinsmiths. He found that although the contract was silent on subcontracting, the discussions that had taken place in grievance-settling meetings and new contract negotiations *had* resulted in an understanding. But it was an understanding of an extremely limited kind. Management had given assurances only that work would not be contracted out when employees on the active payroll or the layoff list who had normally done such work in the past were able to do it "on a quality basis within the time limits necessary to meet the requirements of the company." Furthermore, the company would have to be in a position to do the work at a cost that would be "competitive," using its own equipment.

Mr. Dash said he could not tell from the evidence whether the parties had always observed this understanding in the past, but it was clear to him that the subcontracting of a capital improvement such as was protested in this case was not a violation of management's promise. For one thing, the job had to be completed in ninety days, and the

---

ment of its right to run its business efficiently impaired contract rights of the union paramount to this right."

For another equally clear case, see *Rollway Bearings Company* (United Automobile Workers, AFL–CIO), 39 AAA 13. Ralph E. Kharas said that management had the right, on the retirement of a janitress, to subcontract the work she performed to an outside company, where: (1) The work, although of a permanent and non-emergency nature, involved only one job "and hence did not very materially affect the numerical strength of the bargaining unit employees." (2) Although there was an economic motive for subcontracting, it could not be said that the purpose was to "undercut the wage structure." Furthermore, the timing of the subcontracting, so that no employee was "released, laid off or reassigned," also indicated "good faith" on the part of management. (3) The janitress had to work in a "remote area on the night shift where supervision was not available or was prohibitively expensive." (4) Difficulties had been created by the need to replace the janitress during vacations or absences for illness, and by the occasional need for additional employees for heavy cleaning. Mr. Kharas concluded: "The bargaining unit representative has too little at stake to justify an assertion that the contract, although silent, requires management to make the more inefficient and less economical decision."

5. 10 AAA 21 (see Chap. 1, note 17).

company's tinsmiths—the eight grievants—were already working full time. To be sure, as the union argued, new tinsmiths might have been hired, lower-rated employees might have been promoted, and the grievants might have been given a great deal of overtime. But such measures, Mr. Dash said, went beyond anything the company had promised. "There is absolutely no showing in the record that any such criteria have been followed in the past or that the parties have interpreted their various agreement provisions or understandings as requiring that such steps be taken to avoid the contracting-out of work." The objectives of an enlarged bargaining unit and more extensive overtime schedules may be "worthy," Mr. Dash conceded, but "they should be secured by negotiations and not through arbitration."

## Oral "Understandings" to Favor the Bargaining Unit

In other *Celanese Corporation* cases which were developing at about the same time, arbitrators Carl R. Schedler,[6] Ronald W. Haughton,[7] and Mark L. Kahn,[8] whose views on arbitrability coincided with those of Mr. Dash, came to conclusions on the merits of the cases which were also very similar to his. The strongest argument the union was able to present in the case before Mr. Schedler was that the company had stated several years earlier that management did not "desire" to contract out work that could be done by bargaining unit employees. This was a slim foundation for the union's case, the arbitrator thought. The oral statements relied upon by the union, he said, "are not promises or agreements, but are at most expressions of intent or hope to favor bargaining unit employees." The only concession to the union's position was Mr. Schedler's dicta to the effect that although the contract did not imply a limitation on managerial freedom to subcontract, there was an implication that such action would be taken only in "good faith," that is, "only . . . when it is warranted by existing conditions." The fact that the grievants were fully employed while the capital improvement was executed by an outside firm, and that some

6. *Celanese Corporation of America* (United Mine Workers of America, District 50), 21 AAA 9.

7. *Celanese Corporation of America* (United Mine Workers of America, District 50), 20 AAA 4.

8. *Celanese Corporation of America* (United Mine Workers of America, District 50), 19 AAA 4. See Chapter 1, note 18, for a discussion of these cases.

were even working overtime, the arbitrator concluded, also supported his finding.

Mr. Haughton's decision was similar in effect. The company violated neither the contract nor the "spirit of the understanding" between the parties, he wrote, in subcontracting insulation work at a time when no employees having seniority as insulators were on layoff. The contention that the work should have been performed by those employees on an overtime basis was rejected. An "understanding" between the company and the union reached six years earlier to the effect that the employer would not deprive employees of work they could do "at the same price as an outsider" did not require the employer "to assign people already working full time to work on overtime which it would not otherwise be unreasonable to assign to an outside contractor." It would be "unfair" to interpret a "quite general understanding," not incorporated into specific language, in the manner urged by the union. Furthermore, he concluded, to uphold the union would be to "do violence" to the purpose of the overtime pay provisions, which was to discourage the employer, by means of "a monetary penalty," from scheduling overtime.[9]

## Non-union Subcontractors

Mr. Haughton's case, like the others, involved capital improvements that had been let to an outside firm. Here, however, there was one element not present in the other cases: the union was able to show that electricians brought in by the subcontractor were not members of any union. This was intended to prove bad faith, or absence of good faith, on the part of the Celanese management, but Mr. Haughton was not persuaded. It was all a matter of motive, he said.

The contracting out of electrical work to a non-union contractor *in order* to escape obligations under the agreement and *merely* to take advantage of lower wage rates paid to non-union employees could be viewed as bad faith; I do not find such motivation demonstrated in this case.

9. For other cases in which it was urged that bargaining unit employees should have been permitted to work overtime as an alternative to subcontracting, see *Alan Wood Steel Company* and *Lee Tire & Rubber Company*, discussed in the next chapter.

As did the other arbitrators in this series of cases, Mr. Haughton found that the oral promise to favor bargaining unit members imposed little restriction on management's right to subcontract for good-faith economic reasons.

I find that while the company assured the union of good faith—that it would not "purposely" deprive its bargaining unit employees of work— the company also made it clear to the union that management would accept no direct contractual curb on its right to do so . . . It is also pertinent to *this* case to note that a principal concern of the union was the occurrence of contracting out while employees capable of doing the work were on furlough. . . .[10]

## "Residual Rights" Applied to Subcontracting

One of the most forceful statements in defense of the reserved rights theory as applied to subcontracting was written by Benjamin C. Roberts, in *West Virginia Pulp and Paper Company* (United Papermakers and Paperworkers, AFL–CIO).[11] Where there was no "express provision of the agreement" forbidding contracting out of work, he said, the employer had the right to purchase skids and pallets formerly made within the plant. This right fell within the scope of a clause reserving to management "all the rights, powers and authority customarily exercised by management subject only to the express provisions of the agreement." In view of the management rights clause, the union's reliance on the recognition, job security, seniority, layoff, and wage provisions was not persuasive. As it is undisputed that the employer would be free to subcontract in the absence of a collective bargaining agreement, he said, such subcontracting could be barred only on a showing that it was specifically forbidden by the agreement. "By its very terms, the reservation of company rights . . . made it incumbent upon the union to prove a restriction rather than, as argued by the union, to have the company cite an affirmative permissive provision to contract out." This interpretation was supported by the history of bar-

10. Another case involving subcontracting to a non-union establishment was that of *Narragansett Brewing Company* (International Union of United Brewery, Flour, Cereal, Soft Drink and Distillery Workers of America, AFL–CIO), 28 AAA 11. James J. Healy was the arbitrator. As the contract in that case was not silent on subcontracting, it is discussed more fully in Chapter 3.

11. 22 AAA 1.

gaining, including an unsuccessful attempt by the union to obtain agreement on a clause limiting subcontracting.

The union had better evidence of what it called "bad faith" in this case than is usually presented to arbitrators, but it was still not enough to overcome all the elements that favored management. It seems that the subcontracting of skids took place after a wage increase had been negotiated for employees in the box shop, where the work had formerly been done. This, the union said, was evidence of "unfair dealing," and of the company's intention to "teach the union a lesson" by laying off box shop employees, among whom there was "a high percentage" of union officers. Furthermore, the company did not give its own employees an opportunity to meet the price of the outside company. To these assertions, Mr. Roberts replied:

In considering this serious allegation, note must be taken of the fact that the contract that was signed on May 26, 1959 followed a four months strike. Although the union has urged that there was an incompatibility between having negotiated wage adjustments beyond the general wage increase for the Box Shop classifications and the elimination of inside production of skids and pallets when work resumed, one must be mindful that these wage adjustments, which were among 82 offered by the company, were proposed in December 1958, a month before the strike, and that the company's decision to purchase skids and pallets was made five months later and at the tail end of a lengthy four months strike which patently would have had some adverse effect on its customer relations and competitive position and cause it to seek economies. These, of course, would have to be consistent with its obligations under the contract and not motivated by bad faith intentions. The time lapse between the negotiation of the adjustments and the decision to purchase skids and pallets, coupled with the lengthy intervening strike, does not permit the suggested inference that the company engaged in unfair dealing with the union by bargaining for the wage adjustments on the one hand while simultaneously withholding that it did not intend to recall the Box Shop.

The remaining question, then, is whether the decision to purchase skids and pallets was for economic reasons, as stated by the company, or "to teach the union a lesson" in the Box Shop where there was a high percentage of union officers in proportion to the number employed in that area and was for the purposes of discrimination because of their union activity. [A management witness] has testified that he had concluded, based on the previous purchases of skids and pallets, that there would be a savings in their outside acquisition. Concededly, the skids and pallets that were bought from Pallets, Inc. were made of cheaper material and construction and no effort was made to duplicate this in the Box Shop before concluding that it was more economical to buy them. The financial figures submitted by the company also were not based on comparable construction and admittedly did not include every item of cost that might be allocated to the purchased skids in matching their net cost against that of the manufactured skids. Nevertheless, if the company made its determination based upon inadequate comparisons, but not in bad faith, that decision could not be said to have been made in violation of the non-discrimination provisions of the contract. Even if there were errors in its judgment of the total savings these are not . . . indicia of a lack of good faith. Moreover, it cannot be said that the company was under any duty to have attempted to duplicate the purchased skids before making its final decision on purchasing all of its skids and pallets on the outside when planning for the resumption of operations upon the termination of the strike.[12]

## *"Residual Rights" after* Warrior & Gulf

Mr. Roberts' decision was handed down on July 1, 1960, only a few days after the U.S. Supreme Court's *Warrior & Gulf* decision. Herman A. Gray, in *American Cable and Radio Corporation* (Communications Workers of America, AFL–CIO),[13] decided a subcontracting dispute almost two years after *Warrior & Gulf*. He ruled in the union's favor, partly on the basis of Justice Douglas's dicta in that celebrated case.

The dispute arose when the company, without consulting the union, contracted out the installation of certain automatic switching equipment that it had bought. It was conceded that the installation could have been accomplished by the company's seventeen "shop and installation technicians." The contract contained no bar against subcontracting. Neither did it contain a management rights clause. Management's entire case was therefore based upon the silence of the contract —the residual rights theory.

12. For another case involving the purchase of skids formerly manufactured within the plant, see the award of Leonard A. Keller in *Allied Paper Corporation* (United Papermakers and Paperworkers, AFL–CIO), 8 AAA 18, discussed later in this chapter.

13. 46 AAA 4.

Mr. Gray declared that the residual rights theory was no longer the complete answer it might have been in the past. Referring to the *Warrior & Gulf* case and to decisions of lower courts and of arbitrators, he wrote:

There has been a change in attitude towards this problem. In an earlier day, it was generally held that the fight to contract out was an inherent managerial power which remained untouched unless express language was embodied in the collective agreement imposing a limitation. This is no longer true. As concepts of the purpose, scope and function of the collective agreement have developed and broadened, there has been a growing trend to the opposite, an increasing acceptance of the view that unless there is express language preserving the power to contract out it must be deemed to have been circumscribed by the very existence of a collective agreement.

One does not have to accept all the reasoning of the court decisions, Mr. Gray added, to reach the "end result" that "an unrestricted power to contract out . . . runs counter to the purpose of the collective agreement, to the expectancy to which it gives rise and to the obligations implicit in it." Mr. Gray declined to go any further. He said he would not define the full extent of the company's implied obligations to the union with respect to subcontracting. But he said that, at least, it involved discussion in advance, as had been done in the past.[14]

Although the grievance was upheld, the union's request for monetary relief in the form of additional overtime pay was denied. The grievants had been working full time and even overtime all along, Mr. Gray said. To have assigned the work to the grievants on an overtime basis would have involved "overtime upon overtime to an extent beyond physical endurance." Furthermore, although the work was protracted, it was not of "a continuous nature," and would not lead to future displacement of employees.

### Implications of the Recognition Clause

Although relatively few contracts contain specific language dealing with subcontracting, almost all contain a recognition clause. Inevitably,

14. For a case in which, according to management at any rate, the union was seeking to turn the *Warrior & Gulf* decision into a windfall, see *Gamewell Company*, note 3, pp. 24–25.

the question arises as to what implications, if any, are contained in the provision that describes the bargaining unit and establishes the union's status. Given the large number of *Celanese Corporation* subcontracting cases in which this issue was raised, only four of which we have discussed above, it was perhaps inevitable that the union would find some basis in the dicta of one arbitrator for pressing a grievance to arbitration before another. That is what happened in *Celanese Corporation of America* (Textile Workers Union of America, AFL–CIO).[15]

The union had lost two decisions in the past, but the arbitrators in those cases had stated that it would be improper for management to subcontract work customarily performed by bargaining unit members unless some emergency made it absolutely necessary. As the subcontracting of mechanical construction work in the instant case did not seem to the union to be justified by an emergency, and as bargaining unit maintenance employees had done such work in the past, union representatives thought that at last they had a subcontracting grievance that could be sustained. James J. Healy did not agree.

To begin with, he adopted "as a threshold conclusion" the dicta of the arbitrators in the earlier cases. In fact, even if he had had "reservations" about those statements, he said, he would be inclined to regard them "as part of the relationship" of the parties, because they represent "the evolution of principles" which they accepted in effect by continuing the relevant contract clauses unchanged from one agreement to the next. Nevertheless, Mr. Healy added, he was "mindful" that the contract did not forbid subcontracting and that "it requires more than a recognition clause or an allusion to seniority provisions" if managerial rights to subcontract are to be diminished. But the chief reason the union did not prevail was that Mr. Healy did not find the circumstances they spoke of present in this case. Although bargaining unit employees had occasionally performed tasks similar to that subcontracted, subcontractors had done it more often. For that reason, it could not fall within the concept of work "usually performed" by bargaining unit employees. Furthermore, there was "some degree of urgency" in this capital construction project, and some doubt as to whether the company's own employees could have managed the job. In summary, Mr. Healy wrote, although there appeared to be "some elements" in the case to make the earlier dicta applicable, those ele-

15. 48 AAA 8.

ments were not present "to a forceful enough degree" to justify a finding that the company had violated the contract.

John F. Sullivan, in a case involving the *Borg-Warner Corporation* (International Union, Allied Industrial Workers of America, AFL–CIO),[16] came to a different conclusion about subcontracting limitations, but the facts before him were rather special.

In 1960, the company, having bought its own truck, contracted with a self-employed man, who was also performing landscaping services, to use that vehicle for hauling rubbish away from the plant. Prior to that time, trash had been removed by a contractor who used his own truck. The acquisition of the truck and the change in the contractual arrangement brought about a grievance of a bargaining unit member whose principal job was moving materials by truck and fork lift, but who also "on at least one occasion" did some hauling of trash. He had apparently not objected when rubbish removal was contracted out before, but now that the company had its own truck, he thought the driving assignments should be his.

Mr. Sullivan's decision hinged on the existence of the recognition clause and the fact that the company now had its own truck for hauling. It was a violation of "an implied condition of the recognition clause," he said, to permit the new contractor to do hauling with a company vehicle. The fact that the grievant had performed some trash removal with improvised equipment in the past supported the union's argument that, although it had not protested the subcontracting before, it had not relinquished jurisdiction over the disputed work. "That the union did not protest the action of the company contracting with the [the former contractor] to do such work *using his own equipment* is understandable," Mr. Sullivan wrote. Now that the company had equipment for the job, the union was correct in insisting that hauling be kept in the bargaining unit.[17]

A case that arose at the *Allied Paper Corporation* (United Paper-makers and Paperworkers, AFL–CIO),[18] was more typical of sub-

16. 31 AAA 3.

17. Although the union won the decision, no monetary remedy was awarded. The subcontracting had been "motivated by reasons of economy, in good faith and in the belief that there was no violation of the agreement." Furthermore, no employee in the grievant's classification was then on layoff.

18. 8 AAA 18.

contracting disputes generally. It resulted in an award by Leonard A. Keller, strongly rejecting the view that restrictions could be inferred from the recognition clause, the wage classification section, or other provisions of the agreement. The issue was simply whether the company had the right to purchase from an outside company skids which had formerly been manufactured within the plant. The dispute was arbitrable, Mr. Keller explained, because of "the implied covenant of good faith and fair dealings" inherent in the contract. But that was as far as implications could go.

Because an employer might use the device of subcontracting to subvert the wage agreement, or to lower standards, or eliminate classification and seniority rights, does not establish that he has done so or intends to do so. Before a covenant of good faith and fair dealing can be held to be violated, there must be proof of unfair dealing or bad faith, or at least of the employer's intention to escape his contract. To assert that because subcontracting might lead to this end, it is prohibited, is to assume the very question in issue. In effect, such an assertion would add to the agreement a provision that work once performed by members of the bargaining unit must always be performed by them, regardless of the employer's reasons for letting it out. Such a provision must be added by the parties themselves.

Mr. Keller's discussion of the case made it clear that none of the employees in the box shop, where skids had formerly been manufactured, was laid off as a result of the subcontracting, although some had to be transferred to lower-rated jobs. Whether the decision would have gone the other way if employees *had* been laid off cannot be known for certain, but it seems doubtful in view of Mr. Keller's strong reliance upon the company's good-faith economic reasons.[19]

### The Impact on the Bargaining Unit

In the *Allied Paper* case, as Mr. Keller pointed out, the bargaining unit had not been diminished, nor had any employee lost his job. Occasionally, some adverse effects can be shown to result from subcontracting, but unless those losses are substantial, they may not be

19. Mr. Keller wrote: "In the present case, the company, after mature deliberation and discussion with the union, and after making efforts to improve the box shop operation, determined to subcontract the work. This meant not only substantial savings, but an important improvement in service, and the provision of needed space for paper storage." For another case involving the purchase of

sufficient to overcome the silence of the contract, the peripheral nature of the subcontracted work, and the employer's good faith. A case in point was that of the *Bearings Company of America* (United Steelworkers of America, AFL–CIO).[20] In April 1960, because there was no more work for him in his classification, a maintenance painter was transferred to lower-rated work. Shortly thereafter, management contracted with an outside firm to paint a new addition to its plant facilities. No contract violation was involved, Laurence E. Seibel ruled.

Plainly, the work here in question was temporary in nature and limited in scope, so that its performance by employees of an independent contractor had no impact on the status of the exclusive bargaining agent or the employees. It is equally clear, from the union's own argument, that the company did not contract out such work as a means of undermining the union's wage rates. To my mind, it is also significant that the work in question constitutes work on a new construction project and is not work which is regularly performed by bargaining unit employees; it is not work which is an integral part of the regular business of the company.

## Bargaining History and Past Practice

A layoff situation *was* involved at the *General Aniline and Film Corporation* (Oil, Chemical and Atomic Workers International Union, AFL–CIO),[21] but Dudley E. Whiting still declined to derive limitations of the employer's right to subcontract janitorial services from the recognition clause and from another provision that barred new hiring during periods when employees with seniority were not at work.[22] An influential fact was that the union had sought in negotiations to restrict subcontracting, but management resisted the attempt, and the agreement remained silent. "When a matter has been the subject of negotiation and one party has been unsuccessful in obtaining a desired provision, it is wholly improper for an arbitrator to award that party the same result as a necessary implication of other contract provisions," he concluded.

---

skids formerly manufactured within the plant, see the award of Benjamin C. Roberts in *West Virginia Pulp and Paper Company* (United Papermakers and Paperworkers, AFL–CIO), 22 AAA 1, earlier in this chapter.

20. 27 AAA 14.

21. 36 AAA 7.

22. For another case involving janitorial services and implications of the recognition clause, see note 4, this chapter.

The rule of contract interpretation that holds that an unsuccessful attempt to amend a contract may be used against the party making the attempt has a strong logical appeal. But it also has a negative side, for it discourages attempts by parties to clarify ambiguities.[23] In the *General Aniline and Film* case we saw that rule of construction applied against the union. In a case of the *West Virginia Pulp and Paper Company* (United Papermakers and Paperworkers, AFL–CIO),[24] it was used, in slightly different form, against management. By trying to obtain the union's concurrence in a certain act, the arbitrator ruled, management forfeited the right it might otherwise have had to act unilaterally.

At the Hinde and Dauch Division of the company, there was a "watchman-janitor" who performed the usual security functions, swept up around machines, placed time cards in racks, saw to it that windows were closed at the end of the shift, and executed other chores of that kind. Management had long wanted to remove the watchman from the bargaining unit, and the matter was raised in successive union contract negotiations. But the union always resisted any change. In July 1960, during the most recent contract talks, the company spoke of subcontracting watchman duties to an outside firm, but again the union refused.

Finally, in April 1961, management took unilateral action. The American District Telegraph Company was contracted with for watchman services, employees were told to sweep up around their own machines, a few other chores were given to bargaining unit members, and certain tasks of the abolished job were assigned to a foreman.

The employer relied largely upon a clause that provided for application of seniority "in the event of job abolishment." This seemed to envision the possibility of jobs being discontinued, and as long as the incumbent was given his rights under the contract, management thought no violation was involved.

## Right Lost by Negotiation

Ronald W. Haughton thought otherwise. For one thing, he said, the clause relied upon by the employer related to "wholly doing away"

23. For a comment on this rule of contract interpretation see Chapter 7, note 11.

24. 42 AAA 15.

with a job, not with "removal of the basic elements of a job from the bargaining unit." Furthermore, if that clause gave the employer the power to remove the watchman from the bargaining unit, why did he not do so as far back as 1956, when he began asking for the union's concurrence? "The fact is," Mr. Haughton wrote, "that the company could have acted to take the watchman out from coverage at the expiration of any particular contract since 1956. However, by requesting the right to do so of the union, and by accepting a negative answer, and by including the watchman classification in [the wage classification schedule], it recognized that the classification was part of the contract, and thus acknowledged that it then could not act unilaterally within a contract period to remove it from coverage."

Since the company failed in collective bargaining to accomplish the end of removing the watchman classification and the work performed therein from the coverage of the collective bargaining contract, and absent *specific* contract language, authorizing it to do so, this arbitrator would be exceeding his authority if he were now to sustain the company in an interpretation of the contract, which, on the evidence, is contrary to the way the parties, themselves, have applied it in the past.

The two watchmen, who had been assigned to other work in the plant when the security firm was engaged, were ordered reinstated in their old jobs in accordance with the union's request. However, inasmuch as they had been earning more than their customary watchman rate at the other work, no back pay was awarded.

## Limited Effect of Grievance Settlements

An apparently close causal connection between subcontracting and layoff for lack of work was shown at the *American Enka Corporation* (United Textile Workers of America, AFL–CIO)[25] where, a few weeks after an electrical construction contract was given to a contractor, two bargaining unit electricians were laid off for lack of work. The union thought its case was particularly strong because two earlier grievances protesting subcontracting had been settled to its satisfaction. This, union representatives at the arbitration thought, established a "past practice" that should control in this instance.

25. 34 AAA 14. The arbitrability aspect of this case was discussed in Chapter 1, note 18.

Clarence M. Updegraff was not persuaded. There had also been occasions when the union had not prevailed. Under the circumstances, he pointed out, the two incidents cited by the union fell short of representing a "consistent, uninterrupted, mutually concurred—in past practice" of giving all electrical construction work to the bargaining unit. Moreover, he said:

It seems to be well settled that the day-to-day claims and responses in respect to grievances and in the steps of grievance procedure may not be taken to modify the negotiated contracts between the parties but that the latter should be essentially amended only by formal negotiations and agreements. Matters written and spoken in respect to specific grievances are generally restricted to apply to those grievances only and not to have such broad and far-reaching effect as to amount to formal contractual undertakings, extending or modifying the formal working agreements between the parties.

As do most arbitrators who have to judge the extent of managerial rights to subcontract, Mr. Updegraff took into close consideration the character of the employer's motives. He said that the "evidence does not disclose any purpose, policy or maneuver by the employer to weaken or undermine the union in this case," and that the motive was soundly economic: Maintenance electricians could not do the work "without undue interference with the routine maintenance work and without undue overtime expense." All the union was able to salvage in this case was a subtle hint that the company may not have used the best judgment. "Whether the contracting-out of this electrical work showed good managerial judgment or proper managerial foresight with sympathetic consideration for its regular employees is a matter not before the arbitrator," Mr. Updegraff wrote.

## Binding Past Practice

The past practice at *Eastern Gas and Fuel Associates* (Oil, Chemical and Atomic Workers, AFL–CIO)[26] was of a different kind, with the result that the grievance was upheld—a fairly rare occurrence under contracts containing no specific ban against subcontracting.

It had been the practice not to subcontract maintenance painting until after bargaining unit painters were recalled from layoff. In fact,

26. 10 AAA 13.

painting was subcontracted only once every three years or so, and employees on the payroll were permitted to do that work during the intervening years. Another special fact of this case was that there had been grievances protesting loss of earnings due to subcontracting in the past, and at least one arbitration case, the outcome of which strengthened the union's claim to be consulted before contracts were let. Finally, the contract contained, in addition to the usual recognition and seniority clauses, one provision that stated:

Working conditions and hours in effect on the date of the signing of this agreement may be changed only by consent of both parties. This agreement may not be modified, amended or supplemented without the consent of the union and the company.

and another that said:

The company reserves the right to hire suitable employees. However, the company will first, as far as possible, rehire laid-off union members who are experienced in the job in question or are qualified for the job.

Against this background, A. Howard Myers ruled that despite the silence of the contract on subcontracting, the right of management to hire outside painters to do maintenance work that, "by a long practice of years," had been done by its own employees was "subject to" the quoted provisions of the contract. At the very least, he said, this meant that the re-employment rights of painters (who were then on layoff) were affected, and that the subcontracting constituted a unilateral change in the "conditions of employment" that management was "committed to maintain during the life of the agreement," unless the union's consent was obtained.

The silence of the agreement concerning subcontracting in no way relieves the company of other pertinent contract duties. This conclusion does not deny the company the right to subcontract painting or other work, but it does preclude the cancelling of conflicting employee rights established by agreement, law, and practice. Seniority, bargaining rights, and job rights of the aggrieved men . . . were violated by the company when painting work usually done by them was done by non-unit employees of an outside contractor.

### Plant Security Functions

Often, as we have seen in the *Borg-Warner* case, long-standing sub-contractual relationships are tolerated for many years and then objected to when management makes some change. This was the circumstance also at the *American Sugar Refining Company* (United Packinghouse Workers of America, AFL–CIO).[27] For many years, guard and watchman services were performed by employees of the company. The first union contract, in 1938, provided for "combined watchman and janitor service," while guards were in a different classification, but also within the bargaining unit. About ten years later, guards were removed from the bargaining unit, and the Pinkerton Agency was hired to perform guard services.

The next change occurred in 1956, when the janitor-watchman combination was divided into two jobs, but the contract continued to refer to "janitor-watchman," perhaps through inadvertent failure to correct the contract language. At any rate, ten Pinkerton guards and a captain, employed by the outside company, continued all this time to patrol the grounds and perform the usual plant security functions. At the same time, ten watchmen, members of the bargaining unit, performed fire prevention services during shifts when the Pinkerton men were not on duty.

In September 1960, management decided to eliminate watchman work altogether as a bargaining unit job and to let the outside agency perform all guard and watchman services. By overcoming duplication, the change took 194 hours of work per week out of the bargaining unit. One watchman was pensioned, another was laid off immediately, and eight others were retained, at least temporarily, for other work, under an employment guarantee provision of the contract.

Did the company have the right to make this final change? William E. Simkin said it did in view of the objective of the change, which was "equal or better over-all plant protection with a substantial reduction of the total work force that was required under the dual setup."

Without minimizing the importance of fire protection, the major duties performed by Watchmen were duties not closely related to production. Fire protection is a function for which plant production supervision is not

27. 30 AAA 20.

fully or specifically trained at a relatively small plant and Watchmen had inadequate supervision at this plant. Removal of the fire protection function from the bargaining unit is essentially no different from removal of cafeteria operation from the bargaining unit. If the Company had simply subcontracted the fire protection function . . . with no changes of duties and no combination of work with Guard work, this would be a closer case, despite the "fringe characteristics" of the job as related to production. But when the basic decision was to combine the two jobs with no appreciable increase of Guard manpower and at the same time maintain satisfactory over-all plant protection, the case is much clearer on its merits. It is not possible to conclude that this was an abuse of management rights or that the Union's position as bargaining agent was seriously threatened or "whittled away."

### Effect of NLRB Ruling on Subcontracting Rights

Although he upheld the company on the chief issue, Mr. Simkin rejected the employer's secondary argument that some of the duties of the watchmen should be excluded from the bargaining unit under rules established by the National Labor Relations Board. He wrote: "A substantial question exists as to whether arbitration is the proper forum for decision on this phase of the case . . . In any event, it is quite apparent that the parties made their own decision on this point in 1948, shortly after passage of the Act. At that time, guards were removed from the bargaining unit and watchmen were left in the bargaining unit. A company argument on this point, made some twelve years after the initial decision by the parties and during the term of a labor agreement, can be given no weight in arbitration."

Whether the Taft-Hartley Act's ban against bargaining units which include guards and production workers affects the employer's right to subcontract watchman services also came before Louis A. Crane, at the *Kuhlman Electric Company* (United Automobile Workers, AFL–CIO).[28] It was not a violation to subcontract those services, he said, because guarding the plant was not "an integral aspect of work of members of the production and maintenance bargaining unit." Furthermore, the "tie" between watchmen's duties and the "rights of bargaining unit employees" is "a slender one" in view of the fact that the Taft-Hartley Act prohibits the NLRB from "sanctioning bargaining

28. 13 AAA 3.

units" which include both guards and production and maintenance employees. "While such provisions do not prohibit parties voluntarily from including guards and other employees in a single collective bargaining unit where the National Labor Relations Board has no occasion to intervene, an appeal to the Board would entail separation of such functions from the work of bargaining employees."

Mr. Crane observed that the contract contained a statement that the company would commit "no act calculated to undermine the union." This strengthened his feeling of obligation not to direct the company to keep guards within the bargaining unit, an act that might subject the agreement to attack. Giving that phrase the broadest possible scope, he concluded, and disregarding the apparent good faith of the company, "it is still not possible to find that the shifting of watchmen's functions constituted a basic challenge to the union."[29]

### Reasons for Barring Guards from Unit

Donald A. Crawford also ruled on subcontracting of plant security services at the *Wayne Pump Company* (United Automobile Workers, AFL–CIO)[30] and came to the same conclusion as arbitrators Simkin and Crane. But he explained more fully than did the others the reason for barring guards from units certified by the National Labor Relations Board under the Taft-Hartley Act.

Before dealing with that matter, however, he disposed of the conventional argument that the recognition clause, seniority provisions, and wage classification schedules operated as a restraint on management. None of these provisions is a "guarantee" that a given job will exist, he wrote.

As to the effect of the Taft-Hartley Act and of NLRB rulings under it, Mr. Crawford indicated that he would follow those precedents both as a practical matter, and because the basis for the law's exclusion of plant guards from units of production workers is sound. By subcontracting plant security functions to an outside detective agency, he

29. The union was able to show that guards normally performed some non-guard functions (summoning an electrician, or adjusting a valve on boilers during weekends), but these tasks were held "reasonably incidental" to plant protection work and could therefore be disregarded in this case.

30. 51 AAA 18.

wrote, management "receives the benefits of a trained plant protection force" supervised by "technically competent" personnel, all with specialized knowledge of crime detection. These functions can best be performed, he said, by individuals who need not "look to the union for protection" and who are not subordinate to foremen and supervisors.

When a guard has reason to think that he should question, search, or report a foreman or front office employee, he may believe that he will hurt his situation as an employee if he does. As non-employees, the guards can be rotated and they have the status to deal with professional and supervisory employees with a degree of independence otherwise impossible.

Finally, Mr. Crawford wrote, the plant was too small to justify retaining specialized supervisory personnel necessary to train the three guards who were needed. The losses to the bargaining unit were only *"potential,"* for no janitor-watchman had been laid off during the six months that elapsed between the entrance of the detective agency on the scene and the arbitration hearing. In view of this, the advantage to management in subcontracting was controlling.

### Summary: Acceptable Economic Motives

In most of the cases discussed in this chapter, arbitrators ruled that one of the acceptable criteria of subcontracting, in the absence of contractual restrictions, was a sound economic reason. If all that one meant by this was that some economic advantage must accrue to management, such an injunction would be pointless; it would bar only subcontracting for the purpose of inflicting deliberate harm, even if it harmed the employer as well. Obviously, if there were no economic motive, the issue would not arise at all. As Donald A. Crawford suggested in the *Wayne Pump* case, discussed above, the facts must "demonstrate the existence of compelling logic or economics of operation (other than the wage bill)." The parenthetical remark should not be overlooked, for if the economic advantage in subcontracting were derived from a lower wage rate paid by the outside company, most of the implied restrictions discussed by the arbitrators in the form of dicta would come into force.

The nature of acceptable economic motives for subcontracting was demonstrated by James C. Hill at the *West Virginia Pulp and Paper Company* (United Papermakers and Paperworkers, AFL–CIO).[31] This case was different from most because the arbitrator did not first have to explain to the company why its rights were not unlimited. In fact, Mr. Hill said that the parties themselves had agreed that under certain conditions, subcontracting may "infringe upon the status and integrity of the bargaining unit and the union, or undermine job security and the wage standards." Nevertheless, they were not in agreement as to eight instances of maintenance subcontracting. Before ruling on these instances one by one, Mr. Hill set forth his basis of judgment.[32]

The first was that past practice would be controlling. Although certain work might be within "the competence of employees in the bargaining unit," if the company had contracted such work out in the past, it would be permissible. The union had argued that any practice prior to 1958 was not relevant because layoffs took place in that year. Mr. Hill agreed that it would be an "abuse of the subcontracting rights" to cut the maintenance force and then to contract out the work they were performing. But the facts here were otherwise. The record showed no increase in the volume of subcontracting after 1958, and perhaps a decrease. It followed, therefore, that the layoff of maintenance employees represented a permanent decline in the need for those classifications.[33]

The second criterion for an approvable subcontracting project, Mr. Hill said, was that the need for the work must "vary greatly"

31. 51 AAA 11.
32. The union had asked the arbitrator not only to rule on the specific grievances, but to define "standards and guide lines" for the future. Mr. Hill declined to do this because, he said, there would be "limited value" in such an undertaking to compensate for the "considerable risk" of misunderstanding and misapplication. "The situations are much too varied and complex to permit the laying down of standards by which future cases may be judged. Any generalization may be subject to many exceptions in many different circumstances. The arbitrator can only explain his findings in the given cases for whatever value the parties choose to give them." Nevertheless, as Mr. Hill no doubt suspected himself, the principles he set forth in this case, although derived from and applying to the eight specific instances, did not lack much toward being the "standards and guide lines" the union requested.
33. Mr. Hill said that this was also the conclusion reached by two other arbitrators in previous cases of the same parties.

from time to time, making it impractical for the employer to maintain the "special tools and equipment" and "special skills of workers or supervisors." Also relevant would be "substantial savings in time or costs" and better protection of property against injury.

The question of costs, of course, led to the third criterion—wages. If the savings came about only because the subcontractor paid lower wages, it might be an indication of "an attempt to undermine the wage standards" of the agreement. "Cost savings may be significant and valid where they are based on superior techniques and the specialized experience and equipment of the contractor," he wrote.

Good faith, as every other arbitrator pointed out, was a necessary element. But if one meant by good faith only that the employer acted without malice toward his own employees, Mr. Hill added, it was not a sufficient defense. It is necessary to consider "effects" as well as "intent," he said.

Finally, the "magnitude of the contracted work" may be important. Neither the small cost nor the limited time involved could represent a complete defense, although the "magnitude of the contracted work" might be significant in determining whether an employer could be expected to recall an employee from layoff or hire a new worker. "The employer cannot reasonably be expected to hire an additional employee where the available work would provide only a small fraction of a full-time job," the arbitrator said.

## Applying the Principles

Applying the principles of union contract construction expressed above, Mr. Hill said that the company had the right to subcontract a major roofing repair job that was "larger in scope and different in nature" from the work bargaining unit employees had done. Moreover, by subcontracting, the employer "realized a substantial saving in cost and time"; he "gained access to special equipment, special skills of workmanship, supervision and engineering"; and he was able to obtain guarantees of quality and "protection against property damage." It was also proper to subcontract concrete and cement work of the same kind that had been subcontracted in the past. The union would have had "a solid basis for complaint" if the company had laid off men who were skilled in that kind of work and had then engaged a subcontractor.

But that was not the circumstance here. However, it was an error to "grab the opportunity" of the subcontractor's presence on the premises and have him perform a small job that, according to the evidence, was not part of "an integrated project requiring special skills or equipment of a contractor." Similarly, the contracting out of several welding jobs (with one exception) was justified because special equipment and skills, not possessed by bargaining unit welders, were needed. The one exception was so minor as to be *de minimis*. Also permissible was subcontracting of tile work in the company's lunch room, this work having been "recognized as work of a contractor" by past practice.

The painting of the front office by a subcontractor was "a close case," the arbitrator thought, because no special equipment or cost advantage was involved. But on the other hand, it did involve some plastering. "The record does not show that unit employees had plastering skills." In any event, offices had always been painted by a subcontractor, although the company "formerly employed a maintenance painter as a separate classification." Under the circumstances, this subcontracting project "was a reasonable exercise of managerial discretion and not violative of the agreement." Similarly, although the bargaining unit job was described to include the installation and repair of the sprinkler system and plumbing fixtures, the company had the right to subcontract sprinkler installation, because unit employees had never actually installed new or additional systems, while the contractor was a recognized specialist in this work. Furthermore, subcontracting facilitated insurance approval.

Although the company had all the equipment it needed to grade the parking lot, the amount of work was insufficient to justify recalling an employee from layoff. "The company is not required to hire a man for what would be a small fraction of a full-time job. Taken by itself, this incident [of subcontracting] can hardly be said to have deprived anyone of employment or earnings." An "accumulation" of such minor subcontracting projects could become serious and affect job opportunities of one or more yard laborers, "but nothing of this nature has been shown in the present case."

Finally, Mr. Hill wrote, the fact that the employer had assigned floor-waxing tasks after hours to clerical employees, who were not in the bargaining unit, did not constitute a past practice of having such work done by other than maintenance employees, because that practice had been protested by the union. However, the record in this case "lacks the specificity" to justify an award of relief for past incidents of this kind. That the employer's floor-waxing equipment was broken does not constitute a permanent justification for subcontracting. The company may be expected to repair the old machine or purchase a new one.

# 3

# SUBCONTRACTING: NEGOTIATED RESTRICTIONS

"It is recognized that the company has the right to have work done by outside contractors. However, work performed by employees covered by the agreement will not be contracted out if this will result in the layoff of employees who normally perform such work."

—From a typical union contract

An absolute ban on subcontracting is seldom seen in a collective bargaining agreement. Of 1,687 agreements, each covering more than 1,000 employees, which the Department of Labor studied in 1959, only 378 were found to contain some limitation on managerial rights to subcontract, and in only four of these was the prohibition complete.[1] Such restrictions as are found generally range from the mild ("The company agrees to keep the union informed of the status and scope of its subcontracting program"), to the somewhat confining ("Work performed by employees covered by the agreement will not be contracted-out if this will result in the layoff of employees who normally perform such work"). Most contracts dealing with subcontracting concentrate on the effect it would have upon employment opportunities, present or future.

1. *Subcontracting Clauses in Major Collective Bargaining Agreements*, U.S. Dept. of Labor, Bull. No. 1304, August 1961.

50

## Subcontracting of Job Not Listed in Permissive Clause

Arbitrators and representatives of parties occasionally quote a "canon of contract interpretation" which holds that when particular matters are included in a series, it means that other matters of the same class are excluded. But this rule of construction is not an infallible guide. Matters excluded may also be regarded as questions about which the contract is silent. From this point of view, discussions hinge on either the residual rights theory or the doctrine of implied limitations. Arbitrator Leonard Oppenheim had that range of theories to choose from in a case at the *Southwestern Bell Telephone Company* (Communications Workers of America, AFL–CIO).[2]

The contract here was quite unusual in that it listed five types of work that management had the right to contract out, provided no loss of employment would result. It was further agreed that there would be no strike or lockout over such permissible subcontracting.[3] However, janitorial service was not one of the five jobs listed. Did that mean that the company did not have the right to arrange for a firm specializing in building maintenance to perform that service in a new telephone building? Applying the rule that to include some matters in a series is to exclude others, the union argued that such subcontracting was a violation of the clause. On the other hand, was it a more correct interpretation to say that the contract was silent with respect to subcontracting? And in that event, did the silence speak for management under the residual rights theory, or did it mean that the action still had to be tested against implied limitations standards?

2. 44 AAA 16.
3. The text of the clause read: "The Union and the Company agree there shall be no lockout, stoppage, interruption, slowdown or failure to carry out assigned duties because of allocation of work to contractors as outlined below where such contracting of work to others does not involve the layoff or part-timing of regular employees: The work associated with aerial and underground outside plant comprised of conduit construction and rearrangements, tree cutting and trimming, drayage, and the following pole line construction work: 1. The staking of pole lines; 2. Unloading and hauling material; 3. Pole hole digging; 4. Pole placing on a new line or a line in a new location, consisting of more than ten poles, or extensive replacement on existing rural pole lines; 5. The placing before erection of the pole of brackets or one crossarm (excluding transposition brackets) on only those pole lines covered by paragraph 4."

Mr. Oppenheim supported the union's theory of the case part of the way, but he awarded in favor of management for the practical reasons that, as we have seen, arbitrators often find persuasive. The union was quite right, he said, in stating that the absence of a provision specifically barring subcontracting does not mean that contracting out was automatically permitted. However, the grievance was denied for the following four reasons:

1. "The contracting-out of house service work . . . was not for the purpose of destroying the plant unit";
2. "The contracting was in good faith and for sound reasons of efficiency and economy";
3. "Past practice showed that the company contracted out other types of work as well as house service work"; and
4. "The union [had] attempted repeatedly in negotiations to obtain restrictions upon the company's right to contract out" and had prevailed only with respect to the five types of work specifically mentioned in the clause barring strikes over subcontracting under the specified conditions.

## A Violation Despite Good Faith

Paradoxically, a case turning on a clause that was seemingly one of the least restrictive ended in an award upholding the grievance. This occurred at the *General Electric Company* (Allied Industrial Workers, AFL–CIO).[4]

The contract said only that "there shall be no farming or letting out or transfer of machinery or work for the purpose of curtailing employment in the plant." Interpreting this clause quite literally, management thought that subcontracting would always be permissible if no harm was *intended*. That employment opportunities might in fact be lost by the company's letting work out would not be controlling, as long as the motive was not to do that injury. And specifically in the instant case, management believed that the layoff of a plumber five months earlier could not be relevant to present plans for subcontracting maintenance work. Paul H. Sanders read the clause differently.

He could not believe, he said, that the sole objective of the subcon-

4. 6 AAA 1.

tracting clause was to curb "some sort of unreasonable vindictiveness" on the part of the company.

There is no indication that this was ever a problem or that there was any remote likelihood of the company acting on any such basis. The arbitrator believes that it is much more reasonable to assume that the section was designed to protect normal employment from being curtailed by the contracting process . . . The company need not expand employment opportunity, but it is prohibited from reducing or curtailing normal employment opportunity. Stated more precisely, this means at least that, with regard to work normally being performed in the plant currently, employment opportunity within the plant will be maintained at the normal complement per classification before any of such work is "farmed out."

Thus, the very fact that management's record was characterized by good faith helped to defeat its proposed interpretation of the subcontracting clause.

Somewhat similar was the situation at *Kyova Fiber Pipe Company* (Oil, Chemical and Atomic Workers International Union, AFL–CIO),[5] where management had what appeared to be very wide latitude in purchasing and subcontracting. To begin with, the management rights clause stated that "the right to select and procure raw materials, [and] semi-finished products at the company's discretion . . . shall not be considered to mean subcontracting." All the agreement said about subcontracting was that it would not be done "with the intent and/or purpose of displacing any bargaining unit employee from his normal and usual employment."

In practice, however, the mild restriction proved to be binding. After operating its own trucks for the delivery of pipe, management decided that it would be more economical to use common carriers, as it had done in the more distant past. This left a bargaining unit truck driver without work, and he was eventually transferred to a lower-rated job.

The attorney who presented the company's case before Samuel L. Chalfie described the economic circumstances that impelled the company first to discontinue using common carriers, and then change back again to that means of delivering its products. It seems that when the company was manufacturing clay and cast iron pipes, it had no dif-

5. 38 AAA 20.

ficulty getting good service from common carriers, because their rates, controlled by the Interstate Commerce Commission, were based upon a combination of weight of the load and distance traveled. But in 1957 management began producing fiber pipe, which was much lighter. From that point on, the common carriers became unreliable. The company's decision to operate its own trucks followed logically. But after a few years management was again able to arrange with common carriers who wanted the business of hauling lighter loads. In view of the economic advantage in using a commercial trucker, management argued, the contract with an outside trucking company was not improper. Furthermore, as the company's business was the manufacture of pipe, not trucking, this problem could not properly be regarded as one involving subcontracting at all.

Mr. Chalfie upheld the grievance. It was not controlling, he said, that the object of subcontracting was greater economy. The important fact was that the union contract gave bargaining unit members the right to do the work which was "reasonably embraced within the jobs of the unit."

## The Obligation to Discuss Subcontracting in Advance

When a contract requires only that management discuss its subcontracting plans with the union in advance, permitting the company to proceed with the subcontract even if the union objects, it would seem that the limitation is mild indeed. Nevertheless, back pay was awarded against management of the *Hudson Pulp and Paper Corporation* (International Association of Machinists, AFL–CIO)[6] by Gerald A. Barrett, who found evidence of a violation. There were, however, unusual details in this case.

The contract stated that the company was to discuss "each instance" of intended subcontracting with the union. Complying with this provision, management sought, and obtained, the union's acquiescence in subcontracting of maintenance painting of a new water-treating plant. As the work progressed, however, it became clear that the water level would not be low enough to permit completion of the work as originally contemplated. It seemed logical for management to direct the outside contractor to discontinue work on the original job and finish out his

6. 46 AAA 16.

contract with substitute work. It was this substitute work that became the basis of the union's grievance.

"The substitution of painting work not included in the original company notice requires a finding that the company, however inadvertently, violated the [contract] by proceeding with the outside contracting of painting work for which no notice had been furnished to the union," wrote Mr. Barrett. He added that it was irrelevant that the substituted work was of a similar nature, because the contract called for notice and consultation in each instance of proposed subcontracting. Nor did the fact that the company had the right, ultimately, to proceed with the subcontract, affect this ruling. "It is idle to speculate on the outcome if the company had furnished the required notice and opportunity for consultation."

This case was different from many of its kind in that the union was not only sustained in principle but in its request for a monetary remedy. As the contract gave the arbitrator the right "to order reimbursement of an individual for the loss of earnings resulting from a breach of the contract by the company," Mr. Barrett pointed out, back pay at over-time rates was an appropriate remedy. Moreover, Mr. Barrett explained, the parties had themselves resolved subcontracting grievances in the past by giving employees back wages under identical circumstances.[7]

7. For a case in which management's failure to discuss with the union in advance of subcontracting was held not to warrant monetary or other relief, see the award of Sidney Sugerman in *Alco Products* (United Steelworkers of America, AFL–CIO), 6 AAA 5. Believing that the contractual prohibition of subcontracting without prior discussions did not apply to removal of work to another plant of the company, management did not engage in such discussions. Mr. Sugerman said that was a violation of the agreement. However, the union's requested remedy, consisting of restoration of work, recall of laid-off employees and back pay, was denied. "Such relief might normally be appropriate for breach of an agreement not to subcontract at all, or without the union's prior consent," Mr. Sugerman wrote, "but not for breach of a duty to discuss that which the company is at all times empowered to do anyway . . . It is sufficient that the company be tagged with the finding of violation and a direction in effect to cease and desist from such violations in the future." The fact that the company may have "frankly conceded" breaches of the no-subcontracting-without-discussion provision in the past "circumstances which may or may not have involved vital business decisions" and that it "may have assumed the burden of a cash settlement for some loss of earnings and undertaken to keep the work

## Meeting the Subcontractor's Price

One reason for the discussion-in-advance rule is to give the union an opportunity, perhaps by relaxing work restrictions, to make it possible for the employer to avoid subcontracting. This reason is more often implied than stated. An exception was the case of the *Rockwell Standard Corporation* (United Automobile Workers, AFL–CIO),[8] where the company was required to "consult" with the union in advance of sending a "major job" out of the shop. The contract stated that through such consultation bargaining unit employees would have an opportunity to consider steps that might "keep the job in the plant." The final decision, after the union was consulted, was to rest with management.[9]

David P. Miller was called upon to decide, under that clause, whether the company had the right, after consulting the union, to contract with an outside company for replacement of electrical fixture parts and for the repair of a machine, both tasks being on the premises.

As the disputed work was clearly neither a "major job" nor a job "out of the shop," the case took on some of the characteristics of those that arise under contracts that are silent on subcontracting. Mr. Miller said that whether the company had the right to subcontract did not depend upon the subcontracting clause alone. For one thing, it made a difference whether subcontracting would have the effect of "arbitrarily or unreasonably diminishing" the scope of the bargaining unit. This conclusion, he said, was supported by the practice of the parties themselves. It appeared that they had "argued, denied or settled" subcontracting grievances in the past, not merely on the basis of the

in the unit" does not alter the decision as to the remedy for the violation in this case. For Mr. Sugerman's reasons for regarding transfer of work to another plant as a form of subcontracting, see Chapter 2, note 1.

8. 27 AAA 19.

9. The full text of the clause read: "When occasion arises which necessitates sending a major job, including maintenance and construction, out of the shop for reasons other than lack of suitable equipment in the plant to manufacture the product, the Company agrees to consult with the Union and afford them an opportunity to discuss the reasons for such action and the possibility of so reducing cost as to keep the job in the plant. The final decision, however, shall rest exclusively with the Management."

subcontracting clauses but also on the "applicability of other provisions of the collective agreement."

Furthermore, it made a difference whether the subcontracted work was to be performed away from the shop or on the premises. If the parties had intended no such distinction here, Mr. Miller wrote, they could not have used the phrase "out of the shop," nor would they have referred to "a major job" if they had intended to permit the company to have the final decision as to any type of subcontracting.

But in many ways, the more interesting question was whether subcontracting of work not usually performed by incentive-rated employees was permissible at all. The union's argument had been that only incentive employees are in a position to meet the competition of subcontractors. It was urged that the clause permitting the employer to make the final decision could not apply to hourly rated jobs at all.

The union was not upheld on this point. Mr. Miller said that, however plausible it seemed to permit subcontracting only of jobs paying "flexible" rates, that is not what the contract said.

Returning to the specific incidents of subcontracting, Mr. Miller found for the union on the question of electrical fixtures and for the company on the machine repair work. The disputed work on the fixtures required "minimal electrical skills and took a relatively short time," he said, and was like other "routine and recurrent maintenance jobs" which had always been done within the unit. "To sanction the farming out of such jobs would inevitably result in serious impairment of the bargaining unit," he concluded.[10]

The situation was different with respect to the machine repair job. Involved here was a newly purchased second-hand machine, which required overhaul. This subcontract did not "adversely affect the established scope" of the unit.

The job was unique, or at least an unusual one, for the company's employees. Concededly, its Machine Repairmen had not repaired a [machine] of this type before and were not familiar with some of its operating principles. To that extent, at least, it was not their regular work. The job was, rather, a peculiar and unexpected one of a non-recurrent nature. It did

10. However, here the union's request for a monetary remedy was denied because the company let the contract in the honest belief that a prior arbitration decision justified the interpretation and application the company gave to the grievance.

not fall into the category of the running maintenance repair work normally performed by them, and was one on which the company could not provide the necessary and usual supervisory direction.[11]

### Effect of Subcontracting on Employment

Perhaps the strongest kind of a promise to protect jobs of inside employees was that expressed at *R. D. Werner Company* (International Association of Machinists, AFL–CIO).[12] The contract said plainly:

The company hereby expresses its intent to retain absolutely all work of a machine shop nature in the company machine shop that it possibly can during periods when machinists of this department are on layoff from work.

In January 1961, circumstances developed in which the subcontracting of die manufacturing seemed clearly justified by economic considerations. Management believed that these considerations outweighed even the fact that eight machinists and a helper were then on layoff. The company's view, expressed in a formal brief, was that

. . . the company is required to retain all work of a machine shop nature in its machine shop, while any of its machinists are on layoff, unless it has good, sound and sufficient reasons not to do so. We further submit that, when the cost to the Company of having machine shop work done in its own shop is greater than that charged by an outside contractor, then the Company has good, sound and sufficient reasons for contracting out such work.

At the hearing itself, the company presented testimony about its "precarious financial position" that convinced Clair V. Duff that "further financial deterioration and losses might result in chaos." However, even admitting that an arbitrator must be "realistic" and must be aware that "cost-conscious reappraisal of operating expenses is necessary" if a company is to maintain its position in a competitive industry,

11. The employer's defense in the machine repair issue relied heavily on the cost-reduction provision of the subcontracting clause. Although this part of the grievance was denied, Mr. Miller did not acknowledge that the cost issue was a relevant defense. "I have already held that cost is neither the sole nor a controlling factor judging the propriety of a subcontract which does not fall under [the subcontracting clause]," he wrote.

12. 34 AAA 12.

Mr. Duff said he still had to decide in favor of the union. Not all methods of cost reduction are open to the company when it operates under a collective bargaining agreement, he explained. "The company's action in contracting-out the manufacture of the dies without the union's consent, is a clear violation of the reasonable meaning of [the quoted clause]." He concluded: "If a critical financial crisis arises in the Company and relief from contractual obligations is necessary for survival, such relief must come from negotiations of the parties and not from the mandate of an Arbitrator who has no authority to abrogate the clear and unambiguous contractual provision, which the company agreed to in this contract."

## The Coincidence of Subcontracting and Layoff

The almost inconspicuous three-letter word *now* proved to be a decisive factor at the *Cities Service Oil Company* (Oil, Chemical and Atomic Workers, AFL–CIO).[13] The contract stated: "The company will not contract-out work, which would result in the layoff of any regular employees of the company now performing such work. The company will inform the union concerning the circumstances which result in the company's contracting out work."

On October 16, 1959, the company notified eleven employees that they were to be laid off for lack of work in two weeks. An outside contractor was then doing construction work, and it was admitted that the employees who were scheduled for layoff could have performed construction tasks. But it was also conceded that they were not at that time doing such work.

Focusing attention on the language of the clause restricting management's right to contract out, Ronald W. Haughton said that for a violation to be found, the layoff "must be the *result* of outside contracting," and the work contracted out must have been performed by regular employees "at the time of the layoff." To uphold the union, he added, he would have to read language into the contract which the union had sought, unsuccessfully, to achieve.

While the arbitrator recognizes that the union's written request for [a new subcontracting clause] . . . was undoubtedly only one of many proposals

13. 19 AAA 1.

made by either party, the fact of its having been made, and not having been written into [the contract], must have meaning.

As we have seen, unions rely upon the recognition clause and "the contract as a whole" when prosecuting subcontracting grievances under agreements which are silent on contracting out. The contract in this case was not silent, but the language so clearly favored management that the union saw no advantage to itself in basing the case on the subcontracting clause alone. It was therefore urged upon Mr. Haughton that he judge the grievance in the light of the "totality-of-the-contract." Mr. Haughton declined to do so. That approach would be warranted, he wrote, "if the company deliberately were to undertake to vitiate the contract by subcontracting work . . ." Here, "a bad faith charge is not involved," and in the absence of such a charge, the language of the subcontracting clause "must be applied to each specific case of subcontracting."

## The Question of Ability

Whether bargaining unit employees are capable of doing work that management chooses to subcontract is always a question of fact, as well as of contract interpretation. That was the circumstance in three subcontracting cases heard by Lewis M. Gill. The first was at *Hofmann Industries, Incorporated* (United Steelworkers of America, AFL–CIO),[14] where management was under contractual obligation not to contract out work its own employees were "competent to do." Production workers had occasionally painted the building in the past, and some of these employees were on layoff at the time an outside firm was contracted with. Management, however, had decided some time earlier, after an employee had fallen from a scaffold, not to permit its own workers to do that kind of painting any longer. In other words, they were not "competent" to do the work.

Mr. Gill sustained the grievance. For one thing, he said, a single accident is not enough to support a conclusion that no employees in the unit are able to do the work; accidents may happen on a production line, too. Furthermore, he wrote, production workers who had been assigned to ground-level painting "from time to time" could have

14. 33 AAA 12.

done some of the work, while maintenance employees, who customarily work from ladders and scaffolds, could have been assigned the "high-level painting." Although it is possible that some of the employees on layoff would have been unable or unwilling to do the painting, "it is conceded that the company made no effort to canvass [them] and check their qualifications."[15]

The second subcontracting case that turned on the ability of bargaining unit employees to perform the work came about at the *Reading Tube Company* (United Steelworkers of America, AFL–CIO).[16] Management had farmed out to another company about one hundred hours of work on new parts, the old model of which had been produced within its own plant. The contract prohibited subcontracting of work "normally performed by employees in the bargaining unit" when such employees are "available and competent" to do the work. Giving the contract the most literal interpretation possible, the employer thought that a new model was one which, by definition, had not been worked on by the employees. Mr. Gill interpreted the contract differently:

> The plant machinists had for years made the old-style studs, and one of the machinists had in fact been given an award by the company for working up an experimental model of the new-type, two-piece stud. I think it would be highly unrealistic to say that this was not "work normally performed by employees in the bargaining unit" merely because the design of the stud had been changed . . . The work *could* have been done in the plant, albeit not so economically as on the outside.

In the third of Mr. Gill's ability-and-subcontracting cases, management was sustained, but not without an expression of mild doubt. The case was that of the *Novo Industrial Corporation* (International Union of Electrical, Radio and Machine Workers, AFL–CIO).[17] The problem here, from management's point of view, was that its offices and the public lobby of the building were not being properly cared for

15. Finding an appropriate remedy for the company's violation presented a special problem, because Mr. Gill could not know which employees on layoff could have done "low level painting," and which could have worked from scaffolds. But in view of what he said was a "generally mature and responsible relationship" of the parties, he left it to them to determine who were the four senior laid-off employees who had the ability for the available work. He directed that each of the employees so designated be given three weeks' pay.

16. 23 AAA 11.

17. 26 AAA 17.

by the bargaining unit employee who had been assigned to nighttime cleaning. Finally, an outside firm was engaged to do the work, and the janitor was transferred to the day shift, where he replaced the daytime janitor. The latter was laid off, recalled to another job, and still later laid off again.

The contractual basis of the company's action was disputed by the union. The agreement had barred subcontracting of work when "competitive conditions [are] equal," and when no layoffs would result. The doubt in Mr. Gill's mind was whether dissatisfaction with the state of cleanliness could not have been solved by assigning a more competent employee to the job. But he concluded that "the company's evident frustration in its efforts to keep the offices and lobby clean" was "not without some relevance in the case." Taking into account the employer's good-faith motive, and the rather special meaning the parties had long given to the contractual phrase "competitive conditions being reasonably equal," he denied the grievance. Mr. Gill stated three points as the basis for his decision: "(a) a genuine saving in overall cost and efficiency of operation is involved, (b) the savings in cost are not accomplished by merely getting the work done at rates of pay lower than those in the contract, and (c) there is no indication of any foot-in-the-door approach to a decimation of the bargaining unit."

## Overtime as an Alternative to Subcontracting

Whether bargaining unit employees are able to do the contracted out work is often a matter not only of ability, but of time—and overtime. This was an issue in a case at *Alan Wood Steel Company* (United Steelworkers of America, AFL–CIO),[18] which was decided by Israel Ben Scheiber. The parties stipulated this to be the question for the arbitrator to answer:

On the facts presented and on the past practice, was the contracting-out of the installation of a conveyor by the company a violation of the contract in effect between the parties? If so, what shall the remedy be?

One of the facts presented was the collective bargaining agreement, which stated that "employees will not be deprived of work normally performed by them and for which the equipment and manpower are

18. 11 AAA 11.

available." In defending the subcontract, the employer had argued that he would have had to "rob" crews doing other work in order to install the work with his own employees. Furthermore, he said, the subcontracting involved a "package deal" with an engineering firm for both the purchase and installation of the conveyor system. Mr. Scheiber upheld the grievance on these facts:

1. There was uncontradicted testimony that, for at least thirteen years, "no outside contractor had ever been brought in to build a conveyor," this work always having been done by members of the bargaining unit.

2. A member of the bargaining unit who had done conveyor work in the past was on layoff and looking for work at the time the conveyor was erected by the outside firm.

3. Although other bargaining unit employees who could have worked on the conveyor were employed as laborers (at millwright pay), they were given no overtime, while the contractor's employees worked on Saturdays and on daily overtime.

4. "It was admitted that no emergency existed" and that bargaining unit employees could have erected the conveyor.

The union also won its requested monetary remedy, not a particularly costly one to the company in this case. "The four senior men . . . who suffered because of such violation are entitled to be paid the difference between the pay of the job 14 classification in the master agreement and what they actually received in not being allowed to work for four days on this job."[19]

19. As indicated, the financial consequences to the company for its violation of the contract were slight. One can never be certain whether an arbitrator would have made a different selection from among the available rules of contract interpretation so as to reach a different conclusion, if upholding the grievance might result in a remedy so harsh as to be destructive. Of interest in this connection was an award of Saul Wallen for *Waterbury Companies, Incorporated* (United Automobile Workers, AFL–CIO), 2 AAA 14. The employer, who operated a small tool and die jobbing shop, was under contractual obligations not to subcontract when any worker in a skilled trade was on less than a forty-hour week. Late in March 1958, while his own staff was fully employed, he let a contract for dies to another shop. A week later, however, seventeen of his own employees were laid off for lack of work. The union demanded that the subcontract be cancelled. Mr. Wallen acknowledged that the contract could be

Management of the *Lee Rubber and Tire Company* (United Rubber, Cork, Linoleum and Plastic Workers of America, AFL–CIO)[20] also discovered that it was a violation to subcontract work with the object of avoiding what was thought to be excessive overtime. Under the special circumstances of the case, Saul Wallen said it would not have been unreasonable for the company to let its employees work on Sundays, as well as Saturdays.

The contract was quite restrictive on the matter of subcontracting. Only when "lack of skills or equipment" made it impossible to do a piece of work with inside employees, or when "the nature of the work or time considerations makes it impractical" to favor bargaining unit employees, did the company have the right to contract out. It happened that some machine and equipment repairs were needed in May 1960, and the employees who could have done the work were already getting overtime. The practical solution seemed to be to call in an outside firm to do the work within what management said was a close time schedule.

Analyzing the testimony, Mr. Wallen said that the time schedule turned out to be nothing more than "a desire of management to avoid Sunday work for bargaining unit people." A controlling fact in the decision was the admission that it was not at all unusual for maintenance crews to work "seven days and many more than eight hours per day" during periods of shutdown for major repairs.

Mr. Wallen conceded that there might be occasions when bargaining

---

construed as the union urged, but he thought the consequences would be so harsh that only explicit language would justify it. He wrote: "Had the parties intended to provide for the drastic step of recalling work already let on contract as an alternative to a layoff from the skilled trades group, they would almost certainly have so stated. For the practical burdens of such a step in terms of cost, of interference with projected completion dates and of efficiency would have been apparent. While the language of Appendix V Section 7 might possibly be construed to impose such a requirement, I find that the construction urged by the Company is the more logical on the basis of the language employed and of the realities of industrial life." For a case in which a harsh remedy was thought not warranted merely for an employer's failure to discuss plans for subcontracting with the union, see the *Alco Products* case (note 7, this chapter). On the other hand, for a case in which a violation on the part of the company was found despite a showing of a "precarious" financial position, see the *R. D. Werner* case (note 12, this chapter).

20. 25 AAA 17.

unit employees would be so "deeply involved in routine tasks" as not to be available for "one-shot" millwright jobs. But this was not the case here, because it would have been "wholly reasonable" to have the millwrights and welders work seven days a week on the subcontracted job.[21]

### Protecting Union Standards

Fear that subcontracting to cut-rate firms might cause wages and working conditions within the plant to deteriorate is, of course, inherent in every case. Occasionally, however, labor representatives are concerned not only with union standards in the primary establishment, but with union conditions elsewhere. This is particularly true in industries and among unions where "hot cargoes" and secondary boycotts are an issue. A case in point was the *Narragansett Brewing Company* (International Union of United Brewery, Flour, Cereal, Soft Drink and Distillery Workers of America, AFL–CIO).[22] A contract clause read:

Only Union-made malt shall be used if the same is obtainable. All other Union-made material and supplies shall be given preference provided price, quality, and general conditions are equal.

The facts of the case were not in dispute. When the company changed from wooden cases to returnable fiber cartons in 1950, employees of the company were required to prestitch only the small number of cartons needed for replacement. Most of the cartons were shipped flat to a supplier of glass containers, who stitched them as needed. This procedure continued until early in 1960, when competition forced Narragansett Brewing to switch to forty-bottle cartons, instead of the thirty-six-bottle carton which had, until that time, been standard. To prevent the loss of time involved in shipping cartons from the supplier to the glass company and then back to the brewery,

21. For other cases in which arbitrators ruled that subcontracting was permissible to avoid "overtime on overtime," see the *Celanese* cases, Chapter 2, notes 7 and 8. A significant difference between this case and the others, however, was that the contract at the Celanese Corporation was silent on the matter of subcontracting, while this contained a strong limitation on managerial rights to let others do bargaining unit work.

22. 28 AAA 11.

management decided to let the supplier of cartons deliver them directly to the brewery in the prestitched form. As the supplier of cartons was known to operate a union shop, there did not appear to be any problem.

It was discovered only later that the fiber carton supplier had a wholly owned subsidiary, which was non-union, and that it was the non-union shop that produced the cartons. At first, a union representative protested only that non-union work was involved; later, however, the grievance was broadened to include the claim that all prestitching be done by bargaining unit employees. This is the issue that came before James J. Healy.

Putting aside the non-union matter for the moment and dealing only with subcontracting in general, Mr. Healy said that the union had not demonstrated that prestitching of cartons was peculiarly bargaining unit work. He added that not even the employer's statement that he would favor the bargaining unit if he could altered that fact.

One of the "regular and customary functions of management" has been the arrangement to have most of the stitching of cartons (other than for replacement) done outside the plant . . . The aggrieved have not demonstrated that this was work which traditionally belonged to them. The company statement that had there been enough time it would have tried to have had this work done within the plant cannot be held as an admission that the work "belonged" to [bargaining unit] employees. This was more in the nature of a good-faith acknowledgment that wherever reasonably possible it would give preference to its own people.

As to accepting supplies manufactured by non-union workers, Mr. Healy said the company was deserving only of "a mild rebuke."

The company should make a reasonable investigation to insure that materials will be union-made and then turn to non-union made sources only if price, quality and general conditions are not equal. In the present case, the arbitrator is entirely satisfied that the company believed the work would be union-made . . . But the case should serve as a *caveat* to the company that a condition antecedent to the judgment as to equality among the listed factors is a more careful determination of who is going to do the work. Its remissness in this case does not constitute a violation of contract and to the extent it might be construed as a technical violation, a warning for the future is adequate.

# 4

# EROSION OF THE BARGAINING UNIT

"Jobs, like technological processes, cannot remain static in an industrial society. . . . The contract provides protection for the employees in a variety of circumstances. But it cannot and does not undertake to stop the continuous development of new methods in . . . continuously developing industry."

—HARRY SHULMAN

The separation of work from a bargaining unit takes many forms. Most dramatic of course are subcontracting and the removal of machinery from the plant. In such cases, employees may believe they are the victims not so much of blind, impersonal economic forces, as of a deliberate, perhaps vindictive, policy of management. But no less important from a long-range point of view is the slow, often almost imperceptible, erosion of jobs that occurs in the wake of improved technology. As products and methods of production change, as plants are modernized, and as the flow of work is rationalized, some jobs become more complicated, others become less so, still other jobs disappear, and new ones are created.

Every change of this kind threatens, or at least calls into question, the line drawn by union contract negotiators between one bargaining unit and another, or between a bargaining unit and the non-unit sector of the employer's work force. Give a group leader just a little more authority, and he may be transformed into a foreman. Permit an inspector to exercise more discretion over quality control functions, and a question might be raised as to whether he has not become a salaried employee who, while not quite a supervisor, is not exactly a bargaining unit employee either. Even expediters and factory clerical workers may be redesignated as non-unit employees, if the content of their job changes and if the union does not resist the loss of jobs.

### Quality Control and Inspection

Quality control functions are often on the borderline separating bargaining unit jobs from managerial positions. Even small improvements in the techniques of discovering and correcting flaws in work call into question established practices. A case at *Cadillac Malleable Iron Company* (United Automobile Workers, AFL–CIO)[1] was an example.

The disputed task in this case consisted of selecting random samples of castings, carrying them to a shot-blasting machine, and cleaning them so that flaws could be detected while iron was still being poured. If this were not done, defects would, of course, not be corrected early enough, and much spoilage would result. The practice had been for bargaining unit employees to select samples and clean them, leaving it to supervision to determine whether quality standards were met. There was no doubt that the rank-and-file employees had adequately performed the manual tasks assigned to them, but the old procedures caused the corrective action, when necessary, to be delayed. Finally, management decided to take the whole quality-sampling operation away from the unit and transfer all tasks, manual, visual, and corrective, to supervision.

Louis A. Crane denied the grievance. "Management has the right to check on work being performed by bargaining unit employees," he wrote. "This is an essential part of the management function. Supervisors are not required to depend entirely upon reports from bargaining unit employees to determine the quality of work performed. They may look for themselves. Of necessity, there is some overlap between supervisory and inspection functions." Mr. Crane thought it worth noting

1. 35 AAA 15.

that after finding a sample acceptable, the castings were returned to the floor so that they might be "picked up again and cleaned by bargaining unit employees along with the rest of the run." He concluded that the disputed work had never been done in its entirety by bargaining unit employees, and that "fragmentation of the function" was not practical. "In short, the disputed work is not bargaining unit work. It is part of the supervisory function and may therefore be performed by supervisory employees."

Quite similar in effect was Milton Rubin's decision in *Murray Manufacturing Corporation* (United Automobile Workers, AFL–CIO).[2] In October 1961 the company, which manufactures some seven hundred different items, decided to re-examine its quality control program. It therefore embarked on an "audit," which consisted of a random spot-checking of products already packaged for shipment. This was done by foremen, and brought a protest by bargaining unit inspectors who thought that because they examined products at various stages of the production line, this audit inspection should also have been assigned to them.

Unlike some cases of this kind, management did not try to justify the disputed work assignment by alleging that the inspectors were inefficient. The purpose of the audit was not to check up on bargaining unit employees, it was explained, but rather to see whether established procedures of quality control were adequate.

Commenting on the union's principal argument that the function of supervision is to oversee the work of unit employees, not to do the work themselves, Mr. Rubin wrote:

This principle would be quite correct and could be applied here, if the audit's purpose was to supplement the regular inspection procedure. Then supervision would be performing work manifestly assignable to bargaining unit employees. But I am not convinced that the supervisors' auditing inspection was inspectors' work. Instead, the evidence is more persuasive that the audit, its method and purpose was not a typical or customary inspection procedure included in the bargaining unit.

As did Louis A. Crane in the *Cadillac Malleable Iron Company* case, Mr. Rubin thought it worth noting that opened packages were returned to bargaining unit employees for repackaging, and defective

2. 45 AAA 5.

items were also sent back for repair by rank-and-file workers. Moreover, he observed that although the contract forbade foremen to do bargaining unit work, it specifically permitted work for "the development of new procedures" and "the testing of methods to determine efficiency." The quality audit work seemed clearly sanctioned by this provision.

## Transfer of Group Leadership Tasks to Supervision

The conclusion that managerial work can be recaptured for the non-unit sector was also reached by Peter Seitz in *Robertshaw-Fulton Controls Company* (United Automobile Workers, AFL–CIO).[3] He found it necessary, however, to add that if the employees in the unit who did the managerial work were to be denied the extra pay that goes with group leadership, the removal of managerial tasks must be real and complete, not merely a change of duties on paper.

For a number of years, four employees classified as inspectors assigned operators to their tasks, instructed other inspectors, took responsibility for quality control, and made forecasts of shipments to customers. They were called group leaders and were paid ten cents more per hour than other inspectors. Although their status was recognized in the wage schedule of the union contract, the position of group leader was not listed as a "job" in the company's manual (incorporated by reference in the agreement). In June 1961 management decided, for reasons of better quality control, to discontinue the group leader status of those four employees. They were declared to be inspectors and paid accordingly. At the same time, supervisors, who were not in the bargaining unit, were given the tasks of directing other employees.

The former group leaders protested on two grounds. First, they said, as long as *someone* in the shop was performing tasks that had once been theirs, group leadership status could not be abolished. Furthermore, they were still expected to do some of the work that was more characteristic of group leaders than of ordinary inspectors.

Mr. Seitz upheld the company on the first point, and the union on the second. As the work that group leaders had been expected to do in the past was managerial in nature, he said, there was nothing in the contract to prevent the company from "recapturing" it.

3. 43 AAA 4.

There is no indication in this agreement of a complete and permanent alienation of those functions which are typically managerial in nature ... The provisions in the group leaders' scope ... given a normal reading and without undue stress upon one word or another wrenched from the context, [must] be interpreted as the company argues, rather than the union. That is to say, so long as the company sees fit to require employees to perform pursuant to that "scope", they shall be recognized as group leaders and be compensated accordingly. That authority, however, which has the power to confer group leadership when it sees fit to do so, also has the power to cancel it when it sees fit to do so. Group leadership is not a "job" and group leader is not a job title in the same way as the job titles set forth in Appendix B. It is not a job classification for which there is a job description. It is a special status under which an employee in the bargaining unit takes on some managerial responsibilities, *when the company desires him to do so,* in return for which he gets extra pay.

However, on hearing testimony as to what the former group leaders were doing after their demotion, Mr. Seitz became convinced that the company had not actually abolished group leadership. It seems that the grievants were still doing everything they had done before except assigning tasks to other employees. The reason may be, he said, that management had never taken the trouble to differentiate between group leaders and the top-rated inspectors. In any event, the demotion of the grievants became "a matter of paper forms and words rather than a thing of substance."

In short, it is not enough, *in light of the usages of the past,* for the company to urge the *form* of the change when it eliminates group leadership; it must show that there is a substantive difference in the character of the duties to be performed.

### Transfer of Inspection Work to Foremen

In the case above, as we have seen, the problem was the transfer of group leadership tasks to supervisors and the demotion of group leaders to inspectors. At *Hofmann Industries, Incorporated* (United Steelworkers of America, AFL–CIO),[4] the problem was the abolition of the inspector classification altogether and the transfer of those duties to foremen.

The circumstances were interesting. For a long time, the company

4. 29 AAA 4.

had what management called an "extremely high loss experience" with improperly manufactured parts. One of the reasons for this was that bargaining unit inspectors, who were assigned to different departments and shifts, were inadequately supervised. Some inspection had always been done by foremen, but management finally concluded that it was no longer "economically practical" to let bargaining unit employees do any inspection work at all. Instead, the employer set out to increase "supervisory coverage" by letting foremen perform the "corrective function in the course of inspecting output on the spot." The new arrangement, management believed, would encourage machine operators to check their own work more diligently, something that bargaining unit inspectors had apparently been unable to accomplish.

Eli Rock upheld the union, chiefly on the basis of the contract which, unlike the contract in the *Robertshaw-Fulton Controls* case, contained strong language protecting existing job classifications.[5] He wrote:

Had there been a relatively minor change here in the amount of inspection work done by the supervisors, or had the inspectors not been eliminated, the issue may have been different. The fact is, however, that four full-time inspectors have been removed, and the clear impression left by the evidence is that the work they formerly did is still being performed. . . . It is difficult for me to find that so radical a change in the arrangement of the work, and under which a task formerly at most a shared one between unit and non-unit people becomes totally non-unit, was permitted under the quite clear language and intent of the contract on this subject.[6]

5. The text of the two clauses relied upon by the union read: "Changes in title or methods of pay of positions included in the Bargaining Unit shall not be made for the purpose of eliminating said positions from the Bargaining Unit." And, "Persons not included in the Bargaining Unit covered by this Agreement shall not be permitted to perform any work consistently performed by the employees within the Bargaining Unit except in cases of emergency or extenuating circumstances such as to instruct employees, correct operating difficulties or take the place of absent employees until other maintenance or production employees can be secured."

6. The remedy for this violation—that is, telling the employer what he must do to bring himself into compliance with the contract and the award—presented Mr. Rock with what he said was a "rather complicated" problem. The difficulty was that management had the right to abolish the jobs of inspectors if it wanted no more inspection work done. The arbitrator could therefore not

## Testing

Like controlling quality or inspecting, testing is an activity that might be within or without the bargaining unit, depending upon the purpose for which it is done and the customs that have evolved within the establishment. Two separate grievances at *Ex-Cell-O Corporation* (United Automobile Workers, AFL–CIO),[7] decided in the same arbitration case by Richard Mittenthal, illustrate this point.

The company manufactured, among other things, jet engine fuel nozzles that had to meet rigid tests before they could be shipped to the customer. The design and development of these parts were the responsibility of engineers, who were not in the bargaining unit. After experimental models met specifications, all nozzles were assembled within the unit and tested by a classification of nozzle test men, who were bargaining unit employees.[8]

Late in 1959 one of Ex-Cell-O's customers reported that certain faults were appearing in the fuel nozzles. At first the nozzle was sent to an independent testing laboratory, but the report was inconclusive.

---

simply direct the company to reinstate the inspector jobs and to permit foremen to do only so much inspection work as they had done in the past. As the parties had not discussed the remedy problem themselves, he thought the only practical course would be to refer the matter to them, with the understanding that if they should not be able to resolve the problem, "either party will have the right to refer such unresolved questions back to arbitration." It appears that the parties were able to decide how to implement the award, for the matter did not go to arbitration again.

7. 36 AAA 4.

8. The procedures for testing were of some interest in the case. The arbitrator described them as follows: "A Nozzle Test man performs his work on one of nine test stands in the plant. He places a nozzle in the stand and starts up the equipment so that fuel automatically flows through the nozzle. Then, he checks to see whether the flow angle is correct, whether streakers are forming, and whether the nozzle is swaying. And by reading the flow raters on the face of the test stand, he can quickly determine whether the nozzle's flow characteristics meet specifications. The cycle time for a production test is approximately two minutes. If the nozzle passes these tests, it is ready to be shipped to the customer. If the nozzle does not pass, the Nozzle Test man diagnoses the problem (burrs, dirt, etc.), repairs or cleans the nozzle, and retests it. The Nozzle Test man performs this work not only on production nozzles but on experimental or developmental nozzles as well."

It became evident that a long-term test program would have to be undertaken within the plant. Management thereupon used some of the regular testing equipment and purchased other parts for a special testing stand, called a "hot fuel rig." This work was done by non-unit engineers, the company believing that only in this way could those who were responsible for the design of equipment see how it functioned under operating conditions.

This was the subject of the union's first grievance, which stated:

Non-bargaining unit personnel doing bargaining unit work. . . .

Non-bargaining unit personnel are conducting a nozzle erosion test on an improvised Test Stand and on Test Stand No. X-4, which should be performed by a Nozzle Test Stand Operator. This erosion test may be an Engineering requirement, but the operating of the Test Stand should be performed by Bargaining unit personnel.

Disposition Requested: That the Company stop the Engineers from running the Test Stands and that they pay the most senior Nozzle Test Oper. all lost wages as a result of this operation.

The union did not object to engineers participating in the testing procedures altogether. It was conceded, for instance, that the non-bargaining unit employees may determine test conditions and evaluate results. But the actual operation of the equipment—that is, putting the nozzle in a holder, starting the equipment, and observing it from time to time—was bargaining unit work, the union representative insisted. The union also relied heavily on the fact that nozzle testing, even on experimental or developmental nozzles, had always been done either by nozzle test men or toolmakers, classifications which were in the unit. The company conceded that insofar as the engineers tested nozzles on the conventional testing equipment ("test stand X-4," referred to in the union's grievance), there was a violation. But insofar as operation of special testing equipment was concerned, it was argued, the work was properly performed by engineers.

The second grievance was somewhat related to the first. It involved the testing of test equipment components. As engineers who had designed the fuel control units also created the apparatus for testing them on simulated flight conditions, it seemed logical to management that pumps, valves, filters and regulators, which were purchased as components of the testing equipment, should themselves be tested by engineers. It appeared from the evidence presented at the hearing that this kind of testing had been done by bargaining unit employees until about 1957, and that for the few following years, both engineers and bargaining unit employees had done this work. But by 1959 only engineers were testing components.

## The Object of Testing

In deciding these two issues, Mr. Mittenthal found some merit in each party's views. Engineers had the right to perform testing, he wrote, where the object was "to discover some unknown condition" that caused malfunction, and where the equipment used did not resemble equipment used by bargaining unit employees. Thus, the principal claim of the union in the first grievance was rejected. The company was not obliged to have the "hot fuel rig" operated by bargaining unit members. However, it was a violation, as the company itself conceded, to permit engineers to operate "test stand X-4," which was equipment customarily operated by bargaining unit members. Mr. Mittenthal wrote:

The Agreement contains a Job Classification and Rate Schedule which includes the Nozzle Assembly & Test classification. The Union relies heavily upon the fact that all nozzle testing, even on experimental or developmental nozzles, had been done prior to this dispute by bargaining unit employees, either Nozzle Test men or Toolmakers. But the tests they perform are *entirely different* from the protested tests the engineers performed. *First,* the aggrieved's tests involve a routine determination of a nozzle's flow characteristics to see whether its performance meets specifications. The engineers' tests involved an attempt to discover some unknown condition which had caused the nozzles to erode. Their interest was not in flow characteristics but rather in finding that combination of heat and pressure which would produce erosion. Their tests could hardly be considered routine inasmuch as each test was conducted under a different set of conditions. *Second,* the aggrieved utilize test stands for their work. The Engineers utilized a "hot fuel rig." The latter device, like any piece of equipment designed to hold a part and subject it to a test, might broadly be characterized as a test stand. But it bears little similarity to the test stands which the Nozzle Test men use in their work. Indeed, the tests these men make could not be done on the "hot fuel rig." The "rig" was not built to check the nozzle's performance against set specifications.

It was specially built for purposes of experimentation, that is, to find the cause of nozzle erosion.

It is clear therefore that past practice with respect to nozzle testing has no relevancy here. The nozzle erosion tests were *something new*, something the company had never done before. These tests, unlike the standard flow characteristics test, involved constantly changing temperatures or pressures. They were plainly part of an Engineering *research program*. And the research was conducted on a specially designed piece of equipment which resembles the test stands in neither form nor function. The Nozzle Test men and Toolmakers do run test equipment. But this does not mean that Engineers are precluded in any and all circumstances from running test equipment. I find, on the basis of the evidence before me in this case, that the disputed work was outside the scope of the bargaining unit.

On the other hand, the union was sustained on the second grievance, chiefly on the history of testing in the plant. The fact, asserted by the employer, that components were tested on special equipment did not defeat the union's case here, because the equipment performed the same function as that used by bargaining unit employees. Furthermore, although the company had stated that there were business reasons for letting engineers test components, "little meaningful information" to support that assertion was put before the arbitrator. "Because the company has shown no compelling reason for the assignment of bargaining unit work to engineers, I have no choice but to grant the grievance," he concluded.

## Experimental Engineering Work

Similar issues arose at *Picker X-Ray Corporation* (International Brotherhood of Electrical Workers, AFL–CIO).[9] In the summer of 1961, the Engineering Department undertook development of a new X-ray machine cable that would be more flexible and operate at higher voltages. Ten experimental cables were produced by bargaining unit employees under the supervision of an engineer, who then took them to the laboratory for examination. Finding defects, he requisitioned additional parts and experimented with them until he overcame the difficulty. In the process, he produced twelve usable cables, according to the union; the company said only eight cables were manu-

9. 47 AAA 4.

factured. In any event, it was this production that became the occasion for the union's grievance.

The union called attention to a job description, contained in the contract, that referred to the bargaining unit job of "cable fabricator" as involving the production of cables "of complex design," under the direction of engineers, or with their "cooperation." The union had no objection to the engineer cooperating in the production, but they did not believe he had the right to fabricate work himself.

Maurice E. Nichols decided the case in favor of the company on practical grounds, rather than as a matter of contract interpretation. As he saw it, the engineer had worked "in the interest of insuring a prompt and complete solution to the problem." And in doing so, he "served to release production of the new cable at an earlier date, thereby benefiting production employees."

It seemed to Mr. Nichols that the chief difficulty was that employees who had always worked closely with engineers suddenly found a wall of secrecy blocking their view of what was going on. They were "no longer a part of the team that was building these cables," and they did not know why. Moreover, suspicion was heightened by the company's attempt, shortly before this incident, to negotiate a change in the agreement that would give engineers more freedom to do bargaining unit work. When the union steward, a grievant in this case, filed his protest, the company's answer "was terse to the point of being abrupt." Mr. Nichols concluded: "It is the opinion of the Board [of Arbitration] that, had the company taken a little more pains in choosing words to answer the grievance and in providing an explanation of its problem to the grievants, this issue might not have reached such serious proportions."[10]

### Special-handling Work

For about six years, any interest the union at the *Marco Electric Manufacturing Company* (United Steelworkers of America, AFL–CIO)[11] may have had in certain motor-rebuilding work that was being

10. For another case in which management was chided for contributing toward the magnification of a grievance by inadequate communication with the union, see *National Telefilm Associates,* discussed later in this chapter.

11. 29 AAA 15.

performed by non-unit laboratory technicians, lay dormant. But in November 1960, because unit employees were on layoff, it decided to "sleep on its rights" no longer. A grievance was filed demanding that this work be given only to unit employees.

Involved in this case was not the run-of-the-mill production work, but the building of a relatively few motors to replace others made by production workers at an earlier date. The company had a plausible reason for permitting laboratory personnel to do this work. The task was complex. The only employees in the unit who were able to assemble an entire motor were generally busy with other work. It was therefore more economical to let non-unit personnel do this work. Furthermore, management said, after disclaiming interest in this work for six years, the union had no standing to change the "past practice."

G. Allan Dash, Jr., ruled that the six-year practice could not overcome the clear language of the contract, once the union decided no longer to tolerate that practice. The fact that the union had "slept on its rights," he said, might affect the kind of relief an arbitrator would award, but it would "not usually nullify those rights or cause the arbitrator to rule that they have been negated through disuse."[12]

Finally, Mr. Dash wrote, the lower cost of production under the employer's preferred way of building replacement motors was not controlling.

The test of costs of production is not a criterion under the agreement for determining whether the company is required to have productive work performed by bargaining unit personnel. If such a test were determinative on this point, the company could readily set up a department with different productive techniques and a very low wage scale in which it might well produce some of its motors at much lower costs than it is presently able to do. Obviously, no such arrangement is anticipated under the agreement and no such arrangement can be read into it by the arbitrator through any strained interpretation of a provision thereof.

12. Whether a practice inconsistent with the contract constituted a waiver of a contractual right arises frequently in arbitration. See, for example, *Pittsburgh Metallurgical Company* (United Automobile Workers, AFL–CIO), 6 AAA 6, discussed in Chapter 6, in which an arbitrator ruled that the failure of a company to require employees to perform a task listed in the job description did not constitute a waiver of its right to do so in the future. See also the comment of Harry Shulman, in *Ford Motor Company* (United Automobile Workers, AFL–CIO), 19 LA 237, in Chapter 6.

In keeping with his judgment that the past practice could affect the remedy, but not the finding of a violation as such, Mr. Dash declined to award back pay to an employee for time he was on layoff while laboratory technicians were working. As the union had given the company reason to believe it was not violating the contract, monetary relief would not be equitable, he said.

## Factory Clerical and Service Jobs

The line between managerial positions and bargaining unit jobs is dictated by law only to the extent that the National Labor Relations Board will not certify units which include both rank-and-file workers and guards or foremen. Beyond that, the scope of the bargaining unit —its inclusions and exclusions—is a matter of the judgment of negotiators and the power one may have to impose his will on the other. It may not be sufficient, therefore, for an employer who wants to redesignate as managerial a bargaining unit job during the life of a contract to show that the job duties resemble those that are traditionally outside bargaining units and that more logically belong in the non-unit sector.

A case in point was that of the *Rockwell Standard Corporation* (United Steelworkers of America, AFL–CIO).[13] One of the bargaining unit employees, classified as an adjustment and correspondence clerk, was promoted to chief of the accounts receivable department, a job excluded from the bargaining unit. In this capacity, he continued to perform a substantial part of the job he held in the past. The union's position was that the adjustment and correspondence work could not go with the man; it had to remain in the bargaining unit for a unit employee to perform, if anyone was to do it at all. The company's answer to the grievance was that the disputed tasks always were supervisory in nature and that the promotion restored logic to work relationships.

Donald A. Crawford's award upheld the union completely:

Even on the basis of its premise that the Adjustment and Correspondence Clerk Job is supervisory, the company cannot successfully contend that it could not have bargained away its contractual right under Article

13. 13 AAA 12.

II to exclude this supervisory job, and that it can therefore now unilaterally remove the job from the bargaining unit to correct an alleged error of judgment. The classification in question was established as a bargaining unit job in 1954 and remained so after the renewal of the contract in 1956. Thus the job has been a matter for collective bargaining by the parties, and the company has in fact given up its right to remove the job from the bargaining unit unilaterally. Any problem the company may now have as a result of the job being in the bargaining unit is a matter for discussion and resolution by the parties—especially since the current contract is about to expire.

## Sharing of Record-keeping Tasks

In the *Rockwell Standard* case, the disputed clerical work had been done exclusively within the bargaining unit for a long time. At the *Carlyle Tile Company* (United Stone and Allied Products Workers of America, AFL–CIO),[14] the clerical work had always been shared to a certain extent between foremen and bargaining unit employees. That accounted for a conclusion by Bert L. Luskin different from the one reached by Mr. Crawford.

Mr. Luskin said the company had the right, after instituting a second shift, to let the foreman in charge keep production records, even though the day-shift records were kept by head kiln firemen, who were within the bargaining unit. "Clerical and record-keeping functions are neither exclusive to unit employees nor to foremen or non-unit salaried employees," he wrote.

The fact that the company in some instances assigns duties to unit employees which would be considered supervisory in nature does not, in and of itself, create a condition where similar functions and duties may not thereafter be performed by non-unit employees. . . . The evidence clearly indicates that record-keeping functions similar to those performed by kiln firemen on the first shift were performed by foremen in other departments. The company would have the right to assign certain incidental record-keeping functions to the foreman of a department, rather than to a kiln fireman whose normal duties would be completely unrelated to the record-keeping functions incident to the operation of the fettling crews.

When certain work is neither the exclusive prerogative of unit or non-unit employees, as in the *Rockwell Standard* case, a shift in the volume of that work from the former to the latter is likely to produce

14. 30 AAA 16.

grievances. That is what happened at *The Budd Company* (Independent Workers Union of the Budd Company).[15] The contract said that supervisors would not perform work "regularly performed by non-Supervisory employees" except for instructing new employees or when the work requires a supervisor's "special skills." In the past, foremen had occasionally dispensed supplies, a task principally performed by hourly rated workers. But in May 1958 a new foreman assigned to a department began making this task principally his. This, said Lewis M. Gill, was a contract violation:

> The evidence establishes that the *bulk* of the work *was* performed by the office clerk in the bargaining unit. . . . If the foreman had merely continued to do this work to the same degree that foremen had done it in the past, I think no violation would be established. By the same token, I think there *is* a violation to the extent that the foreman's share of this work has been expanded, and the bargaining unit employees' share of it has diminished.

This brought Mr. Gill to the "rather elusive" question of an appropriate remedy. The union had asked for eighty hours' pay to a factory clerk, then on layoff. This figure was arrived at by estimating that the foreman had spent about one hour a day at the work in question, or five hours per week multiplied by the sixteen weeks which had elapsed since the most recent layoff. The arbitrator said this estimate was "about right," as far as the time spent by the foreman dispensing materials was concerned. The difficulty was, however, that only part of this time represented an expansion of the customary amount of such work done by a foreman:

> No exact calculation is possible here, but my best estimate is that if 80 hours is the *total* amount of time spent by the foreman in handling the supplies, probably about one-half of that time represents a continuation of what the foreman had done in the past, and the rest represents an expansion of the foreman's activities in this area. Under these circumstances, an award of 40 hours' pay to the appropriate bargaining unit employee (identity to be left to the parties), seems in order.

## Overlapping of Unit and Managerial Functions

When certain duties are customarily performed by bargaining unit employees and supervisors, can the company lay off an employee be-

15. 10 AAA 8.

cause there was not enough for her to do and let a supervisor do the small amount of her work that was available? Did this violate a clause that barred foremen and supervisors from work "ordinarily done by hourly rated employees"? These questions were faced squarely by Howard A. Cole at *Micromatic Hone Corporation* (United Automobile Workers, AFL–CIO).[16]

The grievant was a woman in the follow-up classification. Her claim was that her layoff for lack of work in May 1961 was caused by the performance of her tasks by supervisors. Furthermore, it was charged, supervisors continued to do her work while she was out. After taking a great deal of testimony about her duties and those of supervision, Mr. Cole said it was impossible to draw a "precise line" between the two. "While it appears that a hard core of Follow-Up classification work does exist (notwithstanding changes in methods and procedures, including adoption of the IBM system, which could hardly help but lessen the need for Follow-Up personnel), there also appears to be an established and not insubstantial area of overlap between Follow-Up duties and responsibilities and those of supervision. Supervisory performance of work within this overlap area would not necessarily be violative of [the clause relied upon by the union]—this would depend largely upon degree and motive."

It followed from this, he said, that a showing that a supervisor had done some work customarily performed by the grievant would not be enough for a ruling that the company had violated the contract. It would also have to be shown that what supervisors did would have been enough to justify her recall. Such a showing was not made to Mr. Cole's satisfaction, and he denied the grievance.

Overlapping of functions was also a problem at the *Production Steel Company* (United Steelworkers of America, AFL–CIO).[17] Four separate grievances were presented in this case.

For many years, there had been inadequate storage facilities for steel adjacent to the working area. When shipments of coils and other raw materials arrived, they were tagged with the appropriate technical information and stored at a distance from the department where they would be used. When needed, a "stock chaser" would locate the material by tag number, often with the help of a foreman, because the

16. 42 AAA 21.
17. 43 AAA 3.

proper steel was not always easy to find within a short time. On occasion, a foreman would locate the stock himself, without enlisting the services of a bargaining unit employee.

With the enlargement of plant facilities in 1960, it became possible for the company to introduce a more efficient system of storing and locating coils of steel. In a department where this change occurred, foremen began doing virtually all the stock chasing, the company believing that it was advantageous to make use of the supervisors' greater knowledge of the difference in quality between different types of cold rolled steel. This led to the first grievance.

A second grievance involved certain paperwork in connection with maintaining a schedule which indicated the sequence with which coils of steel were sent through an operation, called the "wheelabrator line." Although the schedule itself had always been determined by the foreman, some clerical tasks used to be performed by an expediter in the bargaining unit. The company later found a way of preparing the schedule with the help of office clerical workers, making it unnecessary for expediters to do that work. This, the union stated in its grievance, was an improper transfer of work from unit to non-unit employees.

A third grievance was that two supervisors regularly wrote out stock tags, a task they had performed only infrequently in the past. The company admitted that it was a violation when foremen tagged stock during operations, but that it was proper for them to do so in the stainless steel division, where the tags, used for shipping, had to be typed. In any event, the company said, that work amounted to very little.

Finally, the union complained that foremen were writing out certain reports for recording down time or incorrect setups, tasks which were formerly prepared by production workers. These reports must be accurate, the company replied, and greater accuracy is possible when members of supervision execute them.[18]

The arbitrator was Erwin B. Ellmann. Addressing himself first to the stock-chasing grievance, he said the company erred in believing that this task could be assigned to either unit employees or foremen,

18. The reports in question were discontinued before the arbitration hearing, but company representatives said they might be reintroduced. The arbitrator was therefore asked to rule on this issue, as well as the others.

merely because both had done the work in the past. "Determining what type, size, gauge and particular steel coil may best fill a customer's order," he wrote, "is a managerial responsibility, but once determination has been made and the coil selected, locating the coil in the plant and indicating that it is to be moved can hardly be regarded as a normal function of supervision."

In the course of processing, a coil may have to be moved many times to different plant areas; each time stock chasing—elaborate searching or almost instantaneous selection—must precede such movement. In the usual situation, if the coils have been properly tagged, the employee can complete this operation by simple comparison of the number of the coil on the tag with the number of his order or requisition form. No discretion is required. These repeated functions, part of the routine of the company's business, are of the essence of the production process in an establishment such as this.

Nor was the company's argument persuasive that a foreman could detect errors on tags more easily than a bargaining unit employee. This did not justify a foreman's "ceasing to supervise and starting to perform the work himself," Mr. Ellmann said.

It is not contended that foremen cannot give requested assistance to bargaining unit employees in locating stock or that they may not check on their performance. But the assumption of primary responsibility for stock chasing by foremen, whether this has resulted in lay-offs of bargaining unit personnel or has merely reduced the total work available to union members, is an unwarranted appropriation by supervision. . . .

The second grievance was denied. The company had the right to transfer from the expediter to an office employee the task of preparing the schedule for sending coils through the wheelabrator line, and the task of preparing a similar lineup in connection with mill operations. "The principles which dictate the conclusion that stock chasing is essentially a 'production function' belonging to members of the bargaining unit," he wrote, "compel the contrary conclusion in the case of preparation of wheelabrator and mill line-ups." Although in the past the expediter "exercised a large amount of discretion and did in fact perform functions in connection with the wheelabrator line-up which might well be regarded as managerial," he conceded, this prior practice cannot bind the parties in view of a provision in the agreement stating that all past practices are "merged" into the agreement.

The third grievance, involving the typing of shipping tags, was again decided in favor of the union. Mr. Ellmann wrote:

No functional distinction has been suggested between preparing stock tags and shipping tags. . . . Preparing tags cannot be removed from the bargaining unit because it is more "convenient" for the company. Deviation from the agreement is not to be justified as an accommodation to customers. If the tags must be typed, they must be typed by an employee within the bargaining unit. It may be true, as the company suggests, that there are not a great number of such tags and the time spent in preparing them is insubstantial. In such event, the work can be restored to the bargaining unit with a minimum of dislocation. The matter is not so trifling, however, that it can be overlooked.

Finally, with respect to the fourth grievance, it was held that the company had the right to require foremen to prepare special reports for recording down time and incorrect setups. The union was not upheld in its contention that because these special reports in part duplicated production reports maintained by bargaining unit employees, they constituted bargaining unit work.

In order better to supervise and direct the working forces and perform its managerial responsibilities, the company could certainly have its foremen furnish information needed to evaluate operational efficiency and the performance of bargaining unit employees. Though production reports may have furnished some of this information, it is conceivable the company wished to determine whether there were discrepancies between the reports of the employees and its foremen. The introduction of another report in no way affected the job opportunities of employees within the bargaining unit who prepare production reports.[19]

### Incidental Clerical Tasks

At the *Production Steel Company*, Erwin B. Ellmann ruled that the greater typing ability of non-unit office workers did not necessarily

---

19. No back pay was awarded for the two violations found in this case, because, Mr. Ellmann said, he had not been shown how extensive the violations were, in terms of time spent by foremen at bargaining unit work, or that employees had suffered losses by those violations.

justify removal of that kind of clerical work from the bargaining unit. Samuel H. Jaffee came to a similar conclusion at the *Celanese Corporation of America* (Textile Workers Union of America, AFL–CIO),[20] but he denied the grievance on other grounds.

The issue here arose in the company's Stores Department, manned by bargaining unit employees. It was here that equipment, tools, parts, supplies, and similar items were kept in bins, each with a "locator card," identifying the item and keeping a perpetual inventory. In October 1958 a new inventory control system was installed, making it necessary for new locator cards to be prepared, in one color for items which could be let out only on requisition, in another for no-requisition-required parts. As the preparation of these cards involved a considerable amount of typing, management believed that non-bargaining unit typists in the purchasing department should do the work.

To begin with, wrote Mr. Jaffee, "I discount the fact, upon which the company relies, concerning the expert typing in Purchasing as against the inexpert typing in Stores. If the other circumstances in the case, aside from this one, were such as to make the job in question properly the work of Stores personnel, it does not seem to me that the difference in the quality or speed of the typing work would be particularly material."

The fact of this case which Mr. Jaffee said compelled a decision in favor of management was that the new locator cards were typed from data available only in the Purchasing Department. It was "insufficiently controverted" that the typist copied data onto cards "*not* from the white bin cards," which were available in the Stores Department, but from the "substantially more accurate and up-to-date" data on the "Traveling Purchase Requisition files" available in the Purchasing Department.

A case in which an arbitrator reached a conclusion different from Mr. Ellmann's in *Production Steel Company* was that of *Kerr-McGee Oil Industries, Incorporated* (Oil, Chemical and Atomic Workers, AFL–CIO).[21] Carl R. Schedler was the arbitrator. The issue was whether certain record-keeping tasks which were usually performed by bargaining unit employees in a laboratory could be performed by supervisors.

20. 4 AAA 12.
21. 38 AAA 2.

For some time, testers in the laboratory, who were covered by the collective bargaining agreement, had been required to tally certain data in notebooks periodically throughout the day. About thirty minutes before the end of the shift, they would transfer these entries into a special report form. In August 1960, management decided to discontinue the notebooks. Employees were directed to make their entries on individual sheets. At the end of the day these sheets would be turned over to foremen, who would transfer the data to daily report forms. Thus, bargaining unit employees were deprived of the thirty minutes of record-keeping at the end of the day. However, no loss of employment resulted from this change.

The reason for the new procedures, according to management, was that employees had been guilty of too many inaccuracies and incidents of illegible writing. Mr. Schedler had no doubt that the new system was more efficient. "However," he wrote, "I cannot agree with the company that it can, in the name of increased efficiency, take away work from members of the bargaining unit which they have exclusively and historically performed and assign it to supervisory personnel."

The substitution of a sheet of paper for a notebook does not so alter or change the basic operation in such a manner as to create an entirely new job. If an electrician has consistently repaired an item with a screwdriver and later learns to make the same repair with a pair of pliers, it does not necessarily follow that the job then becomes something for another craft or for supervision. In the instant case the Company has merely supplied the testers with a different or improved tool, and by doing so, it has in no way changed the content of the job.

It will be recalled that in the *Novo Industrial Corporation* case,[22] Lewis M. Gill wondered whether unsatisfactory janitorial service could not have been remedied by assigning a more competent man to the job, rather than by subcontracting. Mr. Gill resolved that doubt in favor of management. Mr. Schedler faced somewhat the same issue here, but his conclusion was that inefficiency was not a valid reason to take bargaining unit work away from regular employees. If employees were making careless or illegible entries, he said, "it shows a lack of skill or instruction and does not justify transferring the work to supervision." Again, Mr. Schedler drew on the skilled trades for analogy: "The fact that a painter leaves exposed spots and streaks

22. See Chapter 3, note 17.

does not justify transferring painting work to supervision. It indicates that the painter lacks skill, or proper instruction or proper supervision."

## Control of Supplies

The line between bargaining unit jobs and non-unit jobs is not always drawn on the basis of careful consideration and planning. Often, it appears where it does because of an improvised decision years ago. When, on more thoughtful reconsideration, an attempt is made to draw the line differently and remove some work from the bargaining unit, resistance is likely to be shown. This was illustrated at *Ball Brothers, Incorporated* (United Glass and Ceramic Workers of North America, AFL–CIO).[23] The job involved in the dispute was that of departmental stockroom attendant, staffed by a millwright, who maintained supplies and performed machine repair tasks normally identified with his classification. In the fall of 1960, in order to achieve better control of supplies, the company established a new, centrally controlled stockroom, and placed a non-bargaining unit employee in charge. To that employee were transferred virtually all the supplies formerly kept by the millwright. The latter continued to be in charge of tools, as against supplies, and certain machine repair functions were given him to compensate for the loss of supply-tending work.

Pressing its grievance to arbitration, the union argued that the departmental stockroom had belonged to the Millwright Department since 1951, that a job description existed that confirmed this, and that employees had bid for the job of stockroom attendant on the assumption that it included all the duties the grievant was performing until the company made the change. In short, the union said, management was violating the contract by transferring millwright work out of the bargaining unit.

The company's answer was that the job description had been drawn up for the sole purpose of considering whether a formal job of stockroom attendant, with its own rate, should be created. Such a job had not been created; instead, millwrights were assigned to the work and paid the millwright rate.

Fred E. Kindig upheld the company, chiefly on management's show-

23. 36 AAA 41.

ing that the stockroom attendant had never been included as a specific job in the formal wage classification manual, which had been agreed to by the parties. "There was also no proof that the job was ever posted other than as a regular millwright job," he wrote, "even though the employees may have had some understanding as to the differences between the millwright job when assigned to the stockroom area as opposed to any other millwright job." The job description upon which the union relied was merely a summary of what the millwright happened to be doing, not a description of a "bona fide job" in the wage structure of the plant.

## Revised Shipping Procedures

Another case pointing up the fact that a practice does not necessarily have to be continued after the reason for it no longer exists was that of the *Helena Rubinstein Company* (Oil, Chemical and Atomic Workers, AFL–CIO).[24] Involved here was a shift of work not to non-unit employees of the company, but to employees of another company. In other respects, however, this case has the same characteristics as others discussed in this chapter.

For a long time, it had been the practice for "bill of lading clerks" employed by the company to fill out all the forms needed for shipping products to customers. Less than 1 per cent of the company's shipments were then prepaid, and most of the small amount of paper work involved in this type of shipment was executed by Railway Express Agency employees, at their own receiving stations. In June 1958, however, Railway Express instituted a new tariff schedule, which made it advantageous for the company to ship a large proportion of its product prepaid. Railway Express personnel would now appear at the company's shipping department and fill out the necessary forms. So much work was transferred to a prepaid basis that Railway Express employees were on the company's premises practically all the time. This led, of course, to a corresponding reduction in the amount of work available to bill-of-lading clerks.

The union lost no time in pointing out that the job description of bill-of-lading clerk, contained in an appendix to the union contract, expressed these duties: "Make out bills of lading and/or receipts and

24. 7 AAA 12.

manifests for all shipments made. Obtain signatures for all merchandise shipped. File all bills of lading and manifests." To the union, this description was conclusive; writing receipts for "all" shipments was bargaining unit work. Furthermore, the union recalled, in the days when collect shipments were the general rule, there nevertheless were occasions when a prepaid pickup would be made on company premises, and bill-of-lading clerks would have prepared the receipts in advance.

Daniel Kornblum resolved the dispute in favor of the employer. He pointed out that there would have been no controversy at all had the shipments been delivered to an American Railway Express depot, with forms filled in there. Furthermore, he wrote, "taking the view of the facts most favorable to the union, the occasions in the past for bill of lading clerks of the employer to prepare such receipts were at most extremely limited." The fact that employer's bill-of-lading clerks were permitted to do this work in the exceptional instances in the past "cannot be held to represent a deferment by the Express Agency to the employer of the former's traditional jurisdiction over this work, if not also its mandatory function and responsibility under the law as a common carrrier." Finally, as to the effect of the job description, upon which the union relied so heavily, the reference to writing of receipts was not controlling, because the receipts in question here were those of the common carrier, not the employer.

### Interunion Rivalry for Jobs

When two or more unions are recognized as representatives of employees on the same premises, the possibility is increased of grievances over out-of-unit transfer of work or of wrongful assignments. This was evident at the *Hudson Pulp and Paper Corporation* (United Papermakers and Paperworkers, AFL–CIO).[25]

The chief circumstance making disputes almost inevitable was that the NLRB had certified Local 565 of the United Papermakers Union for employees in one warehouse, where Kraft paper was stored, and Local 852 of the International Brotherhood of Pulp, Sulphite and Paper Mill Workers, AFL–CIO, for employees in another warehouse on the premises, where tissue products were kept. In March 1960,

25. 24 AAA 21.

Local 565 grieved that the company had transferred Kraft bags to the warehouse operated by Local 852 members, allegedly in violation of a fourteen-year practice, and of "the letter, spirit and intent" of the agreement. The company answered that using warehouse space in the most economical manner was a managerial right not abandoned through negotiations with either union. It also denied an implication of the union argument that there was any advantage, in terms of wage rates, in letting Local 852 employees ship Kraft bags to customers.

Gordon A. Duncan said that the company had always had the right to decide how to store its products. That it warehoused Kraft bags in a particular location for fourteen years did not constitute a waiver of its right to store them elsewhere. "Mere non-use of a right over a period of time does not entail a loss of it," he wrote.

Caution must be exercised in reading into a contract implied terms, and it is not within the power of arbitration in this case to legislate into the contract past practices and customs. No matter how well established a past practice may be, if the principals have not seen fit to incorporate it into written agreement, an impartial arbitrator has no power to alter the contract by so doing. Failure of the company, over a long period of time, to exercise a legitimate function of management does not constitute surrender of the justification to start exercising such right.

Mr. Duncan took the occasion to endorse the reserved rights theory of contract interpretation. He wrote:

A collective bargaining agreement operates as a limitation upon the original right of the employer to establish working conditions, but only to the extent that conditions of employment are thereby established. The pre-existing right of the employer still continues as to all matters not covered by the agreement, and the employer thus has a right to establish or change working conditions for which the contract makes no provision.

Another paper mill, *Scott Paper Company* (United Papermakers and Paperworkers, AFL–CIO)[26] had a somewhat similar problem of keeping clear the line between two unions. For about a dozen years, Local 431 of this union had had jurisdiction over a caretaker job. The company had tried on several occasions to transfer this job to Local 11 of the International Brotherhood of Pulp, Sulphite and Paper Mill Workers, AFL–CIO, which had jurisdiction over "yard" jobs.

26. 4 AAA 20.

But Local 431 would not hear of it. Finally, in September 1958, when the caretaker was about to retire, management declared caretaking no longer necessary and announced that servicing and cleaning of the three locker rooms, which had recently been enlarged and improved, would be performed by a sanitation crew of Local 11 members.

The company asserted these points in justification of its action: (1) The preamble of Local 431's contract guaranteed the company the right to take action to insure profitable operations; (2) there was no contractual bar to eliminating unnecessary jobs and reassigning remaining duties elsewhere; and (3) management had never abandoned its rights merely by permitting the United Papermakers union to take jurisdiction over caretaking. Saul Wallen upheld the union, saying:

These duties were made part of the [grieving local's] bargaining unit by negotiation and agreement. For whatever reasons, the parties saw fit to give jurisdiction over the job involved to [the grieving local] even though at the time they did so, similar duties were being performed . . . under the jurisdiction of [the other local]. The parties are the architects of their own house; having split the cleaning duties between two locals by negotiation and agreement, they can now combine them and place them in one unit only by negotiation and agreement.

## Jurisdiction over New Job

When the *New York Times* (American Newspaper Guild, AFL–CIO)[27] established its Paris edition, new equipment was installed, consisting of a mechanism with a typewriter-like keyboard in New York and a type-casting machine in Paris. Sitting at the keyboard, an operator could transcribe copy into perforated tape which would then transmit impulses across the Atlantic, where linotype slugs would be cast, somewhat as the conventional linotype machine does.

The question immediately arose as to who was to have control over the keyboard operation in New York. With jurisdiction over editorial and clerical workers, many of whom operated typewriters and teletype machines, the American Newspaper Guild claimed the job. But so did the International Typographical Union, whose members operated linotype machines and also worked at keyboards, not vastly different

27. 33 AAA 6.

from that of the new equipment. Management of the *New York Times* decided that the printers' union had a stronger claim to the job, and notices were posted offering training for the prospective "teletypesetter perforator operator" jobs to ITU members. This led to the grievance of the American Newspaper Guild.[28]

Louis Yagoda denied the grievance, chiefly for three reasons:

1. The collective bargaining agreement between the *New York Times* and the American Newspaper Guild did not specifically include the teletypesetter perforator operator job. The recognition clause did contain a blanket phrase, "and kindred groups of employees in miscellaneous departments," but this was clearly less specific than the reference to the job in the printers' contract. Furthermore, the phrase relied upon by the Guild was intended "to pick up employees in various commercial and business departments," rather than to cover editorial workers.

2. "There is no indication that the Guild or its members will be deprived of other contractual rights by a denial to them of jurisdiction over the teletypesetter perforator operation. No jobs were taken away from them in setting up this new operation. Even in terms of future growth possibilities, it was shown that they would not be injured. The manning of transmitting machines, the preparation of copy prior to translating it to tape, and the use of additional editing functions would continue and probably expand the size of Guild jurisdiction."

3. The ITU had a "stronger claim" to the job, not only because it had an apprenticeship program in teletypesetting operating and because its contract specifically included this job, but because there was "humane logic" in giving work to those who had formerly performed the same job in a different way.[29]

---

28. Although the printers' union was clearly an interested bystander in this case, it was not officially a party. The arbitrator's task was primarily to determine whether assigning the job to the typographers violated the contract of the editorial workers.

29. Mr. Yagoda wrote: "The work is the setting up of type electronically rather than that of devising, editing or transmitting news copy. The keyboard—although clearly differing from either the teletype keyboard or the linotype keyboard—nevertheless continues traditional linecasting functions such as 'quadding' and 'justification,' transmitted to the linotyper by means of an electronic message rather than immediately, as heretofore."

Although the third point helped support the decision in favor of the employer, management was not quite happy that the arbitrator had concerned himself with the validity of the ITU's claim. Company representatives would have wanted the grievance denied on the basis of the first two points alone. It was urged that the arbitrator had authority under the contract with the Guild to determine only whether the Guild was entitled to the job, and that his authority did not extend to ruling on whether it was proper to award teletypesetting to the printers. Mr. Yagoda answered that, in view of the company's defense, it would be "somewhat unrealistic and artificial" to ignore the "jurisdictional dispute aspects" of the case.

## Protecting Skilled Crafts

Understandably, the strongest job security provisions are reserved for the skilled crafts. Even the clearest evidence of waste and inefficiency may be insufficient to overcome contract language, where such employees are involved. At *Socony Mobil Oil Company* (Oil, Chemical and Atomic Workers, AFL–CIO),[30] for instance, the contract said that, except in cases of emergency, "no employee excluded from the appropriate unit covered by the terms of this agreement shall be allowed to perform work in any classification included under the terms of this agreement in such a way as to prevent the promotion of qualified employees or cause the demotion of qualified employees."

This clause was invoked by a pipe fitter's helper who protested that on a certain occasion, a boiler maker and his helper, members of another union and unit, had repaired a leak in a pipe line. The company's defense was that no more than fifteen or twenty minutes of pipe fitter work was involved, the rest of the time being occupied in going back and forth to the site of the leak and in waiting for a welder to prepare a clamp. In fact, the company said, what was involved in the alleged out-of-unit classification was really messenger work, not pipe fitting, and the high rates paid to pipe fitters were clearly not justified by the facts.

Earl J. Miller upheld the grievance. That there may be inefficiency in the standard procedures of the establishment, he said, is not relevant in view of the express contractual provision relied upon by the union.

30. 43 AAA 16.

The helper who should have been promoted to perform the work was awarded the difference between what he actually earned for the day and what he would have earned had he been assigned to the disputed work.

The jealous concern of the skilled craftsman for his jurisdiction was also revealed at the *West Virginia Pulp and Paper Company* (International Brotherhood of Electrical Workers, AFL–CIO),[31] where the issue involved no more than replacing electric light bulbs. The grievants, members of the union in this case, were maintenance electricians, who complained that management had encouraged production workers, who were represented by another union, to replace bulbs when they burned out. In the past, operators had occasionally replaced bulbs, especially when a maintenance electrician was not immediately available, but the electricians now feared that this task would be completely lost to them. Moreover, it was argued, these simple tasks are the very work on which apprentices in the electrical craft are trained.

The company relied on the management rights clause and on the fact that the work involved so little skill as not to fall exclusively within the scope of the electricians' jurisdiction. It was also argued that electricians were occupied elsewhere at more critical jobs, from which they ought not to be summoned for trivial reasons.

Paul H. Sanders resolved the dispute in favor of the company for four reasons:

1. Maintenance electricians customarily, but not always, replaced bulbs.

2. Operators were permitted to replace bulbs when electricians were not immediately available.

3. The contract with the union representing electricians reserved all management's rights except those "specifically surrendered" or "abridged by express language."

4. The grieving union was unable to show "that the action taken by the company violates some express provision" of the agreement.

However, the case was not a total loss for the union, for some of the dicta satisfied its needs for craft security. If the tasks in question "had been recognized as belonging exclusively to the Electrical Department," Mr. Sanders concluded, or if they "clearly called for skills and

31. 34 AAA 13.

knowledge of electricians," the recognition clause would probably have operated to restrain management from the change in assignments.[32]

## The Union's "Geographic Jurisdiction"

The scope of a bargaining unit and of the union's claim to jobs is usually determined by the description of work to be done. But where the work is not necessarily confined to one area, geographic boundaries may mark the line of a union's job rights.

*National Telefilm Associates* (International Brotherhood of Electrical Workers, AFL–CIO)[33] operated television station WNTA, Channel 13, in Newark, New Jersey, under a contract clause which recognized the union's right to all work originating "within a fifty-mile radius." But in view of the acknowledged importance to the company of becoming the New York outlet for network programs "which may become available from time to time," the same clause said that the union will not "unreasonably withhold its permission" to accept the "feed" of non-WNTA programs which originated within the fifty-mile area.[34]

32. For another case involving a union's claim that work belonging to its unit was given to employees represented by another union on the premises, see *Ball Brothers Company, Incorporated* (United Glass and Ceramic Workers, AFL–CIO), 12 AAA 2, arbitrated by G. Allan Dash, Jr. The work assignment was not wrongful in this case, he said, bcause it involved an isolated incident of a telephone message going astray. This was the reason the employee in the proper classification was not called to work. The union's reliance on the recognition clause might have had validity, he added, if cross-classification assignments were made in such volume as to cause employees to lose time.

33. 36 AAA 31.

34. The full text of the clause read: "The company recognizes the union's right to jurisdiction over company originations (AM or TV) within a fifty (50) mile radius. The union recognizes the desirability and economic importance of the company being able to serve as the New York outlet for network programs which may be available to it from time to time. In such situations where the originations can occur in the company studio, the company will make every effort to effect this. If this is impossible because of legal, talent or facilities consideration (i.e., picking up the last hour of the NBC Garroway Show), the union will consider on a case-by-case basis and will not unreasonably withhold its permission to accept the feed which will route through the respective control room. This in no way diminishes the union's rights which are herein reaffirmed."

The arbitration case grew out of the "Open End" program on Sunday, October 9, 1960, in which Premier Nikita Khrushchev was interviewed by David Susskind. Since the Russian Premier's movements had been restricted by the U.S. State Department to the island of Manhattan, it was known that the program could not originate in WNTA studios. Other locations were considered, including the Russian headquarters on Park Avenue, the residence in Glen Cove, Long Island, maintained by the Russian Embassy, and studios of television networks in New York City. None was satisfactory to both the Russian and American security officers. Finally, it was decided to originate the program "live" from the United Nations, and feed it through WNTA to a network of 35 television stations and 250 radio stations. The only difficulty with this arrangement—and this was the source of the union's grievance—was that UN regulations precluded the possibility of employing WNTA engineers. It therefore became necessary for the company to obtain the union's concurrence in letting engineers employed by others do the work. The union refused, and remained adamant in its position; its only counter-proposal was that six engineers be assigned to Newark "to perform any work that was available there to them." On the day of the telecast, management finally accepted the proposal and posted a notice saying that the company was "engaging the six men under violent protest." It was also announced that management would institute arbitration proceedings against the union the very next day.

The result was an arbitration case in which the employer was the claimant and the union the respondent—a rather rare occurrence. The issue presented to Israel Ben Scheiber was: "Did the union breach the contract in effect between the parties when it demanded that the station use six engineers who could not be used in the broadcast of the Khrushchev interview on the Open End program on October 9, 1960? If so, what shall the remedy be?"

The company won the award on the principal issue, but not without a rebuke from Mr. Scheiber for the thoughtlessness displayed by management in not informing the union promptly of the problem that was developing. It appeared that the union's representative had first learned of the program on the Thursday morning before the broadcast, when he read about it in a newspaper. That the parties were in daily contact with one another all along only heightened the union's resentment at apparently being taken for granted.[35] Mr. Scheiber believed that this had much to do with the union's intransigent position. Nevertheless, he wrote, "in spite of the provocation," it was the union's obligation under the contract to give consideration to the problem and not unreasonably to withhold permission to conduct the program through technicians cleared for security at the UN. In view of the fact that the "over-whelming public interest in having Mr. Khrushchev on this program cannot be denied," and in view also of the union's past recognition of public interest "as an important factor in a situation such as this," it was the arbitrator's conclusion that "it was not reasonable for the union to impose the condition of assigning six engineers who were not necessary to the transmission of this particular program." The remedy prescribed by Mr. Scheiber was that no pay be given them for their "standby" service.[36]

A case involving the same union and a similar fifty-mile jurisdiction clause arose at the *Metropolitan Broadcasting Division of Metromedia, Incorporated* (International Brotherhood of Electrical Workers, AFL–CIO).[37] Louis Yagoda said that a clause requiring the employer to use bargaining unit engineers employed by radio station WNEW on all programs "originated" by the company within fifty miles did not bar the use of tapes of a U.S. Army briefing session and a speech by West Berlin Mayor Willy Brandt supplied to the station, even though the recording was done within fifty miles by engineers who were not employees of the company.

No violation was involved here, Mr. Yagoda said, because the tapes had not "originated" with the employer. The clause on which the union relied was "apparently designed to keep management from sending

35. For another case in which lack of communication between management and labor was credited with causing a major grievance, see that of the *Picker X-Ray Corporation,* discussed earlier in this chapter.

36. Several other secondary issues were also disposed of in this case. Contrary to the employer's assertion, Mr. Scheiber said, there was no evidence that the union had also violated the no-strike clause by threatening a work stoppage. Nor would the arbitrator rule on whether the union had violated the Lea Act, which forbids coercive practices in broadcasting. Arbitration is not a forum to determine such matters, Mr. Scheiber wrote. Finally, the employer's request for an award directing the union to pay all the costs of the arbitration was denied. "Not only does this request evidence a misunderstanding of the grievance procedure," he wrote, "but to grant it would involve a violation of the contract.

37. 45 AAA 3.

somebody other than a bargaining unit engineer to the place at which the sound originates for the purpose of transposing it to a recording of some nature, such recording to be broadcast eventually or transmitted to other stations or networks for broadcast," he explained. Nevertheless, Mr. Yagoda said there remained a "troublesome element," not completely satisfied by the statement of the reasons for the fifty-mile clause. He expressed the dilemma this way:

If the Agreement is meant to make sure that the employer choose a union engineer whenever he decides to have a tape made (at a point of origin within 50 airline miles of New York City) designed for later broadcast or transmission, can not the employer violate the Agreement by merely *designedly permitting* rather than commanding a non-employee to do the transcribing? Let us say an event occurs, known to the station and regarded by it as worthy of sending over the air to its listeners. The management learns, however, that a recording will be made which can later be translated to station broadcasting speed and put on the air to its listeners. It thereupon makes a choice not to send out its own recording team but sits back until the recording shall have been made and makes arrangements to secure it for broadcast. The question then arises: has not this in reality been "originated by Station WNEW (WNEW-FM)" and "for broadcast by" the station?

This was, of course, a hypothetical question, but Mr. Yagoda said he could not ignore it completely. His answer was that it would have to be shown that the person who did the recording was "purposefully manipulated" by the employer, directly or indirectly for the purpose of avoiding use of bargaining unit employees. In that event, the tape would be deemed to have "originated" with the company after all. Such bad faith was not shown to have been the case here, the arbitrator wrote, although "it is probably true that the station could have sent out an employee with recording equipment to make an independent recording at the same time that [the army officer's speech] was being recorded by army personnel." He concluded, however, that the agreement did not require "a searching out of opportunities to employ engineers attached to the station."

# 5

## JURISDICTION OVER WORK

"Persons not included in the bargaining unit covered by this agreement shall not be permitted to perform any work consistently performed by the employees within the bargaining unit except in cases of emergency or extenuating circumstances such as to instruct employees, correct operating difficulties or take the place of absent employees until other maintenance or production employees can be secured."

—From a union contract clause

In the previous chapter we have seen how, under the impact of improved technology, economic necessity, and managerial innovation, some jobs lose the quality that identified them with the bargaining unit. In some of the cases discussed, the outcome was a permanent loss to the union of jurisdiction over work and people. But the removal of jobs from bargaining units is not the only way work is diminished. There is also the temporary loss that occurs when foremen and supervisors believe that exceptional conditions justify their helping a bargaining unit employee get a job done, or when peripheral tasks, such as inventory-taking, for instance, are assigned to non-unit personnel.

The union's resistance to out-of-unit assignments has less to do with actual losses incurred (often, as we shall see, the losses are trifling, or only hypothetical) than with institutional psychology. Rightly or wrongly, the union feels compelled to act as if the bargaining unit were a beleaguered fortress which, if breached at any point, might be weakened and destroyed.[1] This posture of defense does not, of course, preclude an offensive raid in industrial relations any more than it does in other fields of human activity.[2]

### Production Work by Supervisors

Seldom do collective bargaining agreements impose an absolute ban on foremen doing any kind of production work. Usually, they are per-

1. Management's difficulty in understanding the union's viewpoint was illustrated at *Federal-Mogul-Bower Bearings, Incorporated* (United Rubber, Cork, Linoleum and Plastic Workers of America, AFL–CIO), 33 AAA 21, where the union protested because a leadman changed a fuse that blew on a 400-volt line during the night. It was argued that a maintenance employee should have been called in for the task. Four hours' call-in pay was demanded in his behalf. To the company, this demand was an example of "featherbedding in the extreme." Jacob J. Blair denied the grievance because there was no showing that changing a fuse was the exclusive function of maintenance employees or that what was done could "undermine or jeopardize the wage structure," but he thought that the company's characterization of the grievance was not warranted. He wrote: "It is to be recognized that the union has the responsibility of maintaining work assignments within the various occupations as a means of protecting the negotiated wage scale. In other words, the union is responsible for policing job assignments in order to prevent work done by a higher paid occupation being assigned to employees in a lower paid job. To this extent, the company contention that this is an attempt to get 'something for nothing' is rejected."

2. The eagerness with which unions will lay claim to jobs that come within reach was illustrated at the *American Chain & Cable Company* (United Steelworkers of America, AFL–CIO), 32 AAA 19. The job in question was that of driving a test car, equipped with tire chains, to test and record the performance of the company's product. For many years, this work was done principally by a salaried employee, outside the bargaining unit. However, bargaining unit employees occasionally performed such work in the absence of a salaried employee. In 1959, a regular test driver was given a special assignment, and a bargaining unit employee was given the task. He did the work until September 1960, when the salaried employee returned from his special assignment. At that point, the union grieved that test car driving had become bargaining unit work which could no longer be claimed by the non-unit employee. The company answered that the job would never be transferred to the unit because the findings of the road tests had to be kept confidential. The company would select an occasional employee for test car driving, as long as seniority did not apply, but this did not affect the right of management to keep the job out of the bargaining unit. A seeming weakness in the company's case was the fact that the unit employee who had substituted for the regular test car driver happened

mitted to do non-supervisory work when necessary to meet emergencies or to teach, examine, and experiment. As a practical matter, supervisors are also permitted to do anything that can be regarded as incidental to the managerial function.

Whether non-unit personnel overstepped contractual limits depends upon the facts of the case and upon the interpretation one puts on such words as "teaching," "emergencies," and "incidental." Another source of dispute is the so-called *de minimis* violation. Although management is often as determined as is the union that foremen abstain from production, it seems to be contrary to the nature of some supervisors to see a bottleneck develop and not apply their hands directly. The *de minimis* explanation never satisfies the union; the threat to the integrity of the bargaining unit seems implicit every time foremen cross the line, even for a few minutes of work. Moreover, as in so many areas of union contract administration, the question of good faith may be involved. A supervisor's mistaken judgment that a trifling amount of work was permissible under special circumstances may be one thing. A calculated policy of "whittling away at the bargaining unit" by repeated violations may be quite another.

## "De Minimis" Violations

The cumulative effect of *de minimis* violations was demonstrated in two cases at the *Foote Mineral Company* (Oil, Chemical and

---

to be the senior man. But even this did not defeat the company's case. Lewis M. Gill wrote: "In making that decision, it should be emphasized that I am not called upon to decide whether the job is of the sort which should be in the bargaining unit in view of the nature of the work being performed. My jurisdiction is limited to interpreting and applying the contract terms." Staying within those limits of his authority, the arbitrator ruled that the union had no contractual right to the work in question. For one thing, bargaining unit members had substituted for non-unit personnel on this work in the past without claiming the work as a matter of right. Furthermore, the job had never been listed among the work classifications in the appendix to the contract, nor was a rate negotiated for test driving. The union had one telling point: when one unit employee who was driving was laid off, management assigned another unit employee to the job. But even this, although it did "lend some color" to the union's contention that the job was treated as bargaining unit work, could not be decisive, because the incident took place while the regular salaried test driver was on the special assignment.

Atomic Workers, AFL–CIO). The first[3] was resolved by Laurence E. Seibel; the second[4] was arbitrated by Samuel H. Jaffee.

Although there was a lapse of about fifteen months between the two cases, both turned on the same contract clause, which read: "It is agreed that foremen and supervisors shall not do production work or maintenance work customarily performed by hourly workers, except for the purpose of training and emergencies."

The case before Mr. Seibel came about because management believed it was not improper to let a foreman receive materials for less than fifteen minutes at a time on occasion after 4:30 P.M. or on week ends, when a regular storeroom attendant was not on duty. On such occasions, a foreman who did the storekeeper's work would sometimes enlist another bargaining unit worker to assist him, but this did not make the invasion of the forbidden area, as the union saw it, more acceptable. Although the company had the right to change job content, union representatives conceded, work could not be taken from one classification and given to another on an overtime basis only, with the object of avoiding call-back or overtime pay to the storekeeper.[5] But above all, the union found the company's argument of *de minimis* repugnant. A few minutes of work now and then contained a threat that the volume would grow in the future. Furthermore, by better planning, the work could have been done during regular hours by the person properly classified to do it.

Mr. Seibel agreed with the union. He was not persuaded by the

3. 19 AAA 26.

4. 36 AAA 6.

5. For a subtle, but important, difference between permitted and forbidden work, see *The Standard Products Company* (United Automobile Workers, AFL–CIO), 34 AAA 18. David P. Miller held that it was proper for a supervisor to unlock the tool crib on Friday night so that the "relatively few employees" scheduled for week-end overtime could draw their own tools. However, if the supervisor had issued tools to the others, it *would* have been a violation. Mr. Miller wrote: "The supervisors did not operate the crib or even stay in it. . . . When only a relatively few employees are scheduled to work overtime, the company may, if it chooses, arrange to have each employee secure his own equipment from the crib instead of bringing in a Crib Attendant for whose services there would be comparatively little demand. While this may not always be the most efficient or safest procedure, contractually it is not improper so long as no employee or supervisor assumes the task of servicing others or performs any other regular duty of the Crib Attendant."

employer's view that a small amount of work, since it did not deprive hourly rated workers of jobs, was not within the contract's limitations. Nor did the fact that production might be interrupted if the foreman did not receive the materials constitute an "emergency" within the contract's meaning.

While it is true that the entries into the storeroom appear to be of short duration, they equally appear to be regular and recurring in nature, and, accordingly, it is at best questionable whether the *de minimis* concept advanced by the company is applicable. The better view, in my judgment, is that the contract plainly and unambiguously provides that supervisors shall not perform hourly rated employees' work "except for the purposes of training and emergencies" and that, therefore, the work here in question of a regular and recurring nature should not be performed by supervisors unless in connection with "training and emergencies."

As often happens in such cases, it was not easy to find an appropriate remedy for the violation. The union had asked for compensation to the storekeeper, at the rate that would have applied if he had been called in to do the small amount of "regular and recurring" work. This request was rejected not only because of the "somewhat technical" nature of the violation, but because the contract itself permitted a degree of flexibility and interchangeability in assignment of tasks across classification lines. Furthermore, as supervisors had been performing forbidden work of this kind "for some time" without opposition by the union, "it can hardly be said that the company's violation of the agreement has been purposeful." Thus, the union won a verdict that the company had violated the agreement, but no monetary relief was awarded.

The case before Mr. Jaffee had similar characteristics, and it, too, resulted in a finding that the company's *de minimis* defense was not valid. But unlike Mr. Seibel, who declined to award a monetary remedy, Mr. Jaffee said that the history of *de minimis* violations justified an award of four hours' call-in pay to two grievants.

Management in this case admitted that violations had occurred on two successive days when supervisors did a total of thirty-five minutes of work that normally belonged to employees on layoff. During the grievance discussions preliminary to arbitration, the company argued that, in view of the few minutes involved, no one would have been called in, nor would overtime have been involved for other employees in the plant to whom the work might have been assigned. For these reasons, any monetary award would be a "penalty," which would be beyond the arbitrator's authority to impose.[6] As to this, Mr. Jaffee wrote: "The violations having been conceded, I of course find that they occurred. The only question that is left, then, is what the remedy should be. What this in turn comes down to, as the parties view it, would appear to be a choice between the imposition of a 'penalty,' or the issuance of an award which would constitute only a 'slap on the wrist,' this last on the basis that the amount of time spent on the disputed work was *de minimis*. But even if the fifteen and twenty minutes involved may be considered *de minimis*, I do not think that that principle has application where, as here, violations of this character (presumably also *de minimis*) have occurred repeatedly, and especially where an award to that effect has previously been issued [by Mr. Seibel]. The little *de minimis* 'acorns' have by this time grown into an 'oak' of some size."[7]

## *"Damages" and "Penalties"*

But Mr. Jaffee acknowledged that the company's argument against a "penalty" award did constitute a "difficult aspect of the problem" in that the work forbidden to foremen might have been assigned to

6. For a discussion of the distinction between damages and penalties in labor arbitration, see the award of John R. Abersold, in *Bearings Company of America* (United Steelworkers of America, AFL–CIO), 20 AAA 19. Mr. Abersold said that "unless it can be shown that the employees suffered some *actual loss*," no monetary remedy can be imposed. "The reason for this is that the process of arbitration is designed for the purpose of *compensating* employees for a *loss* which they have sustained by an action of the company which *cannot be sustained* under any provision of the Labor Agreement. Thus, the damages are *compensatory* in nature and may not be *punitive*."

7. See also *Consumers Power Company*, discussed later in this chapter, where David P. Miller wrote of the *de minimis* doctrine: "That principle has only limited applicability in a collective bargaining relationship. It is entirely understandable that a single trifling matter between one-time litigants be treated as '*de minimis*' and dismissed by the courts. But where parties are bound together in a continuing contractual relationship, repeated instances of minor infractions cannot be regarded in the same light. For, not only is the cumulative effect of the repeated violation to be reckoned with, but the repetition in effect becomes a challenge to the established rule or contractually expressed prohibition. Thus it becomes a valid issue which should be resolved by the parties by adjudication

employees in other departments who were then at work. In that event, the cost to the company would have been slight, certainly less than the eight hours of pay the union was seeking. But this question was resolved in favor of the union, chiefly because the company had "scrambled the eggs" and it was no longer possible to unscramble them. "We cannot be sufficiently certain," Mr. Jaffee wrote, "precisely in what way the matter would have been handled had the admitted violations not occurred." Under the circumstances, he concluded, the burden is on the company to prove that less costly procedures would have been followed than calling in employees from layoff. This burden, he said, was not met. In awarding call-in pay to the grievants, Mr. Jaffee was careful to emphasize that he neither regarded the award as a punitive one, nor did he intend that all future violations be remedied that way. "The determination here is based on the facts found in *this* case," he wrote. "In other words, the award does not constitute a precedent that any future violations . . . will result in awards requiring the payment of call-in pay. Each case will have to be determined on its own facts."[8]

---

in their mutually adopted appeals procedure. Valid issues may not be summarily dismissed if the parties are to achieve an harmonious continuing collective bargaining relationship."

8. For another case in which an arbitrator held that the burden was on the employer to justify a less costly award, see *Ball Brothers Company* (United Glass and Ceramic Workers, AFL–CIO), 12 AAA 14, arbitrated by G. Allan Dash, Jr. Conceding that it was an error for a foreman to have done forty minutes of forbidden work, the company had offered to "make whole" an employee with forty minutes' pay. But Mr. Dash said this would be inadequate. The fact that the foreman decided to do the work himself implied that there was no bargaining unit employee on hand capable of performing it. That being so, an employee should have been called in specially, in which case he would be entitled to four hours' call-in pay.

Another case involving an admitted violation and a disputed remedy was that of the *Borg-Warner Corporation* (Allied Industrial Workers of America, AFL–CIO), 21 AAA 6. A foreman having performed certain experimental millwright work for three hours, management offered three hours' pay to a bargaining unit employee. The union demanded three hours at time and a half. When the controversy came to arbitration, Russell N. Sullivan upheld the grievance. The evidence was "uncertain," he said, as to whether the work was done during straight time or overtime. As the area in which it was done was not open to union representatives, the company had the "burden of proof" to show that only straight-time hours were involved. That burden was not met,

Another arbitrator who had occasion to reject a *de minimis* defense under quite similar circumstances was Richard Mittenthal. The case was that of the *Huron Portland Cement Company* (Oil, Chemical and Atomic Workers, AFL–CIO).[9] In fact, Mr. Mittenthal went so far as to say that if violations continued, "it might become necessary for an arbitrator to grant compensation in cases of this character." Presumably, Mr. Mittenthal meant some compensation that would go beyond actual losses, but he did not explain how a monetary award of that kind would escape the defect of being punitive.

As in the *Foote Mineral* case, the contract here limited the scope of a foreman's bargaining unit work rather strictly:

> Employees not subject to this Agreement shall not perform work regularly assigned to the classifications covered under this Agreement, except in cases of emergency or for the purpose of instruction, training, inspection or investigation.

Despite this, it was admitted by the company that supervisors had "lent a hand" to repair crews for a few minutes on several occasions. One of these incidents involved about five minutes' work to finish a job. As it would have taken longer than that to find a repairman to do it, management did not think the offense was serious. Another incident consisted of "cable pulling" by three supervisors, who devoted a total of thirty minutes to the task.

The arbitrator awarded four hours' pay to the senior man on layoff because that is what he would have been paid if he had been called in to do the cable pulling. For the "trifling amount" of repair work done, there was no remedy aside from the possibly futile warning quoted above.

### De Minimis Work Approved

As we have seen, arbitrators are not inclined to approve unauthorized performance of non-supervisory work, even when the losses to the

---

in Mr. Sullivan's judgment. As all millwrights were working full time, and none was on layoff, proper application of the agreement may have necessitated overtime, unless other work was postponed. For all these reasons, the more costly remedy was awarded.

9. 13 AAA 18.

bargaining unit are so slight that no practical remedy is possible. When small amounts of production work are found permissible, it does not signify an endorsement of the *de minimis* defense as such; it is rather a conclusion drawn from the fact that the contracts contained only mild restrictions. In other words, no violations occurred. Two cases may be cited.

At *Consolidated Paper Company* (United Papermakers and Paperworkers, AFL–CIO),[10] foremen were forbidden to do bargaining unit work only if it would "result in lost time or pay to the employees covered by the agreement." Moreover, even if lost time were a consequence, foremen would still be privileged to work "in extreme emergencies to prevent serious company losses."

On a certain Sunday, an overtime day, a paper-making machine was shut down for repair. Five employees, including three millwrights, a pipefitter, and a welder, were assigned to the task. They completed the work within forty minutes of the end of their shift, but apparently not without "an hour or so" of help from the foreman. From the beginning, the union had believed that a fourth millwright should have been asked to work. A grievance was therefore filed, protesting the assistance the foreman had given to the repair crew.

In view of the contract language, the critical issue was whether the work the foreman had done had caused the fourth maintenance man to lose any work. Mark L. Kahn said it had not:

The Arbitrator is satisfied that the millwrights who were at work could have completed their task well within the eight hour shift even if the foreman had entirely avoided all millwright work. Although the maintenance crew finished its work on April 20, 1958, by no later than 1:50 P.M., the men were paid and could have been required to work until 2:30 P.M. on that day. The Arbitrator therefore concludes that the effect of any bargaining unit work the foreman may have done was simply to let the maintenance crew finish up somewhat earlier than would otherwise have been the case, and did not cause [the grievant] to lose work time or pay.

Furthermore, the evidence showed that the foreman had "got into things" only to the extent he customarily did, without objection by the union, during non-overtime hours. The foreman's work was thus "incidental" to his managerial function.

The second case was that of *Cook Electric Company* (United Auto-

10. 13 AAA 19.

mobile Workers, AFL–CIO).[11] Here, too, foremen had wide latitude. They were permitted to spend as much as 20 per cent of their time at bargaining unit work. The difficulty arose because a foreman did "an extremely small amount" of work in three classifications—parts handler, expediter, and tool crib attendant. There were no employees regularly assigned to these classifications because it was expected that very little work would be needed, and the company and union had not been able to agree on how the classifications should be combined with other work to make a full-time job. The result was that when something had to be done from time to time, a foreman did it.

The union did not claim that the foreman had exceeded the 20 per cent limit. The objection was rather that, as no employees were assigned to the classification, it was improper for the foreman to do any part of the work. The practical effect of such work, the union argued, was to let foremen displace senior employees altogether.

Eli Rock was the arbitrator. To begin with, he declined to comment on whether the union was correct in resisting the employer's proposal for combining jobs. But right or wrong, the union's refusal created "an obviously difficult situation" which had to be faced. He wrote:

The essential aspect of the present case, and one which is very difficult to avoid, is the extremely small amount of bargaining unit work done in this particular instance. Regardless of what kind of ruling might eventually emerge on the general question above, it seems clear that the amount of work done by the foreman here was so small and *de minimis* in nature as to make extremely difficult any meaningful remedy to the union, absent a clause which strongly outlaws bargaining unit work by supervision. . . .

The requested remedy here is that the company should pay employees in each of three affected classifications who should have or would have been recalled had the work not been assigned to the foreman. The whole emphasis of the request, and the apparent reason for taking the case to arbitration, seemed to lie in the union's desire to preserve a continuing job, or jobs, for members of the bargaining unit. It is extremely difficult, however, to see how such a remedy could realistically be granted considering the very minimal nature of the work performed in the affected classifications. Nor can it be persuasively argued that the company could have kept such a recalled employee or employees busy by assigning them work (of the same classification) being performed on other shifts. It seems quite clear that the contract does not offer a basis for so directing the

11. 24 AAA 9.

assignment of work, but even if that is not to be regarded as the issue in the present case, it would seem clear that such a transfer of work in the situation of limited work which is here present might only have had the result of causing some layoff on the shift from which the work was transferred.

## The Exception for Emergencies

An emergency, according to one dictionary, is "a sudden need for immediate action." In the industrial environment, however, there are many sudden needs for immediate action that do not necessarily fall within the meaning of "emergency," as the word is used in collective bargaining agreements. A flood, a fire, or an explosion will surely qualify, and if the contract permits foremen to do bargaining unit work in emergencies, it is not likely that objections would be raised following disasters of that kind. But a request from a customer for a rush delivery also calls for immediate action. Is that an emergency such as would justify a foreman's working? Or is it merely one of the normal occurrences of business, to be dealt with in the ordinary way? Furthermore, some emergencies are man-made, and within the power of men to avoid. Where management neglects routine maintenance of a machine, for instance, should the inevitable breakdown during a shift result in "emergency" privileges, in the same manner as an unaccountable breakdown might?[12] These are some of the questions of fact

12. A question of this kind was raised by the union at the *Corn Products Company* (American Federation of Grain Millers, AFL–CIO), 16 AAA 21. A heavy rainfall occurred during one night, and suspecting that part of the plant might be affected, a foreman made an inspection tour about 1:00 A.M. He found the water level in an electrical manhole dangerously high, threatening to cause a short circuit. Furthermore, water was draining into the basement of the plant. Enlisting the help of a production worker, he installed a pump and operated it for thirty minutes.

This would clearly seem to have been the prudent thing to do, for damage to the electrical system might have resulted if pumping had been delayed until the start of the day shift. Nor was it possible to call in a bargaining unit employee within a short time. But the union filed a grievance, based on the assertion that management was aware of the probability of seepage after a heavy rainfall. By failing to take timely precautions, the union argued, the company had forfeited the privilege of relying on the "emergency" exception to the rule of barring foremen from production work.

Bert L. Luskin, who arbitrated the case, found the facts not exactly as the

and interpretation that arise in disputes over performance of rank-and-file work by supervisors.

## Predictable "Emergencies"

The distinction between an urgent production problem and an emergency was drawn by A. August Lanna, II, in a case of the *Gulf States Paper Corporation* (United Papermakers and Paperworkers, AFL–CIO).[13] The contract here was silent on the question of foremen working, but it was company practice not to permit them to do bargaining unit work except in emergencies. One Sunday morning in October 1960, a supervisor assisted in the removal of a water cooler from a certain area so that the place might be used for storage of paper. The supervisor had known several days earlier that this task would have to be done, and he reported the need to his own supervisor. But somehow, the water cooler was not removed in advance. As it might have idled about fifteen employees not to use that space for storage, the supervisor applied himself to the task of disconnecting the pipes. The job took a few minutes. As it was admitted that such work would ordinarily be done by a pipefitter, the union's grievance asked that the pipefitter, who had not been called in to work that Sunday, be given call-in pay.

Mr. Lanna said that an emergency could be defined only "as a situation which becomes prevalent as of an immediate instant and requires immediate action to prevent losses which might affect both the employer and employees." Because the company knew at least a

---

union had portrayed them. The dangerous condition had been "closely checked," he said, and had been corrected on all occasions "when it became evident that the pit had to be pumped out in order to keep the water from flowing into the conduit. . . . In substance, it is the opinion of the arbitrator that the condition which existed required immediate attention to the extent that the water should have been pumped out as quickly as possible in order to avoid or prevent the possibility of serious and extensive damage. In view of the fact that sufficient unit employees were not available to perform the function, and in view of the fact that the work should not have been delayed until the start of the first shift or until unit employees could be called in or perform the work, the supervisor was justified in performing the 30 minutes of manual functions within the permissive language of Article IV, Section 15."

13. 34 AAA 2.

week in advance that the water cooler would have to be moved, and as it knew the consequences of not moving it before Sunday, this was no emergency.[14]

A ruling to the same effect—that only circumstances "which the company could not foresee and/or avoid" constitute emergencies—was handed down by Howard A. Cole at the *Parsons Corporation* (United Automobile Workers, AFL–CIO).[15] The grievance was filed because a foreman had worked for about twenty minutes on each of two successive days during which the regular employee, who would normally have done that work, was on temporary assignment to another shift to help fill an order for the Navy. There was nothing wrong with that transfer, Mr. Cole wrote, but having put it into effect, the company "had a real obligation to plan and carry out operations in a manner which would, so far as possible, make unnecessary the performance of [the work in question] on the first shift."

As the forbidden work was done on two successive days, the question was raised as to whether this alone excluded reliance on the emergency provision. Mr. Cole answered that repetition by itself did not mean there was no emergency any more than a single occurrence meant that there was.

Whether a given situation does or does not fall within the coverage of the emergency exception . . . can only be determined in light of the particular facts and circumstances of that situation. For example, use of the emergency exception on three successive days would not be automatically and necessarily improper, any more than its use on a single day would be automatically and necessarily proper. While frequency of resort to the exception may be a relevant factor to consider, in the final analysis each case must stand on its own.[16]

14. It had also been urged by management that, as only a few minutes of work were at issue, and as no high skills were involved, the grievance ought to be dismissed as *de minimis*. Mr. Lanna said the *de minimis* doctrine would have applied only if the company did not have prior knowledge of the work to be done. Call-in pay was awarded in this case not to either of the two grievants, but to an employee who, according to Mr. Lanna, had a prior claim to the work. The arbitrator's authority to award monetary relief in favor of an employee who did not grieve was derived from the contract.

15. 27 AAA 1.

16. The remedy problem in this case was of some interest. The union had sought call-in pay for the employee next in line for overtime, but there was evidence that a motion had been passed at a union meeting to penalize em-

## Repeated Emergencies

Whether repetition of an incident precluded the existence of an emergency also arose at the *Celanese Corporation of America* (Textile Workers Union of America, AFL–CIO),[17] where a drain line became clogged, causing water to back up and soak several hundred bales of cotton. It became necessary for a foreman to examine each bale and determine which had to be scrapped. All the trucking and rebaling incidental to this operation was performed by warehouse employees, but some slitting open of bales, weighing, and handling of the material was done by the foreman.

The union grieved, demanding fifteen hours' pay at time-and-a-half for an employee next in line for overtime when the incident occurred. The company rejected the grievance, citing a "company policy" adopted nine years earlier, to which the union had allegedly agreed, that foremen could engage in production work "as a temporary measure in case of emergency."

While this grievance was pending a second incident occurred. It seems that a sprinkler head broke in the same area, wetting close to two hundred bales. The process of weighing, examining, and determining which bales could be salvaged was repeated by the foreman, bringing the total of bargaining unit work performed by him to thirty-one hours.

When the matter came before Samuel H. Jaffee, the union argued that even if the first incident could be considered an "emergency," the same could not be said of the second. Apparently, the union was most concerned about the weighing operation, a task normally performed by hourly rated employees. Three questions were before the arbitrator: (1) Had the union agreed to the policy statement cited by the company? (2) Did each of the flooding incidents constitute an emergency? (3) Could the weighing of bales have been separated from

ployees accepting overtime assignments while others were on layoff. As some employees had accepted overtime since the adoption of that resolution, while others declined, the award directing four hours' call-in pay to the appropriate bargaining unit employee was made contingent upon his submitting an affidavit to the company stating that he would have reported for work had he been called.

17. 14 AAA 2.

the managerial tasks performed by the supervisor? The arbitrator upheld the company on all points:

1. It is unnecessary to determine whether the policy referred to above, claimed to have been agreed to, is still in existence. Even if it is not, it is the general rule that a supervisor can in any event do unit work "as a temporary measure in case of emergency." So to this extent the policy changed nothing.

2. Do we have an "emergency" here? I see no escape from the conclusion that there was an emergency in both incidents. The fact that it happened twice made the second incident no less an emergency on the facts presented. Among these facts were (a) that time was of the essence, and (b) the large amount of money involved in connection with salvage operations. The fact that the flooding happened twice did not convert the abnormal into the normal.

3. I conclude on the facts peculiar to this case that it was impracticable to require [the foreman] to have separated the weighing from the rest of the work, and that, on the whole, the weighing portion of the work was in any event *de minimis*.

## Scheduling Problems and Emergencies

There is often an element of urgency about scheduling a crew for work, and the unexpected failure of some employees to report may create what management regards as an emergency, and what the union believes is merely the consequence of excessively "tight" scheduling, without enough allowance for extra help. That was the situation at the *Celanese Corporation of America* (United Construction Workers).[18]

The union's case, in essence, was that management had created its own emergency by scheduling only thirty-one employees for a shift that required a minimum of twenty-nine employees to operate. Such a schedule was too tight, the union argued. It did not leave room for normal absenteeism. Thus, when only twenty-eight employees appeared, the foreman substituted for the absent man to keep the shift running.

The company's defense was based on the contract, which read:

It is agreed that supervisory employees, excluded from the bargaining unit, shall not perform work usually performed by the production . . .

18. 3 AAA 15.

employees of the bargaining unit, except: 1. In case of emergency . . .
2. In the absence of regular employees when no other qualified employee
is available. . . .

and on the fact that there seemed to be a concerted refusal of employees on an earlier shift to "double over" and fill the vacant job.

Although scheduling of thirty-one employees for a shift requiring
at least twenty-nine might be "tight," Samuel H. Jaffee ruled, the
company could not be blamed for not anticipating a "concerted refusal" of employees on other shifts to respond to a work call.

At any rate, I cannot on the evidence before me find that there existed
a "company-created emergency" in the only sense that might be an effective answer to the company's reliance on [the quoted contract clause]—
that, right or wrong, it deliberately or perhaps recklessly brought about
the situation which resulted in the events of the night of July 19.

## No Emergency When Employees Could Have Been Scheduled

As we have seen, the controlling fact in the *Celanese* case was that
management could not know in advance that a concerted refusal to
report for work would take place. At *T. B. Wood's Sons Company*
(United Automobile Workers, AFL–CIO),[19] the problem was not absenteeism, but defective work. But here, the company could have
scheduled men for the work. The failure to do so was therefore held
against management.

Lewis M. Gill said that the discovery on a Friday that certain pieces
intended for delivery the following Monday were defective, and the
scheduled absence of production workers on the day when the defects
were discovered, did not constitute an emergency within the meaning
of a clause barring foremen from non-emergency work. It was therefore a violation for the night shift foreman to have repaired the work
himself. The contract, Mr. Gill wrote, "plainly refers to a type of
situation where the regular employees cannot do the work in the time
available," making it necessary for the foreman to "pitch in and get it
done." Either a day shift or a night shift worker should have been
called in to do the work, he concluded.[20]

19. 29 AAA 10.
20. This award would normally have included back pay to an employee, but
Mr. Gill thought that "considerations of equity" and "common fairness" barred

## De Minimis Emergencies

In some of the cases discussed above, management knew in advance exactly what had to be done and could have made arrangements other than to have supervisors do production work. That is why the defense of emergency was disallowed. At the *Alan Wood Steel Company* (United Steelworkers of America, AFL–CIO)[21] management knew only in a general way that certain tasks had to be done, but could not know exactly when the need would arise. Nevertheless, this knowledge was sufficient to result in an adverse decision on the question of emergency work.

The task took only about five minutes; it consisted of dislodging a jam of ore being carried from a mine to a mill. This was done by burning out the clogged metal with torch equipment. The union's grievance quickly followed, asking that four hours' call-in pay be given to a bargaining unit welder. The company's answer was that it did not encourage foremen to do non-supervisory work, but that the grievance should be denied because: (1) it was *de minimis,* involving only five minutes of work; (2) foremen had done such work off and on for about fifteen years without protest on the part of the union; and (3) an emergency made the work necessary.

Addressing himself first to the third point, Sidney Sugerman said that although the "precise timing and extent" of the work could not be anticipated, it was, by its "repetitiveness," a "natural expectation."

---

monetary relief because of special circumstances. It seems that the foreman, before undertaking the work, had obtained the approval of a union committeeman. The union later argued that no individual had the right to approve contract violations, and Mr. Gill said this statement was "quite right as a general principle." But he pointed out that the contract gives committeemen broad authority to settle grievances "with or without" the aggrieved employee. "The broad purpose of encouraging settlement of complaints through the Steward or Committeeman has some definite pertinence here," he wrote. "I think it is at least arguable that if the Steward and Committeeman are thus given authority to settle complaints, they may well have authority to waive a strict enforcement of the contract." As the arbitrator did not award pay to anyone, it was not necessary for him to rule on whether a day shift or a night shift employee was entitled to the relief.

21. 39 AAA 3.

For that reason, it could not be regarded as an emergency within the contract's meaning.

It is the opinion of the undersigned that the mill shift foreman was not protected by the contract in doing the burning work. Despite what he may have done previously in that connection without union complaint, whether the latter had notice of it or not, he was forbidden by contract to engage in such work clearly belonging to members of the bargaining unit.

In fact, wrote Mr. Sugerman, that the company could assert a past practice in favor of foremen doing this work itself "undercuts the argument of 'emergency.'" Finally, he wrote, it is "inaccurate" to speak of *de minimis* violations of this kind, for it "is of a type commonly regarded as substantial and serious in industrial relations." Four hours' call-in pay was awarded.

Perhaps the most frustrating case, from management's point of view, was that of *Borg-Warner Corporation* (United Automobile Workers, AFL–CIO),[22] for here the company was found in violation of the contract, although it is difficult to see what the company might have done under the circumstances that would not have breached the agreement. The difficulty was that the contract clause, which barred foremen from production work, simply did not permit of exceptions for the kind of circumstance that arose.

The protested incident occurred on the night shift. Normally, an employee on the day shift filled propane tanks in preparation for the night crew. On this occasion, however, he forgot. However, the tanks had to be filled if the employees were to do any work. The night shift foreman first tried to get a bargaining unit employee to perform the task, but all said they did not know how. As he himself had never filled propane tanks, and was not sure he knew how, he telephoned one of the supervisors and received instructions, which he obeyed. While filling the tank, one of the bargaining unit employees, who had said he could not do the work, stood by and offered advice, revealing thereby that he was not as innocent of experience as he had pretended.

The whole operation took eight or nine minutes. Nevertheless, a grievance was filed, asking that call-in pay be given to an employee who, according to the union, should have been called in to do the

22. 51 AAA 14.

work. The employer's defense was threefold: First, it was said, the failure of the first-shift employee to do his job created an "emergency," in that the night shift could not work without the fuel. Secondly, the amount of work done was *de minimis*. And finally, it was argued that the union could not prove that the person named as the grievant would have been called in, in any event. Under the circumstances, no monetary relief should be awarded.

The difficulty with the company's position, John F. Sembower said, was that the contract did list some exceptions to the ban on work by foremen, but emergencies were not among those exceptions. The lapse was all the more significant in that the call-in pay section did refer to emergencies as a circumstance relieving management of its obligation, which proved that the parties had not been unaware of the possibility of such occurrences. Mr. Sembower went on to say that, to a certain extent, an exception for emergencies could be implied in any agreement. But in that event, the definition of emergency would have to be a very narrow one, limited to "fires, catastrophies and threatened disasters," and other circumstances which similarly defy "intelligent anticipation." In the case before him, he wrote, the foreman thought he faced a "desperate situation," but it was not an emergency "in the strict sense of the word."

The *de minimis* defense was also rejected. In fact, Mr. Sembower thought it inconsistent of the company to plead emergency and *de minimis* at the same time. Finally, he ruled that the lack of absolute proof that the grievant was the person to be called in did not matter. There was such a "strong inference" that he was next in line to be called in that the objection had to be overruled. Besides, the company had not raised this point during grievance processing, which was another reason that the defect in the union's case, if it was a defect, could not be controlling.

### Teaching and Testing

Some jobs are best taught by practical demonstration. It is perhaps for this reason that many contracts that forbid supervisors to work do permit them to take over a production job for the purpose of teaching rank-and-filers, or to test the effectiveness of production techniques.

An unusual question was raised at the *American Bosch Arma Mississippi Corporation* (International Union of Electrical, Radio and Machine Workers, AFL–CIO).[23] Could a supervisor invoke the privilege of working while teaching, where the employee being taught was not under his direct supervision? It seems that a manufacturing superintendent worked with a bargaining unit employee for a short time to develop a new system of packing magnetos without damaging identification plates or chipping paint. The union believed that he went beyond proper limits in the work he did, but its alternative objection was that, as the superintendent was not in direct charge of the employee, he was not authorized to work under any circumstances.

"There was no evidence," wrote Douglas B. Maggs in answer to that argument, "that only an employee's immediate supervisor, his foreman, is authorized under the parties' agreement to assign work to, or direct, or instruct an employee." Consequently, the supervisor's work could not "for that reason alone" be held a violation of the contract. Furthermore, instruction of employees was concededly necessary because the work involved was on a product never before manufactured by the company. Although the union was correct in its contention that other supervisors would not have thought it necessary to do as much bargaining unit work as the supervisor in question did, he was nevertheless "motivated . . . solely by a purpose to instruct" the employee concerned. "Some persons find it necessary, when instructing others how to do something, to demonstrate how it should be done—to say 'Do it this way.' Others believe they can instruct chiefly by words, with little or no demonstration." The supervisor whose work was protested "is a person who believes that he can achieve little by instructing chiefly by words." The production work he did approached the "maximum permissible," but he did not exceed that maximum.

## Tasks "Incidental" to Supervisory Duties

It is not always easy to tell whether a supervisor is doing only work incidental to his supervisory functions or is encroaching on the bargaining unit. The reason is that the line drawn by union contracts between unit and non-unit functions is frequently an arbitrary one.

23. 25 AAA 13.

Moreover, observing the limits it imposes sometimes seems to violate common sense.

A case in point was that of the *Oxford Paper Company* (United Papermakers and Paperworkers, AFL–CIO),[24] where there was no clear-cut contractual restriction on the type of work a foreman might do. Arbitrator Saul Wallen held that an acting foreman had not violated the agreement when he performed certain repair and maintenance operations while getting a machine ready for production. "The fact that duties of a similar nature were sometimes performed by foremen" in the past was one factor in the company's favor. Another was the "emergency nature" of the repairs, although the need for repairs was "foreseeable," and "greater prudence" might have been shown in assigning another production worker to the repair task. Mr. Wallen concluded: "This grievance arose out of the fact that [the acting foreman] impresses the men in the unit as a little too 'eager beaver' and that he fails to exercise the forbearance that other supervisors have shown under similar circumstances. While he was close to the line drawn by company policy between proper and improper activities for foremen, I do not believe he crossed it on the occasion complained of."

Another case having the same characteristics was that of the *Consumers Power Company* (Utility Workers of America, AFL–CIO),[25] arbitrated by David P. Miller. It seems that a sales supervisor, who customarily drove his station wagon between Royal Oak and East Detroit, one day delivered a product that was believed to be needed there. Deliveries were the work of bargaining unit employees, of course, but as the sales supervisor was driving between the two locations anyway, and as the product was needed to complete a sale, it did not occur to him that having the item in the back of his station wagon made a difference. It seemed "incidental" to his supervisory duties, and therefore permissible.

Mr. Miller said the supervisor had erred. The clause barring supervisors from bargaining unit work, he wrote, makes no exception for unit work "incidental" to supervisory functions. He urged upon management "intelligent application" of contractual restrictions, and upon the union "avoidance of picayune complaints and overzealous policing

24. 5 AAA 16.
25. 45 AAA 8.

which might impair the efficient functioning of the organization." But he did uphold the grievance.

## "Checking Out" Production Standards

If employees are disturbed at the sight of foremen working, even when the object is to test and improve productive techniques, how much more distressed they must be when the object of the foreman's work is to determine whether bargaining unit employees are deliberately holding back production. That was the circumstance at the *Yale & Towne Manufacturing Company* (International Association of Machinists, AFL–CIO).[26]

For about a week, the employees of a certain department and management found themselves at odds over production standards. The former thought a speedup was in progress; the latter believed there was a deliberate slowdown among welders and frame assemblers. Finally, an incident occurred that led to the disciplinary suspension of virtually an entire shift. In order to gather facts on the basis of which the suspensions would either be revoked or sustained, the company's director of industrial relations asked five supervisors of the department to perform some of the work on Sunday and "check out" the production standards. There were on hand some unit employees who had not been suspended, but the director did not believe they had the skill for the work required, nor did he believe they could be trusted under the circumstances to work at the proper pace.

Each of the supervisors did a day's work, but as it happened, their findings were never used, for a two-week work stoppage began; by the time it ended, the data the supervisors assembled were no longer needed. Nevertheless, the union filed a grievance protesting the work done by the supervisors that Sunday.

G. Allan Dash, Jr., said the work was privileged under a clause permitting supervisors to meet "emergencies," providing such work is "kept to a minimum."[27]

26. 34 AAA 20.

27. The text of the relevant clause read: "The work jurisdiction of supervisory employees shall be limited to the allocation of work, direction, instruction and training of employees. Work of a productive nature that may be necessary in carrying out their duties and in meeting emergencies shall be kept to a minimum. The Union may question as grievances, circumstances that

The record in this case shows that management concluded that the employees . . . had not given the protested standards a fair trial and was convinced that they were engaging in a concerted slow-down of work in an attempt to sustain their contention that the protested standards were inadequate. As a consequence of that conclusion management decided that it was not required to follow the several remaining steps of [the clause governing protested standards] to check out the adequacy of the protested standards. Instead, it determined to charge virtually the entire Department with a concerted slow-down and to suspend almost the whole work force of the Department. This was a drastic step to take, but was one which supervision had the right to take under . . . the agreement with, of course, the accompanying requirement to defend its action as being based upon "good and sufficient cause" if later called upon to do so. . . . When management decided to check out the protested standards on Sunday, September 25, 1960, solely to decide if it was correct in its act of suspending the mass of . . . employees for an alleged concerted slow-down of work, it certainly was proceeding with prudence. . . . In reaching this conclusion the arbitrator accepts the company's statement that the check study was not made to sustain its position concerning the adequacy of the protested work standards.

Mr. Dash concluded that the work in question was not of a "productive nature." It was rather a response to an emergency situation, it being "wholly unrealistic" to believe that the "checking out" of standards could have been accomplished by bargaining unit employees.

### Inventory Work

Once a year or so, when inventory is taken, work becomes available which is often not clearly within the scope of the collective bargaining agreement. There are many reasons for this ambiguity. One is that some contracts cover *employees,* not work. Other contracts that do identify work as "belonging" to bargaining unit members ordinarily refer to the normal production tasks and often do not mention inventory work at all. Employees assigned to these special tasks are usually working out of their normal classifications or, at any rate, working at

---

involve unreasonable productive work performed by employees not covered by this Agreement as it applies to work usually done by employees covered by this Agreement."

other than usual jobs. Furthermore, inventory-taking also requires the participation of salaried clerical workers and supervisors, who do not often find themselves in the shop working so closely with production workers. Finally, inventory occurs most often either when the plant is shut down for that purpose, or on week-ends when the plant is not otherwise operating. And so, in addition to questions as to whether non-unit personnel are taking work from the bargaining unit, issues arise as to the order of layoff, recall rights, and the observance of the contractual method of distributing overtime. Some typical cases involving the union's claim of jurisdiction over inventory-taking follow.

## Inventory Work Not Exclusively for Unit Employees

The fact that a union contract specifically mentions a type of work, and requires that preference be given to seniors when and if such work is given to unit employees does not necessarily establish that work as the exclusive right of unit employees. This was a holding in a case at the *Simmons Company* (Upholsterers' International Union of North America, AFL–CIO).[28] The dispute involved the taking of inventory, which management had assigned in part to bargaining unit members, and in part to office personnel. The contract said only that "when employees are selected for inventory work, the selection shall be made by applying [a combination of seniority and ability]."

Did this mean that inventory work had the same status as production work? The union thought so, but Robert G. McIntosh did not. He wrote:

There is nothing in [the inventory clause] that states that the company will give the inventory work to the employees in the bargaining unit, but merely sets out the method by which they will be selected in the event the company does use them. True, the union is recognized as the exclusive bargaining agent, but that does not mean that all the work will be given to members of the union. . . . Inventory is not normally production work and would not ordinarily be an exclusive function of the bargaining unit unless the parties, by contract, specifically state it so.[29]

28. 35 AAA 7.
29. Mr. McIntosh also said that the procedures followed by management in taking inventory on this occasion were no different from those it had observed in the past. This fact contributed to the decision in favor of the company.

The contract at the *Kysor Heating Company* (United Automobile Workers, AFL–CIO),[30] contained two provisions that, applied to an inventory problem, seemed to be in conflict. The first said that half the employees needed for inventory-taking would be selected on the basis of seniority, the other half on the basis of ability. The other provision, which did not deal specifically with inventory work, said that foremen whose departments consisted of fewer than six employees would be permitted to do bargaining unit work. How, then, did these two clauses apply at a time when only one person was needed for inventory in a department where the foreman was not forbidden to do bargaining unit work? The union believed seniority applied, in which case, the steward, with superseniority rights, should have been called in. The company interpreted the contract to mean that only if there was more work than the foreman could handle was there any need to assign a unit employee at all. This brought the steward's grievance before William Haber.

As the union conceded that the foreman could have been the *second* employee assigned to inventory, if two had been needed, the question really seemed to turn on whether the inventory clause of the contract, relied upon by the union, invalidated the provision permitting foremen to do bargaining unit work. On this critical point, the company was upheld. The union's interpretation "strains the meaning" of the inventory clause, he wrote. "The requirement that one-half of the number needed for inventory should be selected in accord with seniority and the remaining half without reference to seniority, is intended to refer to bargaining unit employees and not to the foreman." Mr. Haber was helped to this conclusion by the fact that the practice of having a foreman take inventory in that department by himself "has apparently prevailed since 1953 without protest by the union."

### Inventory on Overtime Day

At the *Electric Storage Battery Company* (International Union of Electrical, Radio and Machine Workers, AFL–CIO),[31] the contract required that overtime "be distributed among all hourly paid employees of that job classification as evenly as is reasonably practicable on a

30. 27 AAA 2.
31. 16 AAA 6.

quarterly basis; subject, however, to requirements of production." When the need for taking inventory in the "boosting" department arose, management directed that a "booster attendant" from the shipping and receiving department do the work on an overtime day. The grievant, who was both in the booster classification and assigned to the boosting area, claimed that the work should have been given to him. Bert L. Luskin ruled that this assignment was not a violation of the contract because inventory work was "not the normal type of work which is considered to come within the regular duties performed" by the grievant. Furthermore, he said, the requirement that overtime be allocated evenly among employees in a classification "does not necessarily require that the work be assigned to a particular classification where the work is not normally required to be performed by the employees in the classification in question." In this case, as the employee who performed the eight hours of inventory work on overtime was classified as a booster attendant, a similar period of overtime would have to be given in the future to the grievant. But the assignment of the work to the employee from the shipping department was not in itself an error.

## Within the Scope of the Agreement

Whether inventory work comes within the purview of an overtime distribution clause also arose at the *American Can Company, Dixie Cup Division* (United Papermakers and Paperworkers, AFL–CIO),[32] but this time with a decision different from that in the *Electric Storage Battery* case.

On a Saturday, the employer had assigned five first-shift employees to what was to have been five hours of inventory work, but which actually took eight to nine hours. This, according to the union, was a violation of a clause providing that "when operations are scheduled for Saturday, the first and second shifts will each be five hour shifts. . . ." Under this clause, the union contended, the first-shift crew should have been permitted to work only five hours, the remainder going to a similar crew from the second shift.

Management's answer was that the quoted language applied to machine operations only and governed procedures not applicable

32. 4 AAA 17.

where only one shift was scheduled on inventory. Furthermore, it was said, the union's position would make any misjudgment of the estimated time for the work unreasonably costly.

John Perry Horlacher found this defense weak. First of all, if the overtime distribution provision did not apply to non-machine-operating employees, there was no clause that did cover their conditions of work. "It seems a little odd that there could have been a deliberate mutual intent to produce such a result." The language of the overtime clause is "inclusive," not "restrictive." There would have to be "rather compelling reasons" for excluding some employees from coverage of this clause. It was probably true, as management representatives asserted at the arbitration hearing, that the five-hours-on-Saturday provision came about because the parties wanted to avoid longer shifts in the machine operations. "It does not automatically follow, however, as the company argument implies, that the provision must be limited in its application to the principal occasion which brought it into being." He went on to say:

A rule or principle stated in the general form carries with it a presumption of general applicability. This of course can be rebutted but it is not sufficient for rebutting the presumption to prove that the rule grew out of situation X and thereby infer that it applies only to X. This *may* be the case. But if the rule is inclusively framed, the evidence that it does not apply also to Y or Z ought to be pretty clear and convincing.

Furthermore, to uphold the company's interpretation would be to rob other provisions of the agreement, dealing with "time allocation for shifts other than the first," of meaning. "The principle that the construction of one clause of a contract should give the fullest effect to the entire agreement and not nullify or impair some other provision would in this instance favor the broad construction."[33]

33. While upholding the union's view that second-shift employees should have been called in for the three or four additional hours it took to complete inventory, Mr. Horlacher made it clear that the decision would have been different if fewer hours had been needed.

# 6

# THE INTEGRITY OF JOBS AND
# CLASSIFICATIONS

"The company will exercise its right to require any employee, for purposes of efficiency, to perform any task which is necessary to the ful-
fillment of urgent or essential work . . ."

—From a company's statement in answer
to an out-of-classification grievance

If one were to judge only by the typical management prerogative
clause, it would seem that employers should have little difficulty in
adjusting job duties to the changing needs of the business. The right
"to direct the work forces" would certainly appear to include the
power to rearrange job duties, add new classifications, abolish others,
and leave still other jobs unfilled when they are vacated in one way
or another. Yet, managerial authority to do all these things is not
unlimited. For one thing, the prerogative clause usually contains the
saving phrase that rights will be exercised "subject to other provisions
of the agreement." And even if the proviso is omitted, there is always
the doctrine of implied limitations to contend with. Implications drawn
from negotiated rates, job classifications,[1] job descriptions, or depart-

1. One difficulty in administering job security clauses is that grievants, and
occasionally negotiators, confuse "jobs" with "classifications." The distinction
between the two words arose in a case of the *Copeland Refrigerator Corporation* (International Union of Electrical, Radio and Machine Workers, AFL–

127

mental seniority may not be sufficient to overcome management's right to change job content in all cases. But possible implications do at least serve to establish the arbitrator's jurisdiction over job classification disputes, and the arbitration risk by itself may lead to a more cautious approach than management would otherwise take.

Moreover, contracts often explicitly limit the employer's right to change jobs. In some, for instance, technological change or an alteration in the method of production must have occurred since the contract was last negotiated before the employer can do away with or change an established classification. One object of such provisions, of course, is to prevent the employer from escaping from a bargain that has turned out to be onerous. But quite apart from contractual limitations, implied or expressed, the worker's resistance to change is also something to be reckoned with.[2] To the wage earner, a job is not

---

CIO), 46 AAA 14, where several employees had sought to assert their seniority to resist transfer from one job to another within the same classification. Patrick J. Fisher wrote: "The company has the unquestioned right to assign tasks or jobs within job classifications. In fact, it has *always* transferred employees from one assignment to another within given job classifications. Under this contract, the employees' bid rights become vested in classifications, not jobs. It is significant that during the last contract negotiations the union advanced a proposal which would restrict the company's right to make such assignments within classifications. The company objected and the proposal did not become a part of the contract."

2. An alteration in customary work assignments often brings on two almost instinctive reactions on the part of unions: the first is to resist any change, and the second is to retain control over as much work as possible. Both were evident at *Strick Trailers* (United Automobile Workers, AFL–CIO), 13 AAA 8. The facts, as described by the arbitrator, Lawrence R. Van Deusen, were simple. In January 1959, certain record-keeping tasks were assigned to a time-keeper in the machine shop. At the time, this employee protested that these tasks were unfamiliar to him and were not within his classification. Overruled on this point, he performed those tasks as directed. Three months later, however, the clerical functions were taken away from him and given to an employee who was not in the bargaining unit. Instead, additional timekeeping duties were given the timekeeper. Again he protested, this time asserting that the clerical tasks, although burdensome, belonged to him and could not be transferred out of the unit. Mr. Van Deusen defined the question before him as follows: "Has the company violated the agreement with the union by taking away assigned functions from the timekeeping classification and assigning them to a classification outside the union?" He saw no violation of the agreement, but for very special reasons. "If the assigned work which was withdrawn had

merely a collection of tasks. He tends to think of a job as "his" in the proprietary sense,[3] and the higher his skill, the more profound the sense of possession is. Not surprisingly, as will be seen in many of the cases discussed below, management sometimes waits for the death or retirement of an incumbent before undertaking changes that were apparently long overdue.[4] But some changes cannot wait upon natural attrition; they are dictated by stern reality in a competitive economy.

---

become an historic function, then there would be a violation of the contract," Mr. Van Deusen wrote. As the work had not become an historic function, its removal became "an exercise of the management function and, therefore, not a violation of the agreement." Moreover, he said, the grievant knew, when the clerical tasks were given to him, that the assignment was experimental, subject to change. It was also significant that "job security" was not an issue in this case, no layoffs having occurred in the timekeeping department.

3. For one example of how jealously employees guard their craft "rights," see *Massey-Ferguson, Incorporated* (United Automobile Workers, AFL-CIO), 48 AAA 18. An experimental mechanic (a bargaining unit employee) on the second shift was preparing an experimental tractor to be photographed. Because bare metal would not photograph well, he sprayed a two-inch strip across a small area, using a pressurized paint can available to almost anyone in the shop. The task took ten minutes. When the regular spray painter of the first shift learned of this, he filed a grievance in which he said he should have been given that work. Boaz Siegel wrote: "The amount of work performed by the experimental mechanic on Friday, January 12, 1962, was so small as to come within the doctrine referred to in the judicial system as '*de minimis*.' No modern industrial enterprise can operate if some small straying from strict lines of job classification is not permitted. The amount of time consumed in performing the work in question and the character of the work itself is so small as to be unworthy of an arbitration. If the event complained of by the union was one of a series of incidents of similar character, if the union had charged that this was part of a deliberate course of conduct by the company to undermine the collective bargaining agreement, perhaps the facts would give rise to a matter justifying the use of the arbitral process. Not only was this not charged in the case at hand, but further, the union did not rebut the testimony of the company that no supervisor instructed the experimental mechanic, a member of the bargaining unit, to perform the work in question. Accordingly, it is the opinion of the arbitrator that Grievance No. 37 involves so small a complaint that it does not constitute a breach of the collective bargaining agreement and the parties and the arbitrator are required to overlook it."

4. See, for example, *Chesapeake Corporation of Virginia* (International Brotherhood of Pulp, Sulphite and Paper Mill Workers, AFL–CIO), 8 AAA 14, where, for many years, gear motor repair work had been done by a millwright. The need for such work was declining, and management would have preferred

## The Effect of Negotiated Wage Schedules

In a sense, no collective bargaining agreement is completely silent on the matter of job classifications. The reason is that practically every contract requires the payment of certain rates. And rates are generally keyed to jobs. Does this, then, have the effect of perpetuating listed jobs for the duration of the agreement, or does the wage schedule merely mean that the indicated rates will be paid when and if management chooses to run those particular jobs? This is one of the central questions in administering union contracts. It also appears to be a question which, more than any other, divides arbitrators. However, in evaluating the remarks of arbitrators on this matter, the reader should remember that the question seldom arises in pure form. Many factors combine to lead an arbitrator to his conclusion. One can never be certain that even the strongest language in favor of a theory of contract interpretation would have prevailed if the past practice, the nature of the job descriptions, the presence or absence of a management rights clause, or any one of a number of other factors had not contributed to the final decision.

One case which illustrates the influence of negotiated wage schedules along with other factors was that of *The Warner Company* (United Cement, Lime and Gypsum Workers, AFL–CIO).[5] As far back as

---

to assign the primary responsibility for disassembly, diagnosis, and reassembly to electricians, who could call upon other crafts for help when necessary. But nothing was done until the millwright resigned. Seizing what it thought was an opportunity, management instituted the work assignment change. Unfortunately from the company's viewpoint, however, the contract required that craftsmen be employed in their own classifications, performing duties generally associated with those crafts. Management tried to overcome the effect of this provision by citing its "full employment policy," but Gerald A. Barrett, who arbitrated the dispute, did not believe full employment was the real motive. The purpose the company had in mind was rather, he said, to reorganize the work "as a result of [the millwright's] resignation." He saw no contractual authority for this. "The company possesses the power to exercise such flexibility in assignments as is authorized by the contract and by the past practice at its plant, and it is granted such power in Section X. The company does not possess the right to exercise unlimited flexibility so as to permanently assign work to one craft which has traditionally been performed by another craft."

5. 46 AAA 20.

the 1940s, the company maintained two job classifications, one known as "dust collector operator," and the other as "stone end helper." Both classifications were continued over a period that included at least six new contract negotiations, and four employees actually performed in each classification. They were at all times paid the rates that the prevailing contract said were to be given on those jobs. Later, however, management undertook a cost-cutting program, made necessary by competition. When a new management took over late in 1961, efforts in this direction were intensified, and one result was a decision that the two classifications were no longer needed on each shift. The job duties of each could be performed by one employee without undue burden, it was thought. And so a new classification, called "stone end and dust collector man" was created, and the union was so informed.

Presenting the issue before William N. Loucks, the union set forth seven arguments:

1. The contract contains no management prerogative clause. It must be presumed from that fact that the negotiators intended management to have no rights other than those explicitly stated.

2. Each of the abolished jobs was at that time "part and parcel of the classification system" of the agreement.

3. Arbitrators have held that a job classification and seniority system stands as a barrier against unilateral change by the employer.

4. The distinction drawn in the contract between "jobs" and "classifications" makes the total elimination of the latter "most clearly a violation."

5. The company's notification of the union did not satisfy the contractual requirement of consultation in advance.[6]

6. The contractual requirement of notice to the union is of secondary interest in this discussion, but it does shed some light on problems of adjusting jobs to changing needs under collective bargaining. The arbitrator wrote that a letter given to the union on October 26, 1961, in which it was announced that two job classifications "[would] be abolished," effective November 6, did not satisfy the contractual requirement that "when jobs are discontinued or abolished, the Policy Committee will be notified and the plan discussed by the parties before such action is taken." In order to uphold the company's assertion that the letter complied with its contractual obligation, "it would have to be held that the contract provision means nothing more than giving notice of the abolishment of a job or jobs some time before the effective date of such abolishment . . . The bare words of the provision in question make it

6. The clause stating that "each job shall be given and retain a definite name and qualification" also signified the intent to continue classifications.

7. A provision for discontinuing jobs within classifications under certain conditions, without any reference to discontinuing classifications, makes it clear that the latter may not be done.

The company's chief arguments were an even dozen:

1. It is one of the "residual rights" of management, often upheld by arbitrators, to abolish job classifications and create new ones for "a proper business objective."

2. There was a great deal of common labor involved in both of the combined jobs.

3. With the decline in the volume of work, it cannot be denied that there is not enough for eight men to do.

4. The two jobs selected for a combination classification were not only similar to begin with, but they became more similar as time went on.

5. Arbitrators have held that the right of management to change classifications on the basis of new technology or methods of production is not diminished by the fact that the changes were gradual, rather than dramatic.

6. Even without technological change, the decline in the amount of available work is in itself justification for combining the jobs, and it does not matter that the decline began before the most recent agreement.

7. Arbitrators have rejected the view that a listing of rates and job classifications amounts to a "freeze" of jobs.

8. Several sections of the agreement, in making provision for

---

clear that the parties intended that the Policy Committee get something more in the company notice than a mere opportunity to learn that the company decision *had been made* and *would become effective* on some stated future date. . . . It clearly implies that the union is to be given an opportunity to discuss the matter with the company *before* the company has definitely decided what it is going to do." Nor did other cases, cited by the company, support its position that the "notice" in this case was the same as that which the union had accepted without question in the past in similar cases. The cited cases "did not involve . . . the type of explicit, accomplished-fact-notification the company issued in the instant case. . . ."

new jobs and for the elimination of old ones under certain conditions (after notice to the union), prove that the parties contemplated such action being taken.

9. The notice-to-the union requirement of the contract was satisfied.

10. The contract referred to "creating" jobs, and arbitrators have held that one of the ways of doing that is to combine jobs.

11. Jobs have been combined in the past many times without objection by the union.

12. "The right which management has to combine jobs does not spring from a Management Rights clause. It is a basic reserved right of management. The right is inherent."

Mr. Loucks said that as the company had not complied with the obligation to consult the union, he had it within his power to order restoration of the two classifications, regardless of other considerations. But both parties had indicated that they wanted a decision on the "substantive question." He therefore undertook his own analysis of the issue, and came to the conclusion that the union was largely correct.

*The Obligation to Maintain Classifications*

The listing in the contract of job classification titles and rates "per se" commits the parties to maintain those classifications, he wrote. For this he had three reasons:

1. The contract did not specifically spell out management's right to abolish classifications.

2. No "technological or other change" had occurred, unforeseen at the time of the last negotiations, which was of sufficient gravity to make it "imperative" that the jobs be combined.

3. More specifically, all the business reasons the company had cited for the changes were either known at the time of negotiations or could have been forecast.

The arbitrator has been offered no explanation as to why management could not, or did not, seek to abolish the two job classifications and merge their job duties into a new job classification during the [contract] negotiations. . . . Clearly . . . these factors were then visible, their importance to the company was then clear, and means of adapting to them job classifications to be listed in the agreement should then have been negotiated—or, at least, the company should now be able . . . to show that it *proposed* some means of coping with them in the contract being negotiated.[7]

The union's sixth point, that the contract required every job "to retain a definite name," was particularly well taken. It would not be a "tortured interpretation" of that clause, Mr. Loucks agreed, to hold

7. For another award pointing up the fact that changes in methods of production must have *followed* the most recent contract negotiations if they are to be used as a basis for changing job content or rates, see *Worthington Corporation* (United Steelworkers of America, AFL–CIO), 10 AAA 4, where Donald A. Crawford required the company to reinstate old standards. He wrote: "The company is correct when it says that [the contract] provides no specific time limit within which it must adjust standards to changed conditions and methods, products, tools and the like. But the right granted the company by [the contract] to keep its standards on a proper basis imposes the normal or reasonable expectancy that it will exercise that right upon a contemporary basis. To sustain the company position is to hold that standards established by the company, accepted by the union, in effect for a substantial period of time, including contract renewals, and apparently quite satisfactory to the company, were not permanent standards protected by the agreement. Such a ruling—in the absence of a clear understanding that the company could delay revising standards for process changes indefinitely—is not reasonable. Each party has the right to expect that the other will go forward and exercise the rights bestowed upon it by the contract's terms."

To the same effect was S. Herbert Unterberger's decision in *The Bassick Company* (International Union of Electrical, Radio and Machine Workers, AFL–CIO), 7 AAA 7. "When the language in [the clause relating to incentive rates] was agreed upon and included in the collective bargaining agreement in the early 1950's it was the clear intent of the parties to stabilize the permanent rates then in effect. At the same time, provision was made for changes in those rates if a change in operation, methods, etc., takes place. Read in context, it is obvious that the parties meant this to apply to future changes. It would be extraordinary, indeed, and thoroughly unlikely, that they meant this to encompass a change in operations, methods or equipment . . . which, at that time, had already occurred as much as ten years earlier." In this case, the company had stated, in justification of the change, that the original time study records were lost. Mr. Unterberger said this made no difference. Management could not become "the beneficiary of its own negligence."

See also *Columbia Broadcasting System, Incorporated* (United Electrical, Radio and Machine Workers of America, Independent), 28 AAA 19, where Jules J. Justin ruled that a job had not been changed sufficiently since the last wage negotiations to justify reclassification.

See also *Morse Chain Company* (International Association of Machinists,

that it means that, once given a name, as a job is in the contract, it "shall be retained for the term of that agreement." On the other hand, the company's evidence did not satisfy Mr. Loucks that the union had agreed to similar action in the past.

The details of these four cases, which are the only ones the company has offered in support of its assertions with respect to past practice, do not permit the arbitrator to conclude that past practice created or demonstrated the existence of a contractual unilateral company right to abolish a job classification and combine its job duties with those of another job classification. Clearly, if the company informs the union of an impending or proposed action of that sort and there is a specific settlement between the parties as to what is to be done—as there apparently was in the first of the . . . four cases, or there is no recorded final objection by the union—as there apparently was none in the last three cases, the mere fact that the company proceeds to effectuate its original or a modified proposal does not demonstrate that the company is using a *unilateral right* to proceed to abolish and combine in a case where the union does object to and oppose the company action. What the company seeks from the arbitrator in the instant case is a decision that it has the right to proceed unilaterally despite the union's opposition to abolishment of the job classifications involved and combination of the job duties thereof into a newly created job classification. The arbitrator does not find in the four cases cited by the company any demonstration of the existence in fact of such unilateral power prior to the initiation of the instant case.

But the union's victory in this case was not complete. The award directed the employer to reinstate the two classifications and to reimburse employees who were working in those classifications for losses they may have suffered. But the union had also asked the arbitrator to restore four jobs in each classification. This the arbitrator refused to do because, he said, it was not within his authority "to determine how many employees the company must have in each job classification." He did say, however, that his refusal of the union's request in this respect was without prejudice to the union's right to press a new

---

AFL–CIO), 44 AAA 18, where the union claimed that a shutdown of another plant of the company and the consequent increase in the number of parts handled by the instant plant justified an upgrading of certain jobs. Daniel C. Williams said that a substantial increase in work had taken place, but only that part of the increase which followed the effective date of the contract could be taken into account in the new job evaluation.

grievance alleging that the company, subsequent to the award, was maintaining fewer jobs in either or both classifications than it was obligated to do under the agreement.[8]

An attempt to combine two jobs into one was also an issue that came before Peter Di Leone at the *Harbison-Walker Refractories Company* (United Stone and Allied Products Workers, AFL–CIO).[9] Here, too, "implications" were drawn from the wage classification schedule, but not such strong implications as would amount to a "guarantee" that jobs would always exist.

Management here had not undertaken a fundamental reorganization of work. Nothing more seemed to be involved than a combining of two jobs so that the incumbents would work two days at one and three days at another. Contract provisions were also different. One clause, relied upon by the union, stated that wage rates and job classifications would be maintained for the duration of the agreement. This clause seemed to favor the union. Another provision required negotiation of rates for "new and/or changed job classifications and new methods or substantial addition to existing classifications." The latter clause seemed to favor management, at least in the sense that it showed that the negotiators had contemplated the possibility of job changes during the life of the agreement.

It was on the second clause that management relied in an attempt to combine the duties of two classifications during a period when there was not enough work to provide full time for both. One of the jobs was "motor blower," the other was "greaser." According to the com-

8. The events subsequent to the issuance of the award are not known, but it is at least possible that although the employer was not upheld on the questions of principle involved in this case, he may have prevailed in practice, if his object was merely to reduce by four men the number of employees in the two disputed classifications. Management had said that the duties of the two classifications were similar (point 4 in the statement of management's view). Assuming that the volume of work supported only four employees, it would seem that by classifying two as dust collector operators and two as stone end helpers, but letting all four do exactly what they would be doing if their classification were "stone end and dust collector man," management would, in effect, be having its way. Whether this would continue to be so if the volume of work increased is, of course, another question. If management's purpose had been to use a favorable decision in this case as a basis for changes to be put into effect later, the defeat here would be of greater consequence.

9. 32 AAA 2.

pany, a "reappraisal" of the two jobs was required because of a reduction in the amount of work available. The result was to create one classification called "motor blower-greaser," and to assign employees so classified to one job for two days and another for three days each week, paying them on the basis of the kind of work done.

Mr. Di Leone drew some implications from the existence of the wage schedule of the contract. But he thought it important to emphasize that the implications could not be carried to the point of providing a "guarantee" that the indicated work would be offered at all times. The critical fact, he said, was whether technological and method changes had occurred.

Technological changes, the implementation of new processes and a number of other factors may cause the elimination of the job altogether or it may affect it materially. It would be wrong to say that the company is obligated to retain the displaced worker on this job under these circumstances. The right to make these changes rests with the company which includes the right to make decisions to abolish, change or combine jobs and if these decisions are made because of sound operating business practices and are free from any capricious or discriminatory motive, the union cannot be heard to complain.

In the instant case, however, no technological changes were made and no new processes were introduced. This fact distinguishes the instant case from those cited by the company. [The grievant] now performs the exact duties as a greaser when he greases three days a week and the same is true when he performs the motor blower duties, except that they are performed two days a week.

To uphold the company in this case, Mr. Di Leone concluded, would make a "nullity" of the job classifications and rates negotiated by the parties. "Nowhere in this agreement is there a provision which gives the company this right."

A transfer of duties from one classification to another was involved in the *Hellerton Manufacturing Company* case (United Automobile Workers, AFL–CIO),[10] but again it was not based on any technological change. The outcome of this case, as of the *Harbison-Walker* case, was adverse to management.

The problem centered around an operation called "plug tamping,"

10. 28 AAA 20.

performed by female machine operators on a spark plug manufacturing line. Prior to the change, two "material supply men" and two "major set-up and repairmen" were assigned to eighteen machines. The former brought material to the machines and removed the plugs when the tamping operation was completed; the latter were responsible for adjusting machines and making repairs.

In January 1960 the company enlarged the size of the bins from which the operators drew their work. This made it possible, management thought, to eliminate one of the supply men. In addition, the task of removing the trays of completed work was given to the setup men. This reduced still further the work of supply men. This change became the subject of a grievance, which eventually reached Aaron Horvitz.

"The contract not only shows a recognition of job classifications," he wrote, "but specifically evidences an acceptance by the parties that differences must exist between those classifications. The wage scale is tied into the classification system and the differences in rates must be based upon the different functions and duties performed within these classifications. The rates agreed upon after negotiations must reflect the money consideration the parties have placed upon the accumulated duties performed by employees within each classification. If that is so, to permit the company unilaterally during the agreement to add duties to a classification by removing them from another would violate the result achieved when a rate was mutually assigned to the combined set of duties that existed when the rate was agreed upon. If this type of unilateral action were permitted, it would render meaningless the entire rate structure of the contract."[11]

Moreover, Mr. Horvitz found limitations of managerial rights in the job bidding system provided for in the agreement.

An employee exercises his seniority rights based upon the job as it then exists. If after bidding the company has the right to change the job, the successful bidder may have accepted a job that he might not have wanted

11. A parenthetical issue was raised in this case by management's reliance on the fact that no formal job descriptions existed. This made no difference, Mr. Horvitz said, because "the duties of the jobs in question had remained unaltered for many years." As the negotiators had considered these particular jobs when they determined rates, "unilateral adjustment of the work is no different from unilateral adjustment of the rate. . . ."

and have given up a job, to which he cannot return, which he actually prefers.

In this case, Mr. Horvitz said he was specifically not saying what his conclusion would have been if the company had tried to establish a new classification and had offered to negotiate a rate with the union, instead of merely taking work from one classification and giving it to another. "If that had occurred, the new job would have been opened for bid and the rate subject to negotiation. The company, however, did not choose that route and I am not passing thereon one way or another."[12]

## The Doctrine of Implied Limitations

One of the most outspoken opinions in favor of the doctrine that the wage schedule implies limitations on managerial rights to change job classifications was expressed by Robert P. Brecht, in *Conoflow Corporation* (Machinists and Instrument Workers, Independent).[13] The contract at this company contained so strong a management rights clause that the employer was content to hinge his entire case on it. But strong as the clause was, Mr. Brecht held that the company had no right to transfer a certain metal-working operation, known as "precision lapping," from the Valve and Motor Department to the Machinist Department.

The management rights clause, with the employer's underscoring added, read:

*The union agrees* that the *function of management belongs solely to the company,* and that *it will not interfere with the company's free exercise* of this function subject to the provisions of this agreement. The functions of management include, among others: The right to select and to hire new employees; to direct the working force; to formulate reasonable plant rules not inconsistent with the provisions of this agreement; to suspend

12. Mr. Horvitz arbitrated a case at the *American Radiator and Standard Sanitary Corporation* (International Union of Electrical, Radio and Machine Workers, AFL–CIO), 18 AAA 9, which, unlike the *Hellerton* case, did involve a technological change. Not surprisingly, in view of what he wrote in the *Hellerton* case, the decision was in favor of the company. The *American Radiator* case is discussed more fully in Chapter 8.

13. 34 AAA 11.

or to discharge for just cause; to transfer employees because of lack of work or other reasons consistent with efficient operation; *to assign work to employees;* to decide the number and location of its facilities; to determine the products to be manufactured, *including the means and the processes of manufacturing;* and *to introduce new and improved production methods or facilities,* exclusive of any incentive methods of pay unless negotiated. *Nothing contained in this Section shall contravene the positive provisions of this agreement.*

Mr. Brecht upheld the grievance. The significance of the clause cited by the employer was "quite limited," he said. It could not be used for "reshuffling of job content" or altering "the framework of operating practices." He conceded that the company had shown a logical basis for the transfer of the work, but this showing was "almost incidental" to management's chief argument that the management rights clause gave it unlimited power.

Effective, positive provisions of the agreement that limit this broadly interpreted right, he wrote, are found in an appendix to the contract which establishes the "rate structure." This constituted more than a "pegging out of rates," he declared. "It includes as well a series of job titles associated with these rates and it may properly be presumed that this section . . . must be taken seriously and must be given meaning."

Job titles are not created in a void. It is true that there are no job descriptions that detail the job content of each classification of work, but this in no way justifies the conclusion that the job content behind each is an open question, subject to the company's redefinition by its own unilateral action. . . . If the company were at liberty under its right to assign work to reconstitute the work element of jobs, the whole fabric of job titles would become meaningless.

Furthermore, Mr. Brecht wrote, certain departments were identified in the contract (although without details as to the jobs performed in each), and this identification implied that "customary practice" will determine where work is to be performed. True, he said, the work in question here overlapped two departments, but that did not give the employer the right to transfer the overlapping work permanently to either department. If this was to be done, the union's concurrence had to be obtained.

The only solace management may have extracted from this case was Mr. Brecht's dictum that a "different matter" would have been presented if management had shown that the transfer of precision lapping had been made necessary by "new and improved production methods and facilities." This, however, had not been the company's position. "The basic stand of the company was its right to assign work to employees, unqualified and unrestrained and inclusive of job content changes, without benefit of improved facilities or methods," he stated.

## A Contrary View on the Effect of Wage Schedules

A viewpoint directly contrary to Mr. Brecht's was expressed by John Perry Horlacher in *American Chain and Cable Company* (United Steelworkers of America, AFL–CIO).[14] In fact, the company cited to Mr. Horlacher a prior decision of Mr. Brecht for the same parties, in which the latter had expressed views similar to those stated in the *Conoflow* decision. Mr. Horlacher acknowledged that the circumstances of the cited case were comparable, but he said he thought Mr. Brecht's views were mistaken, and he chose not to follow them. He said he preferred the viewpoints expressed by Ralph T. Seward and Sylvester Garrett in two steel industry arbitration cases.[15]

In any event, Mr. Horlacher undertook his own analysis of the issues of this case. He found that following a survey conducted by an outside management consultant firm ("a carpet-bagging outfit that caused all the trouble," according to the union), the company decided to put into effect what it called a "prescheduling production control system." The purpose was to produce a more even flow of production from job to job and from one department to another. The execution of this plan involved the combination of some jobs, the elimination of several old classifications, and the introduction of some new ones. The total effect was to improve service with fewer employees. The excess workers were laid off in accordance with the normal procedure for reduction in force.

Replying to the union's grievance,[16] the company cited two clauses that it interpreted to justify the change. The first stated, in part:

14. 51 AAA 16.
15. Ralph T. Seward, *Kaiser Aluminum and Chemical Corporation*, 8 SAB 5195, 5196 (1959), and Sylvester Garrett, *United States Steel Corporation*, 2 SAB 1217 (1953).
16. The grievance read: "The union is protesting the company's action in the foundry. The company abolished mutually agreed-to job descriptions with-

When changes are made in equipment, method of processing, material processed, or quality or production standards which would result in a substantial change in job duties or requirements . . . adjustments of hourly and incentive rates may be required. In such cases new wage rates shall be installed in the following manner . . .

The second clause said that "in the event an employee's job becomes obsolete, he shall be dealt with in the same manner as a laid-off employee."

The union, relying upon a favorable decision it had obtained from Mr. Brecht some time earlier, insisted that the fixed rates of the contract indicated that the classifications related to those rates were similarly "frozen."

Mr. Horlacher's decision upheld management. Where there was nothing "documented in the contract" to prevent the employer from changing contractual job classifications, he wrote, and where the contract contained several provisions that established procedures in the event jobs are changed or become "obsolete," the employer had the right, after installing a new system for the flow of work, to eliminate job classifications and to reassign the duties of abolished jobs to other classifications. That a clause permitting establishment of new rates in the event of changes in jobs did not specifically list the new production system as one of the circumstances permitting such changes did not mean, as the union had asserted, that the job classifications could not be abolished in this case.

The rate schedule, which formed such an important part of the union's case, was not controlling, Mr. Horlacher said, because it was intended to protect wage rates, not job classifications.

If it were intended to freeze the job classifications these provisions should read "All job classifications and the rates applied to them shall remain in effect for the duration of the contract. Neither job classifications nor rates shall be changed except as permitted in this Agreement." But the focal point of the provisions as written is *rates* and the patent intent is to protect rate integrity. If a worker performs the duties specified in the description for job classification X, he is to be paid the rate listed in Schedule A for X. But to say because a rate is specified for job category X that this

---

out abolishing the work attendant to the description. The union demands that the company abide with the mutual agreement."

job as a *classification* cannot be eliminated from the job structure or in any way changed is to have the tail wag the dog. . . .

The listed rate must be paid only when an incumbent holds that particular job and performs only and precisely the duties attached to it. If he performs those duties plus some other duties in a different job duty combination, clearly some other and different rate may be appropriate. Rate integrity—the important consideration—is maintained.

## Implications of the Seniority Clause

In many cases of this kind, unions have argued (and arbitrators have agreed) that seniority rights fixed in contracts, as well as wage schedules, impose limitations on the employer's right to take actions not specifically forbidden. Here, in a sense, management converted that rule of contract interpretation to its own advantage. Since the parties negotiated a clause permitting rates to change when "methods of processing" are altered and to apply seniority rules to employees whose jobs became "obsolete," management representatives argued, such changes must have been contemplated by the negotiators. These were relevant points, Mr. Horlacher agreed. And he specifically rejected the union's contentions that jobs could not become obsolete while the duties still remained to be performed, or that the new production control system was not a "method of processing" within the meaning of the agreement.

The union's characterization of Section 13-v as irrelevant assumes that a job classification becomes obsolete only when the job tasks which comprise the classification no longer exist. The company's reference to this section assumes that a classification may be obsolete because a more efficient organization of the continuing work tasks has rendered the old organization undesirable and therefore dispensable.

The latter is a legitimate use of "obsolete." It is the sense used every day in referring to machinery. A machine is obsolete because a better machine has been developed and not because the job the machine was built to do no longer exists. . . .

. . . the phrase "method of processing" cannot be given the restricted meaning the union imputes to it. The System the company installed can with accuracy be described as a change in the "method of processing" the stuff manufactured in the company's foundry operations. And the other phrases concerning equipment, material and production standard changes connote the technological or physical type change in processing, so that if "method of processing" meant the same thing and nothing more it would be redundant in some degree. The way in which work tasks are organized and related to the workers who perform them is pretty clearly a matter of the method of processing whatever is produced.

Finally, Mr. Horlacher emphasized that a decision in favor of management would not, as the union had feared, make the contract "worthless." Nor would it "empty seniority rights of all their meaning." He explained that the contract cannot guarantee any particular level of jobs, but it does throw "real protection" about the jobs which the operating needs of the company warrant. "Seniority rights do give senior employees preferential status with respect to those jobs that exist," he concluded.

## Security versus Flexibility

Facing the same issues, Richard Mittenthal's decision in *Thompson Electric Welder Company* (United Automobile Workers, AFL–CIO)[17] was very similar to that of Mr. Horlacher. This case involved the consolidation of departments and the consequent reassignment of duties. Management was able to show economic necessity for the change, which may have had something to do with the forceful language Mr. Mittenthal used, although the decision itself turned on his interpretation of the contract as a whole.

As usual in such cases, the company had relied upon the management rights clause, and the union had countered with the assertion that the contract contained a job classification schedule. Mr. Mittenthal's resolution of the conflict was:

Work content and hence the classifications themselves cannot always remain stable in face of technological improvements or a substantial decline in business. . . . Nothing in the agreement suggests that the parties intended to freeze departments or classifications. . . . It does not follow [from the presence of the job classification schedule] that the parties meant to keep those classifications intact for the life of the agreement or to prohibit management from combining them in appropriate circum-

17. 42 AAA 1.

stances. This schedule, in the absence of any evidence that it was intended to have some broader significance, must be viewed simply as setting forth the applicable rate of pay to employees who hold a given classification.

Mr. Mittenthal added, however, that "management rights are not unqualified." They may not be exercised in such a way as to discriminate against the union or to violate the provisions of the agreement. From this point of view, management was found to have violated the contract in one respect. In consolidating departments, a "Crew Leader A" was downgraded to a B classification, apparently because the department he was transferred into never had a Class A man assigned to it before. But the evidence showed that he was doing "essentially the same" work before and after the transfer. The award directed the company to restore him to his proper classification.

### Necessity Versus Convenience

In the case discussed above, management was able to show economic necessity for a change in job duties. There are times, however, when what is alleged to be necessary proves to be merely convenient. Sanford H. Kadish had occasion to call attention to the difference between the two concepts in a case of the *Sutherland Paper Company* (United Papermakers and Paperworkers, AFL-CIO).[18]

The contract said that job content could be changed "when it becomes necessary" because of changes in methods of operation. The employer thought this provision clearly applied to a problem that had arisen in one of the departments where paper was rolled onto spools or "cores." To make packing and shipping operations efficient, it was decided to use the same spools for all sizes of rolls. This made it no longer necessary to stop the machines as often so that millwrights could change cores and transmissions. Furthermore, management believed millwrights could be dispensed with altogether, as far as these tasks were concerned. Operators were told to perform these occasional duties themselves. This amounted to a considerable saving, especially on shifts where millwrights were not readily available.

Mr. Kadish had no doubt that the new work assignments were

18. 51 AAA 20.

much more efficient, but he pointed out that economy of operations was not the criteria of the contract. Instead, the contract referred to changes that become "necessary."

It does not seem to me that the elimination of the need to change the spindles, resulting from the conversion to uniform core sizes, made necessary the assignment of the duty of changing transmissions to the operators. . . . I can understand that from the company's point of view it would be more convenient and economical to have the operators change the transmissions, since it would save having to pay three hours' call-in pay to millwrights for doing a job the operators could do in ten to fifteen minutes. But [the clause permitting changes in job content] does not authorize the company to change job duties wherever considerations of convenience and economy so indicate. It is solely where the described changes of operations require it that this may be done.

While acknowledging that his decision in favor of the union meant that the company had to continue an uneconomical practice, Mr. Kadish pointed out that he was not imposing a new burden on management. The "asserted inconvenience and expense," he said, also existed in the past when millwrights had to be called in for the sole purpose of performing that slight task. The company and the union were not in agreement as to how often that took place, but the arbitrator was convinced that, at the least, it was not an unusual occurrence. Finally, Mr. Kadish said his decision could not be affected by the company's citation of a "general pupose" clause which referred to "economy of operations." That clause, he said, might have "some relevance" in construing an ambiguous provision of the agreement, but there was nothing ambiguous here. The contract permitted changes in job duties only when "necessary," and convenient as it would be to make those changes, no absolute necessity was shown.

### Elimination of Classifications

In the division between arbitrators as to the significance of the wage rate schedule, Jay W. Murphy sided with the "many well considered opinions that stand for the proposition that, unless a contract provides to the contrary, the employer has the power to change or eliminate job classifications and to combine jobs by unilateral action, provided this is done in good faith." He made that statement in the case of *Crown*

*Zellerbach Corporation* (United Papermakers and Paperworkers, AFL–CIO).[19] It was therefore not a violation, he said, for the company to eliminate the classification "scrap pick up" and transfer the duties to another classification. He specifically agreed with the company that the wage schedule, which listed job titles, but not descriptions, was intended only to prescribe rates for a job when it is running and that no guarantee that the job would continue could be inferred. Other relevant facts favoring management's position were the "abundant past practice" of keeping the job titles of discontinued jobs in the wage schedule (paying the appropriate rate when the work must be performed) and the presence of a management rights clause.[20]

A slight variation of the implications-of-the-wage-schedule problem arose at the *Standard Packaging Corporation* (United Papermakers and Paperworkers, AFL–CIO).[21] In negotiating the most recent contract, the union had urged inclusion of a statement that the wage rates listed in a special schedule "shall be considered part of this agreement." The employer saw no objection, and the phrase was added to the contract. This incident was recalled by the union in November 1961, when the company decided to eliminate the "counter (female)" classification, reassigning the duties to a higher classification and transferring the incumbents to lower-rated jobs. As the union saw it, the wage classification schedule, which included the "counter (female)" job, was now part of the contract by reference, and no longer subject to elimination at the will of one party alone.

Thomas Kennedy upheld the company. By agreeing to the language urged during negotiations by the union, he said, management was "simply recognizing a condition which previously existed." The rights expressed in the management prerogative clause (". . . to change assignments . . .") was therefore not diminished by the new language.

19. 46 AAA 3.

20. A second issue in this case was whether the company had the right to assign to "printer slotter operators" the scrap pickup tasks of the discontinued jobs. The operators had objected that the task was "menial," and that they would lose incentive earnings. The first objection, Mr. Murphy said, was not valid, because the pickup duties were "immediately and intimately connected with the performance of the printer slotter work," and could be made incidental to the grievants' jobs. As for earnings, the evidence convinced the arbitrator that the operators had ample idle time for the additional task.

21. 48 AAA 9.

There is no evidence to support the position that when this management agreed to Schedule "A" it had reason to believe that its right to eliminate classifications and to alter job content would be so restricted. On the contrary, management had reason to believe that the intention of Schedule "A" was the usual intention of such a schedule, that is, simply to indicate the rates which must be paid for the various classifications so long as their work content remains the same as at the time when the agreement was signed.

## Past Practice

In many of the cases discussed in this chapter, past practice was asserted as an argument by one party or the other. This is understandable, for, in a sense, every change in work assignment or in the content of a job represents a departure from the practice immediately preceding that change. But not every kind of past practice is binding upon the parties. The duration of the practice is, of course, important. But the more critical question is whether it represented an *agreement* that work assignments must be made only a certain way, or whether management always had the freedom to assign tasks unilaterally, and just happened to prefer one way to another. As the late Harry Shulman, dean of Yale Law School, wrote in a case he arbitrated for the *Ford Motor Company* (United Automobile Workers, AFL–CIO),[22] "the relevant item of significance is not the nature of the particular method but the managerial freedom with respect to it."

At *Crompton & Knowles* (United Steelworkers of America, AFL–CIO),[23] for instance, an arbitrator judged that unless the company was permitted to change past practice, management would be "hopelessly hamstrung" in its function. For more than a decade, it had been the practice for virtually all the welding in the maintenance department to be done by arc welders, who were regularly assigned to the forge shop. This practice suited the arc welders very well, for it gave them some security against layoff and even provided overtime on occasion. As their own jobs were incentive-rated, the arc welders were paid average hourly earnings when they were transferred to maintenance welding for the company's convenience. When they were given maintenance welding as an alternative to layoff, they received a special day rate.

22. 19 LA 237.
23. 24 AAA 13.

In 1959, however, management decided that this arrangement was unsatisfactory. A new job of "welder all around" was declared vacant in the Maintenance Department, and employees were invited to bid for it. The job was filled with the senior bidder.

The union's grievance was that this was not a "bona fide vacancy" within the meaning of the contract because the arc welders, who had done the work for fifteen years, were available. Furthermore, it was argued, by settling grievances over the rates to be paid arc welders when they were assigned to maintenance department work, the company had officially recognized the past practice as binding.

The company denied that anything more was involved in earlier grievance settlements than determination of rates. In any event, whatever rights the arc welders thought they had must yield to the management rights clause, which gave the employer the right to manage the plant and "direct the work forces."

Frank E. A. Sanders resolved the dispute in management's favor and rejected the view that only the development of a new machine or process could overcome the binding effect of past practice.

It seems to me that the approach of the union is somewhat too narrow. Where the company, in discharge of its responsibility for running the plant, decides to change a certain established procedure to bring about greater efficiency, and where this does not run counter to the express provisions of the contract, the basic question . . . is whether the company's action has been arbitrary or unreasonable. Of course, past practice is a factor in considering this question. But the mere fact that the new procedure runs counter to the prevailing practice cannot alone make the company's action arbitrary and unreasonable. In other words, if the company is not to be hopelessly hamstrung in its job of managing the plant, it must be given reasonable freedom to adopt such changes in operating procedures as it deems to be in the interest of greater efficiency and productivity.

### The Effect of Job Descriptions

In disputes over the addition of duties to jobs or the removal of elements from classifications, the formal, written job descriptions are, of course, vital. Some statements are merely a listing of tasks which employees happen to be performing at the time. Others are descriptions of tasks which may properly be assigned to employees, notwithstanding that those duties were not performed at the time the description was composed. In a sense, the latter type of job description is like a reserved rights clause of the contract; it preserves the right of the employer to add duties to jobs when such action becomes necessary.

A case in point was the job description of "truck-driver" at the *Pittsburgh Metallurgical Company* (United Automobile Workers, AFL–CIO).[24] Back in 1954, the job was described to include "change oil, clean, lubricate, fuel, change tires, or any other duties necessary for self-sustaining truck operation."[25] But until December 1957, maintenance mechanics lubricated all trucks, and truck drivers were not required to do so. At that time, however, an employee who had been downgraded to truck driver was asked to lubricate the vehicle he had been operating. The maintenance department steward promptly filed a grievance.

It was controlling in Bert L. Luskin's decision that "the job description clearly and unequivocally established the right of the company to require a truck driver to lubricate the truck he was operating." That drivers had not been previously asked to do that work, he said, did not mean that the company had "forever waived" its right. It would have been improper to ask a driver to grease a vehicle he was not operating, he cautioned, but that was not the circumstance here. Finally, he wrote, if the union believed the job description was inaccurate, "a grievance should have been filed within a reasonable period of time after its issuance on February 6, 1954, even though the specific duty in question had not been assigned to the driver."

## Tasks Not Included in Job Descriptions

Where formal job descriptions exist, they generally constitute the boundary lines for work assignments. But it is seldom possible to compose a statement that includes every detail of a job. Moreover, because management generally wants some flexibility in work assignments, job descriptions often contain statements to the effect that employees may be called upon to perform tasks related or similar to those outlined

24. 6 AAA 6.
25. The union had not specifically approved this job description or others written at about the same time. Mr. Luskin concluded from the evidence that they remained in force and in effect only as "guides and standards for deter-

explicitly.[26] But even with those precautions, disputes arise over out-of-classification assignments, as one did at the *Cleveland Pneumatic Tool Company* (Aerol Aircraft Employees' Association, Independent).[27]

It was the grievance of the union that the company had laid off hand truckers and had required assemblers, subassemblers, and radial

---

mining the respective duties of employees in each of the classifications covered by the job descriptions."

26. See, for example, *American Bosch Arma Mississippi Corporation* (International Union of Electrical, Radio and Machine Workers, AFL–CIO), 36 AAA 10, where the job description manual stated that "descriptions are general in nature and not limited to work covered in the job description." The grievance in this case, although involving a trifling amount of work, was not without interest. For a number of years, the company had been trying to simplify the task of replacing hooks on a machine which automatically dipped small parts into a plating solution. This had been done by skilled workmen, who had to drill holes into a bar and attach hooks by silver soldering. Finally, a way was found to accomplish this by no more than a simple turn of a screw with a screwdriver. This task was thereupon taken away from maintenance employees and given to the employees who operated the plating machines. The union protested in behalf of the former. The work was "historically" theirs, it was argued, and it did not fall within the job description of platers. Steven T. Bladek dismissed the grievance, pointing out that the right to "transfer and assign work" was specifically mentioned in the management prerogative clause. However, he said, "had the assignment of the new duties to the plater resulted in an excessive work load, or impaired incentive earnings, a different conclusion would have to be reached."

The meaning of the phrase "similar or related" was also an issue in a case of the *Consumers Power Company* (Michigan State Utility Workers Council, AFL–CIO), 49 AAA 10, but it is at least possible that resentment over the presence of a subcontractor on the premises had as much to do with the grievance as misunderstanding of the meaning of that word. Where the agreed-upon job manual required employees to perform work "similar or related" to the listed job duties, David P. Miller ruled, the company had the right to require a mechanic, who ordinarily inspected his own mechanical construction and maintenance work, to inspect the construction work performed by an outside contractor. The fact that the grievant's job classification did not specifically include such inspection work was not controlling, because the disputed work was neither "dissimilar" nor "unrelated" to the grievant's job. The union's contention that the job description places "reasonable walls" around a classification, and that the work should have been assigned to a classification the duties of which specifically included inspection work was not upheld. Mr. Miller said that the reasonable walls theory fails to support the union's view because "there is a similarity of function and duties" in the two kinds of inspection work. "It is

drill operators to do their own hand trucking. Union spokesmen made it a point to say that they had no objection to those classifications doing that work as such, but not when hand truckers were on furlough for lack of work. They put before the arbitrator, Frank R. Uible, official descriptions of all the jobs concerned, and pointed out that trucking was not mentioned in any but material-handling jobs.

---

not unreasonable to conclude that inspection of the work done by a contractor is in the nature of 'similar or related work' which the job description . . . contemplated. . . ." Furthermore, he added, the employer's interpretation was supported by past practice. Although the union was right in stating that the past practice, of which it had no knowledge, could not supersede "clear and unambiguous" contract language, Mr. Miller found no conflict between the practice and the contract in this case. "Rather, the practice serves to bolster the conclusion that the protested assignment is not improper." Nor was the union persuasive in its argument that the practice arose only because employees did not know it was improper. It seemed to the arbitrator "more credible" that the employees did not find the assignments now disputed "alien" or "unrelated" to their work. "While this, of course, does not mean that an individual employee's view about his work determines its propriety, it surely must indicate, where there is no clear prohibition against its assignment to his classification and where the work is in fact similar to other work he concededly may perform, that the practice of assigning it to him does have some reasonable basis."

Even broadly written job descriptions impose limits on the kinds of duties that may be added. For instance, at the *Storer Broadcasting Company* (American Federation of Television and Radio Artists, AFL–CIO), 42 AAA 17, the contract permitted the employer to require that staff announcers perform (in addition to their major duties) "such routine duties as they have been in the practice of performing" and such "other services" as are "consonant" with their employment. Management thought that keeping a daily television log required by the Federal Communications Commission was such an added duty. This log had formerly been kept at this station by engineers, although in the industry generally, it was announcers who maintained that record. Harry J. Dworkin agreed with the union that the addition of this task to the duties of announcers was not within the job description. Evidence of industry practice does not provide a basis "for departure from the express contract language," he wrote. "In construing the language of the contract, it must be assumed that the contracting parties were concerned at the time of negotiation with the conditions of employment affecting announcers in the employ of the company, as distinguished from announcers in the industry generally. When the parties in their contract referred to the 'routine duties' of staff announcers, they necessarily contemplated duties which the announcers employed by [this station] had been performing, as distinguished from the practices of other stations, or in the television industry." Nor can the reassignment of duties be regarded as

The company's defense was twofold: (1) Assemblers, subassemblers, and radial drill operators had always done incidental hand trucking; and (2) in any event, the contract did not prohibit such work assignments, when undertaken for good-faith economic reasons.

On hearing testimony as to what the assemblers and machine operators had actually done, Mr. Uible concluded that a small amount of trucking was, as management had said, an incidental part of all the jobs.

> It is recognized that job descriptions do not as a rule set forth all the detail of a job. . . . In this case, it is clear that over the years, by practice, minor movements have become as truly a function of these several job classifications as though they were fully set forth in the job description. . . . Since this practice . . . has been done openly and for many years, your arbitrator holds that they have become a part of the job duties of these several classifications, and will not be disturbed.

Nor was Mr. Uible persuaded by the union's assertion that the absence of a hand trucker for some months without a corresponding reduction in other classifications disturbed the normal relationship in

---

being "consonant with" the grievants' employment as staff announcers. "The term 'consonant' is defined as meaning 'congruous,' 'in harmony with', and 'consistent with.' The established past practice, without deviation, is that transmitter engineers perform the duties of keeping the log . . . Although the contract is drafted so as to provide some flexibility in the assignment of duties, by the same token it prescribes limitations as regards the type and character of the duties which may be added. In the light of the evidence as to past practice, and the duties involved in keeping the log, the arbitrator must conclude that such duties are incongruous with the duties of announcers, and therefore are not 'consonant' with their employment." Management in this case had cited several cases in which it was held by arbitrators that employers may alter job content without prior negotiation with the union. Mr. Dworkin found those citations not persuasive because they "almost invariably" resulted from cases, unlike this one, in which the contract contained no explicit restrictions on managerial freedom. He wrote: "The cases . . . make it clear that the employer's judgment may not be challenged where the contract does not expressly or impliedly restrict the right to increase the job content of a particular job. Such matters as job content, work load, duties and responsibilities of employees, are proper terms of employment which may be regulated by contract. . . . Substantial changes in job content and duties may be challenged, and are arbitrable, where they involve the interpretation and application of the contract terms."

27. 34 AAA 4.

the work force. The evidence convinced him that there had been times in the past when truckers were assigned, and other times when they were not. And so the grievance was dismissed.

But the employer was not upheld in all the views he expressed in the course of the arbitration. Management had insisted that it had the right to lay off employees and permanently assign their duties to employees in other classifications. Mr. Uible denied that. "To add a new primary function to an already established job classification is to create thereby a new occupation," he wrote. He added, however, that he saw no evidence that the company had done that in any of the incidents called to his attention by this grievance.

The problems of "intentionally" limited job descriptions and past practice were also present at the *Iowa Manufacturing Company* (International Association of Machinists, AFL–CIO),[28] where towmotor operators were asked to assist in loading and unloading operations and to do some work in the hookman and expediter classifications. Walter L. Daykin said the following findings of fact were "clearly justified":

1. The jobs in the plant were intentionally described "only . . . in a limited manner."

2. The company was not trying to reclassify towmotor operators to hookmen or expediters, but only to obtain their assistance in loading and unloading, when necessary.

3. The amount of time spent at the allegedly alien tasks "will be relatively small."

4. The principal function of towmotor operators is to operate tractors, but "it is also clear that over the years these operators have voluntarily assisted in the loading and unloading of their towmotors."

Mr. Daykin's conclusion was that "a precedent had been established by these past practices of the company and union that towmotor operators are not to function in the hookmen and expediter classifications, but they are to assist in a limited way in the loading and unloading of their tractors." He added that this type of assistance was commonly expected of towmotor operators in other industries and plants.[29]

28. 17 AAA 16.
29. For another case involving towmotor operation as an incidental duty added to a receiving clerk's job, see *Eaton Manufacturing Company* (United

## Assignment of Duties Not Inconsistent with Job Evaluation

The importance of job descriptions that leave room for changes that are not inconsistent with a general job evaluation plan was pointed up at the *Chapman Valve Manufacturing Company* (International Union of Electrical, Radio and Machine Workers, AFL–CIO).[30] The grievance, which came before James J. Healy, protested the requirement that time cards, formerly maintained by time clerks, be filled out by production workers.

Controlling in this case, according to Mr. Healy, was the fact that the job description in the contract carried the "standard notation" that it covers the "most significant" duties of the job but does not exclude other occasional work assignments not mentioned, the inclusion of which would be in conformity with the factor degrees assigned to each job. The question, then, was whether the additional duties assigned to production workers were encompassed within this "catch-all" phrase. The union, of course, said they were not and that the duties could be added to the contractual job description only by common consent.

Upholding the company, Mr. Healy said that production workers could be made to fill out their own time cards as an additional duty, and that no new job description was required thereby. He gave four reasons:

---

Automobile Workers, AFL–CIO), 26 AAA 2. Parker C. Williams held that where the contract required employees to perform all duties "specified or implied" in their job descriptions, the assignment of towmotor operation as a task incidental to the duties of the receiving clerk did not require the establishment of a new classification. For the same reason, he said, the employer was not obligated to negotiate the new assignment with the union. The union's position would have "some merit" if the receiving clerk were required to operate towmotors "in the same manner and to the same extent as required by the Towmotor Operator job descriptions." On the contrary, the receiving clerk was required to use the towmotor only in his own area and had no authority to use that equipment in any manner not incidental to receiving clerk duties. Furthermore, some "overlapping" of duties of the two classifications "had existed for a number of years." Finally, Mr. Williams wrote, this interpretation is consistent with past practice, during which the employer "consistently adhered" to the position taken in this case.

30. 41 AAA 11.

*First,* although it is true that the filling out of job cards occupied 60% of the time of 8 Time Clerks, it is equally true that the diffusion of this responsibility—done now somewhat differently—to hundreds of employees means that the duty is a very incidental and minor part of the total duties of any given operator. It is a duty, of course. But any reasonable person would have to construe it as a relatively minor addition. *Second,* the union did not demonstrate to the satisfaction of the undersigned that the absorption of this minor duty by any operators would be inconsistent with the factor degrees assigned to the jobs of such operators. . . . *Third,* a fact glossed over by the union, but nevertheless established by the testimony, is that not *all* of the work done by Time Clerks in processing the cards . . . has been transferred to the many bargaining unit employees. . . . *Fourth,* a close study of the transferred duties warrants a finding that they involve little extra work for a particular operator. In the course of a day they take little time. In addition, they are "occasional" by any comparison with normal or basic duties.[31]

## Addition of Unskilled Task

Almost by definition, an unskilled task is one which anyone can do. But whether such a task can be added to anyone's job is a matter of union contract interpretation. At the *Sprague Meter Company* (International Union of Electrical, Radio and Machine Workers, AFL–CIO),[32] a grievance was filed because management wanted stock room clerks to pack the company's products into standard-sized boxes, tasks they had not previously been asked to perform. The union pointed out that the stock clerks' job description said nothing about packing, but William W. Waite held that to be of little consequence. The disputed task was "below the maximum skill requirement" of either job, he said. And the contract did not limit the employer's right to transfer jobs, in the interests of efficiency, so long as the over-all requirements of the jobs are not changed. "Few job descriptions contain a complete catalogue of all tasks which operators may be called on to perform,"

---

31. A secondary issue in the case was whether the company had the right to transfer certain duties of time clerks to members of supervision. "The net transfer of duties in this direction was so slight as to be disregarded under the *de minimis* doctrine," Mr. Healy wrote.

32. 42 AAA 19.

he generalized, "so the omission of specific statements on the kind of packing performed is not necessarily critical."[33]

## Non-negotiated Job Descriptions

Where job descriptions were determined without the union's participation, where the contract did not forbid management to alter work assignments, and where the contract contained provisions which indicated that the negotiators had anticipated the possibility that jobs would be changed, the basic ingredients seemed to be on hand for a management victory in an out-of-classification work assignment dispute. At the *Oxford Paper Company* (United Papermakers and Paperworkers, AFL–CIO)[34] all these elements were present, plus the additional fact, favoring the company, that no layoff of employees was involved in the disputed work assignment.

The grievance was filed by "beater helpers," one of whose tasks was to collect scrap paper, or "broke," from several machines and dispose of it in a machine, called a "broke hog," that disintegrates it for reuse. The job description, composed unilaterally by management, made it clear that this task was primarily that of beater helpers. But in another department there were cutter helpers who also had to dispose of broke. Although their job description mentioned the emptying of "broke boxes" into the machine, it was the practice, since 1955, for them only to haul the boxes into the beater room or directly to the broke hog, leaving it to the beater helpers to dump the scrap into the chute leading to the disintegrator.

In the summer of 1958 management decided to require the cutting room helpers to empty their boxes, as well as to haul them to the machine. This caused the beater helpers to file a grievance, which eventually came before Saul Wallen.

"May the company assign to the cutter helpers, as it did three years ago, the task of moving some of the broke from their own department to another department?" he asked. He answered:

33. It seems probable that the union's real object in this case was to obtain a higher wage rate for the stock clerks, not to prevent the addition of packing duties to their tasks. In any event, the grievance was denied.

34. 3 AAA 16.

No agreement provision seems to withhold from management the right to reasonably alter job content. There are here no negotiated job descriptions. In the absence of such limitation, this right to determine the content of jobs appears to be reserved to management under Article 1 Section 4 which vests in the company "the management of the work." Clearly, the determination of which classification shall perform what tasks falls within this right.

Furthermore, Article II Section I B impliedly recognizes the right to change job content by barring adjustments in wage rates during the agreements term except "where there has been a substantial change in job content. . . ." Where such a change is made the company is obligated to bargain with the union not about the fact of the change but about the rate to be paid for the changed job.

Now the task complained of (emptying broke boxes in the "B" machine hog) is also done by Beater Helpers and is in fact a major element of their job. Did the company violate any agreement provisions by having the same task done by two classifications? Again the answer is in the negative. It is not improper to set up two jobs with common tasks. What occurs here is that Beater Helpers dump broke from the paper machines while Cutter Helpers dump broke from the Cutting Department. Beater Helpers have no natural monopoly on putting broke in a hog even if the hog is located in the Paper Machine Department. It is a task which may be assigned to others as well.

The only question left was how this change of assignment would affect seniority rights. Under the circumstances of the case, not at all, said Mr. Wallen, because beater helpers were not laid off or deprived of Sunday overtime work opportunities. Nor did the slight addition of duties to the tasks of cutter helpers "frustrate the creation of another job to which someone might have been promoted." Whether the decision would have been different if seniority rights had been involved remains an unanswered question.

## Negotiated Job Description

At the *National Vulcanized Fibre Company* (International Brotherhood of Pulp, Sulphite and Paper Mill Workers, AFL–CIO),[35] on the other hand, the job description *was* negotiated. This was influential in

35. 8 AAA 17.

the decision by Charles H. Lanier, Jr., barring the company from requiring a truck driver to perform the additional duty of moving rolls of paper, by hand truck, from the unloading dock to a storage area some two hundred feet away on another floor. The negotiated job description had included a phrase stating that a driver might have to perform "all other duties incidental to the job," but Mr. Lanier did not think the added duties could be called incidental. Nor did the management rights clause justify the kind of work assignment made. Precisely because job descriptions were negotiated, they must be considered "as part of the contract." The description therefore limited the "discretionary action of management." The company had called attention to another truck driver in the plant who *was* customarily required to do hand trucking, but Mr. Lanier found an important difference between the two driving jobs. The latter's job description did say that the incumbent was expected "to assist and direct loading and unloading of the truck," a phrase that was lacking in the grievant's job description. Furthermore, the two driving jobs were different in other respects as well; the grievant was an over-the-road driver and had no helper assigned to him, while the other driver operated only within a one-half mile range, and had two helpers.

## Posted Job Descriptions

It will be recalled that in the *Hellerton* case, discussed above, Aaron Horvitz held that the obligation to continue assigning tasks to certain jobs could be implied from the job bidding system. The point was that employees had claimed vacancies on the basis of established job descriptions, and that it would be inequitable to leave them stranded, in a sense, in jobs they would not have sought. Somewhat the same reasoning was put forward by Carl A. Warns, Jr., in another case of the *Oxford Paper Company* (United Papermakers and Paperworkers, AFL–CIO).[36] He ruled that when employees, acting with the union's consent, had bid for a new job on the basis of the job description posted by the employer, it reflected an "expectation" that the job would be performed as described.

The issue here was whether the company had the right to require employees in a new classification of "instrument mechanic" to install

36. 44 AAA 11.

panel boards, work which the union claimed was formerly done by pipefitters and electricians. The union did not deny that a new classification had to be established; it was just a matter of whether the company could take the disputed work away from other crafts, compose a new job description, and set new rates, all without the union's participation.

The company's answer was that the writing of job descriptions was exclusively a managerial function and that actions similar to those complained of here were taken in the past without protest by the union. Furthermore, it was argued, the union had assented to bidding for the new classification on the basis of the company's job description and had permitted seven of its members to participate in the bidding.

Mr. Warns said he agreed with the union "in principle" that the listing in the contract of skilled occupations and the wage provisions carry the "reasonable expectation" that the usual job duties will be performed by those crafts. But this is not to say, he added, that there cannot be changes and a realignment of job duties "in the interest of keeping the plant running under the impact of changed conditions and equipment." It all depended, he said, on whether the company could bear the "burden" of showing the necessity for those changes. In this case, the employer had done just that.

It is true that the job description and job evaluation reflect no formal approval by the union. And it is equally true that Article XI, Section A, clearly states that "the Job Evaluation and Job Descriptions agreed upon in writing between the parties on August 27, 1953, as amended through October 5, 1961, shall remain the basis of job evaluations and job descriptions for all present and any new jobs in this plant. . . ." This is unambiguous when it states that the "agreement" of the parties "in writing" shall be the basis of new jobs. But the fact that there is no evidence of a formal acceptance of the job description and evaluation by the union, does not mean that the union has not accepted the duties and evaluation in fact by their actions. The job was first posted on December 2, 1960, and posted again on May 12, 1961. The job was filled by a unit employee. The basis of the posting was the job description introduced into the evidence, and the rate of pay, from the record, was based upon the job evaluation relied upon by the company here. Installation of the instrument panels was undoubtedly a task considered by the company in evaluating the job since it is listed on the job description. The rate was accepted by the employee who was awarded the job with no evidence of a grievance processed to arbitration on the point prior to the one now under consideration.

That the posting of the job description and the bidding occurred before the current contract was negotiated strengthened the company's position. Even though the current contract did not list the classification of instrument mechanic or state its rate (an omission which the company attributed to oversight, but which the union said was significant), the acceptance by the employees "through job posting and job assignment for a period of many months prior to the writing of the present grievance," reflects an "informal acceptance of the job duty" as described by management, Mr. Warns declared. The grievance was therefore denied.

### Temporary Out-of-classification Assignments

In all the cases discussed earlier in this chapter, management sought (and succeeded most of the time) to add permanently to or subtract from the customary set of tasks that had been included within jobs or classifications. There are many occasions, however, when there is no dispute about who "normally" performs what jobs. The only problem is that the usual procedure for work assignments seems impractical or impossible. Contracts often permit temporary out-of-classification assignments under limited circumstances. Even where no explicit restrictions are present, the usual doctrine of implied limitations may be invoked. And so the question arises, in grievance form, as to whether the explicit or implied limitations of the contract were breached.

On May 29, 1949, for instance, management of the *West Virginia Pulp and Paper Company* (International Brotherhood of Electrical Workers, AFL–CIO)[37] issued a "policy statement" saying that from that time on electricians would be responsible for all work performed on motors and electrical equipment, except in emergencies or when special handling is required, in which case employees in the mechanical department would assist. About ten years later, the first grievance protesting violation of that policy was filed. The union objected because employees other than electricians were asked, on a certain occasion, to carry a motor from the electric shop to the job site.

37. 16 AAA 20.

Management urged James A. Morris to adopt its own interpretation of the policy statement, which was that electrical work would not "normally" be given to others, but that the absence of contractual limitations on managerial rights to vary job assignments should be held to mean that the policy statement was not absolutely binding in all cases.

Mr. Morris did not agree with that interpretation. No emergency existed, he pointed out, nor was special handling required. The task could have been assigned to electricians just as easily as to others. Under the circumstances, he said, a decision that management's action was reasonable "would negate to a significant degree the understanding of the parties with regard to the handling of motors."

If deviation from past practice and understanding may occur under routine conditions, then the policy becomes one of whatever the supervisor decides in each situation is the policy.

### Protection of Skilled Craft Lines

Somewhat similar issues were presented at the *St. Joe Paper Company* (International Association of Machinists, AFL–CIO).[38] Here, too, the aggrieved employees were skilled craftsmen, which may have had something to do with the decision in favor of the union.

Actually, two crafts were involved, boilermakers and millwrights. Both were working side by side during the first week of a two-week shutdown for lack of work. During the second week, however, the boilermakers were laid off, and only the millwrights were in the shop. They had been kept on for some machine repair work, but they also did some maintenance work on the boilers. The union had had no objection to millwrights doing such work when boilermakers were in the plant. But it was a violation, it believed, to send them home and let the millwrights work at the boilers alone.

Management responded with the traditional argument: The work in question belonged to either craft, and as there were no contractual restrictions of managerial freedom to assign work, any assignment to one of the two crafts, or to a combination of both, was proper.

James C. Vadakin's analysis was that despite the absence of "rigid work jurisdiction concepts" in the contract, it was an error to overlook

38. 41 AAA 16.

the distinction between primary tasks and secondary or incidental tasks. Although either craft might do boiler maintenance work, that was the "primary" task of boilermakers. Unless that were taken into account, he said, the seniority clause would be rendered "worthless." To fail to recognize the stronger right of boilermakers to that work, "and to view the whole question as a management prerogative to be exercised as seen fit on any particular occasion," he concluded, "would create uncertainty as to who possessed seniority rights" and negate those rights.

## Job Rights of Unskilled Classifications

When management acknowledges that the "principle of job rights" applies, enforcement of those rights is not limited to skilled classifications. This was a ruling of Sanford H. Kadish at the *Sutherland Paper Company* (United Papermakers and Paperworkers, AFL–CIO).[39] It seems that on four separate occasions, while several maintenance truck drivers were on layoff, two drivers from other departments, and two from a unit represented by another union, were permitted to haul work and materials from the maintenance shop and to perform certain other trucking operations usually assigned to maintenance department employees. Responding to the grievance filed by the maintenance drivers, the company pointed out that the contract was silent as to whether work customarily given to certain employees had to be given to them and to no others. But management did concede that "there is a principle of job rights that operates in the plant" and that this principle applies also to drivers "at least up to a point."

This admission was the controlling fact in Mr. Kadish's decision upholding the grievance. It was also supported by another "most important" concession, namely, that if no drivers were available in the plant, the grievants, rather than any other employees, would have been called in.

It would not be plausible to hold that job rights exist to the extent of requiring that [the grievants] be called in in preference to other drivers, but not to the extent that they need be called in when other drivers are on duty. If they have a claim to the work in the one case, it follows that they have it in the other.

39. 48 AAA 5.

Moreover, that truck driving is not a "specialized craft, like that of a millwright," did not mean, as the company had argued, that out-of-classification and out-of-unit assignments could be made. "The company has conceded that only maintenance truck drivers may use stores trucks and that maintenance truck drivers would have to be called in to do their work in preference to other drivers when someone has to be called in."[40]

## Use of Equipment as a Test of Assignment

A worker's job and classification are often identified by the equipment he uses, and it is sometimes prima facie evidence of an out-of-classification assignment when a man is asked to work at another's machine. But what happens when a worker uses someone else's machine without having been asked by supervision to do so? This question was dealt with at the *Murray Manufacturing Company* (United Automobile Workers, AFL-CIO),[41] where an apparently proper assignment of an employee to "miscellaneous clean-up work" on overtime was converted to a wrongful out-of-classification assignment by that employee's preference for one piece of equipment over another.

The employee should have used a lift jack in his work. But he liked the towmotor better, and it was not otherwise needed. On learning that "his" machine had been used, the towmotor operator said he should have been called in for the overtime. Management answered that the company had not directed the employee to use that piece of equipment; he had taken it on his own. Furthermore, the employer said,

---

40. A curious reversal of roles appeared in this case. When unions demand something not clearly authorized by the contract, they sometimes rely upon preambles or other clauses which state that the object of the contract is to create harmony between the employer and employees. This time, the company called attention to the "general purpose" clause, which spoke of "advancing the economic welfare of the company and its employees" and of the need for economy of operation. Mr. Kadish was not persuaded. "It must be recognized that this provision is not a substantive term of the contract," he wrote. Moreover, as the quoted language included the phrase *"and its employees,"* the economic welfare of the employees could not be subordinated to that of the employer when the two are in conflict.

41. 36 AAA 12.

use of the towmotor was only incidental to the primary clean-up work involved. Harry J. Dworkin said that management could not escape responsibility for the use of equipment, nor could it avoid the consequences of an out-of-classification assignment. "There is no contractual intent which would warrant the inclusion in the duties of the miscellaneous classification the type of work normally performed by the towmotor operator," he wrote.

On the other hand, Robert P. Brecht, in *Asten-Hill Manufacturing Company* (Asten-Hill Textile Workers Independent Organization),[42] held it was not a violation of the contract to permit an employee, who did not customarily operate a lift truck, to operate it on overtime for the purpose of raising another employee to a piece of equipment that had to be repaired. A grievance of a material handler was therefore denied. By no stretch of the imagination, the arbitrator wrote, could the raising of an employee be considered part of the material handler's job, particularly as other employees in the plant had occasionally used the lift truck. Moreover, material handlers were not assigned to all shifts. To uphold the grievance would give the grievant a basis for claiming a job on any shift he wanted. "It simply will not do to take one aspect of a job, in this instance the operation of a [lift truck], and give it controlling and overwhelming significance," he concluded.

## "Day-after-day" Assignment

Management of the *Whirlpool Corporation* (International Association of Machinists, AFL–CIO)[43] had rather wide latitude in determining job content and the classifications that were needed. Although employees normally worked in their own classifications, there was no restriction against assigning them to other work when necessary. However, there was an "understanding" reached in discussion of a job evaluation plan, but not expressed in the agreement, that an employee who is asked to perform "two grades of work" on a regular "day-after-day assignment basis," would be recommended by the Industrial Engineering Department for upgrading to a higher classification.

In 1960 a Class Eight employee filed a grievance in which he stated

42. 38 AAA 5.
43. 28 AAA 21.

that for several months he had been performing additional duties in a higher classification. He demanded that he be classified accordingly. Management thereupon agreed to pay him retroactively, but discontinued the additional assignments, and denied the requested upgrading. This brought two questions before Ronald W. Haughton: Did the company have the right to discontinue assigning higher-grade work to him when he filed his grievance? Was the grievant entitled to permanent upgrading?

The purpose of the grievance, Mr. Haughton wrote, was to bring an out-of-classification assignment to management's attention. That done, it still remained for management to decide whether to continue the higher assignments and reclassify the employee or to discontinue them. In any event, the grievant was entitled to pay for his past performance.

. . . [The employee's grievance] could result in the continuation of the work and the payment of a higher grade, or it could serve as a spur to the company to exercise its right of assignment so as not to assign an employee on two grades of work on a regular day-after-day assignment basis. . . . Since there is nothing in the contract which requires the company to *continue* to assign an employee on a regular basis to two different grades of work once he has been so assigned regularly, and since the company has the right to assign, absent specific contract language to the contrary, the finding must be to deny the grievance.

Furthermore, Mr. Haughton pointed out in a footnote, the "understanding" of the parties was only that, if the day-to-day work continued, the industrial engineers would "recommend" the employee for upgrading. This would not bind management to accept the recommendation. In that case, if the higher assignments continued, "a legitimate question of the appropriate classification could be taken up through the grievance procedure by the union."

### Interchangeability of Tasks

During negotiations for a new contract at *Atlas Chemical Industries, Incorporated* (Oil, Chemical and Atomic Workers, AFL–CIO),[44] the parties agreed upon a clause that said: "In order to fully utilize manpower during standby operations, diesel mechanics and garage

44. AAA 3.

mechanics will work together to perform the duties of either classification as directed by supervision. When a garage mechanic is assigned duties in the diesel mechanic classification, the diesel rate will be paid during the time assigned."

It took only three days after the signing of the contract for a dispute to arise over the meaning of the word "together" in that clause. It seems that, believing the clause gave it broad powers to effect out-of-classification assignments, management assigned to a diesel mechanic the work of a garage mechanic who was then on vacation. The union read the clause differently. The two types of mechanics could work "together" and do each other's work only when both classifications were physically present, it argued.

Arbitrator Jay W. Murphy agreed with the union's view. Where the contract as a whole seeks to maintain classification identities, giving effect to principles of seniority, he wrote, the evidence should be "pretty compelling" to warrant a finding that the union had voluntarily given up that valuable claim. The history of bargaining helped Mr. Murphy reach this decision. Before the quoted clause was adopted, management representatives had urged language that did not include the word "together," and contained, instead, the phrase "will work as one unit." That phrase was, in fact, similar to language that had been used elsewhere in the contract to permit interchangeability of tasks for millwrights and repairmen. But the company's language did not prevail in the contract, and the union's did. "It may well be true that the company thought the union substitute proposal meant basically the same as the company's original intention," Mr. Murphy observed. But the history of bargaining showed that the union meant more than a verbal substitution. The fact that union representatives insisted on the use of the word "together" should have placed management "on notice" that the company would not have as much flexibility here as it had with repairmen and millwrights.

# 7

## WORK-LOAD DISPUTES

"There have been vast improvements in producing steel since the installation of the new jet burners. . . . Since that time we feel that we have received an inequitable bonus. Therefore, we ask that this problem be corrected at once."

—From a union's grievance

"A fair day's work for a fair day's pay" is perhaps the most platitudinous phrase in the lexicon of industrial relations. Work is, of course, the *quid pro quo* for wages. But both are also independently affected by all the other matters, including the non-economic ones, that labor and management representatives bargain about. It is doubtful whether that universally accepted statement means more today, or offers more guidance, than it did before the collective bargaining era.

Plainly, a fair day's work is any reasonable amount the employer can enforce. And a fair day's pay is whatever bargain the union has been able to achieve. Presumably, both sides of the equation are brought into an acceptable balance at the moment the collective bargaining agreement is concluded. But the balance is a precarious one, in need of constant readjustment, for it may be upset by economic circumstances over which neither party has full control.

168

### Increasing Output Requirements on Hourly Rated Jobs

Basic to most work-load grievances is conflict between the union's view that hourly rates were negotiated on the assumption that the volume and intensity of work would continue in the future as in the past, and the employer's belief that output requirements may be increased without negotiating new rates. This clash of views was illustrated at the *American Chain and Cable Company* (The Allison Employees' Independent Union).[1] Although both the company and the union had wanted an incentive system installed, and although some fruitful discussions had taken place toward that end, the employees were still on an hourly rated basis when the current contract was negotiated. Meanwhile, however, management restudied certain jobs and determined that sixty units per hour was to be the standard of production for employees who, until that time, had been producing fewer units.

The union argued that the wage scale had been negotiated on the assumption that a certain level of production was standard. To increase that standard would therefore amount to a reduction in wages. Moreover, it was urged, this unilateral action by the company also violated the recognition clause.

This reasoning, wrote Lloyd H. Bailer, was fallacious. In answering the specific points made by the union about the wage structure of the company and past practice, Mr. Bailer also took the occasion for general comments on managerial rights to require "a fair day's work effort."

It may be said, in general, that where employees are compensated on the basis of flat wage rates (whether hourly or daily), the employer is entitled to require a fair day's work effort. When it is found that a reasonable amount of output is not being obtained, the employer is entitled to require an increase in output to a reasonable level, and to take disciplinary action if this result is not achieved. When an employee is paid on a purely piece rate basis, and particularly where there is no minimum wage guarantee, any unwarranted waste of work time naturally decreases the amount of wages which the employer must pay him. In a sense, the employee is penalizing himself. But when an employee

1. 7 AAA 22.

enjoying a flat hourly or daily rate engages in unjustified waste of work time, the employer is penalized by having to pay for work not performed. The fact that an employee is paid a flat hourly rate requires the presumption that he is giving a full hour's work for a full hour's pay, so long as the employer makes available sufficient work for him to do.

The union's position in this case is essentially that the parties have bargained a particular output standard for the present hourly rates of pay, with the result that there is an established piece rate structure which represents the hourly rate divided by the hourly output. When management increased the production standard without increasing hourly rates, according to the union's argument, it reduced the piece rates which were bargained by the parties. While the union has not expressly stated what has just been said, this is the substance of its contention, for only in this sense is it possible to assert, as the union has done, that management reduced the established wage rates. Thus, while the union asserts that it is opposed to the introduction of any type of incentive system, it nevertheless utilizes the argument that wages are geared to output at the subject establishment.

The parties' contract makes no reference to production standards or to piece rates. In view of this fact, I do not think that the past practice of reaching agreement on standards of output requires the conclusion that in the absence of the union's concurrence management may not increase the level of required output, even though this new level is a reasonable one.[2]

Mr. Bailer made it clear that his conclusions that output requirements could go up without an increase in rates applied because the new standards were reasonable. The union had not been able to support its contention that sixty units per hour was an "impossible" standard. "The company's engineering studies had been submitted to

2. For a similar expression of views, see the award of Robert G. Howlett in *Atlas Press Company* (United Steelworkers of America, AFL–CIO), 11 AAA 7. He said that the setting of "norms of work loads for hourly paid employees" was a "necessary management function," exercised since the "earliest existence of the employer-employee relationship." If this were not the case, he said, "every employee could set his own pace, and a most ineffective operation, and possibly even business failure, would result. The issue is not whether management has the power to establish standards or norms or expected work loads, but whether the establishment of a particular standard or norm or expected work load is reasonable under the existent conditions."

the union," Mr. Bailer pointed out. "In the light of these facts, I am unable to say that this rate of production is unreasonable. It therefore must be concluded that management did not violate the agreement in introducing this new standard."[3]

## No Rate Adjustment Warranted by Equalized Work Load

It is not always possible to know, from a reading of arbitral awards alone, whether the real purpose of a work-load grievance is to protest a work assignment which is believed to be onerous, or to exert pressure for a higher rate of pay. A case illustrating this ambiguity was that of *Borg-Warner Corporation* (Allied Industrial Workers of America, AFL–CIO).[4]

The issue did not appear to be of great consequence. In January 1960, the foreman instructed welding machine operators on the day shift to file their own welding tips, just as second-shift welders were doing. Separate grievances were filed protesting the assignment and asking for a rate adjustment. They were consolidated in a joint submission of this question to Bert L. Luskin.

Did the action of the company in assigning the filing of welding tips to employees in the Operator, Fabricating, General classification in Dept. 11 violate the Agreement or result in some employee or employees being unfairly treated?

3. This case came to arbitration in the form of the union's protest against the imposition of discipline on two employees who failed to meet the new production standards. The discipline was not upheld, for reasons not relevant to the present discussion. For another case in which management's right to increase output requirements was upheld, see *Johnson and Johnson* (Textile Workers Union of America, AFL–CIO), 16 AAA 5. George Moskowitz said it was an error to issue a warning notice to an employee for spending almost twice the estimated time on a job where that employee had not been told what the estimate was. Mr. Moskowitz wrote: "An employer has the right to set reasonable standards or guides by which to measure a 'fair day's work' in return for a 'fair day's pay.' . . . But it is one thing for the employer to use its planning estimates for its own scheduling purposes and cost computations, and quite another to use such estimates as a basis for warning, reprimand or discipline when neither knowledge of, nor agreement with such estimates is brought home to the employees or their bargaining representatives."

4. 23 AAA 2.

Should the Arbitrator find for the union, he is authorized to make the proper pay adjustment to the eligible employees.

No factual issues divided the parties here. It was agreed that set-up men had filed welding tips on the day shift, and that operators performed that task on the second shift, on which there were no setup men. Furthermore, management agreed that the filing and re-adjustment of welding tips, when incidental to a model changeover, would be done by setup men as before. And so nothing was involved but the small amount of such work during production "whenever it becomes necessary . . . in order that the machine may operate . . . efficiently and safely."

The contract, Mr. Luskin ruled, "must be construed in a consistent manner so that it may have equal effect . . . regardless of the shift on which the work is performed." If second-shift operators, using the same machines, could perform this "simple manual function," so could the first-shift men.

## *"Reasonable Production Levels" after Abolition of Incentive System*

The same issue which came before the arbitrators in the two cases discussed immediately above appeared in even sharper form before James J. Healy at the *Clarostat Manufacturing Company* (International Union of Electrical, Radio and Machine Workers, AFL–CIO).[5] At the union's insistence, an unsatisfactory incentive plan had been abolished. The question then remained as to whether management could expect the employees to work for time rates at the same pace that prevailed under incentives. Mr. Healy's answer was that management could still insist upon reasonable standards of production, but it would not be reasonable to expect quite as much production after the change in wage plans as before. In short, the employer must not expect that the abolition of the incentive system would "inure to the company's benefit."

This conclusion, he said, followed particularly from the fact that it was management's fault that the incentive system was defective.

Assignment of blame has a purpose. In considering the problem at hand, the company must recognize that some of the bad habits it protests

5. 46 AAA 19.

were the product of earlier remissness. . . . Even if high earnings were a function of loose standards and not necessarily indicative of high performance, the company would not be reasonable to expect maintenance of performance at a much lower (hourly rate) earning.[6]

### Reduction in Crew Size

Just as the reference to a job in the contract is no guarantee that the job will continue unchanged, so does the reference to the composition of a crew give no assurance that the composition will not be altered. This conclusion was illustrated at *The Asplundh Tree Expert Company* (International Brotherhood of Electrical Workers, AFL–CIO).[7]

The contract said that three-man "bucket" crews, assigned to clearing the right-of-way for electric power lines, would consist of a foreman, at least one top-rated trimmer and one other trimmer, whose rate would depend upon his experience. Did this clause bar the company from reducing the size of the crews to two? William N. Loucks answered the question in the negative. "There is nothing in this provision which suggests in any way that the company's use of bucket crews is limited to three man crews," he wrote. "In order to hold that this provision *excludes* the use of two-man crews, the [arbitrator] would have to read into this contract provision words which plainly are not there. If it were the parties' mutual intent, as the union asks the [arbitrator] to find, that this provision controls the *size* as well as the composition of the bucket crew, surely this control would have been added by specificity and not by mere 'intent,' as the union now contends."

6. The procedure in this case was somewhat unusual. The parties had stipulated that the arbitrator could, if he so desired, retain jurisdiction for a limited period. Mr. Healy chose to do so for the following reasons: (1) to permit the establishment of guides to insure "fairness and reasonableness" of expected levels of performance; (2) because "the validity of general guides can be tested only by reference to particular jobs," and (3) because "the present atmosphere of suspicion requires for a limited time" the presence of a neutral to evolve a "fair approach" to proper levels of performance. Accordingly, the parties were directed to meet with the arbitrator on a specified date for the purpose of working out procedures for the expeditious handling of problems which might arise.

7. 39 AAA 9.

The history of bargaining in this case also supported the conclusion reached as a matter of contract interpretation. It appeared to Mr. Loucks that the union had signed the contract in its present form with the intention of seeking to obtain, through arbitration, the control of crew size it had not been able to achieve in negotiations.[8]

Whether the size of a crew may be reduced is not always a question of contract interpretation. At times the issue is simply one of fact: Does the reduced crew size result in an excessive burden on the remaining members? This question was raised at the *Carpenter Steel Company* (United Steelworkers of America, AFL–CIO)[9] and was answered in management's favor by Monroe Berkowitz.

For a number of years, the company had employed three setup men, who performed their work on four machines. In January 1960, in order to improve the flow of materials, one of the machines and the operator were removed to another area. This left two setup men to work on three machines, and to perform certain other tasks. Six months later, management decided to transfer one of the setup men, leaving it to the sole survivor in this department to perform setups on all three machines. When necessary, he was permitted to call upon a foreman for assistance.

Mr. Berkowitz found no unreasonable burden imposed on employees by the new ratio of operators to machines. He wrote:

The evidence about the extent of the workload was confined in the main to the average number of set-ups during certain periods. While this evidence cannot be conclusive since the set-up man has other duties to perform, it does lend support to the company's contention that the remaining set-up man will not normally be overburdened with work. . . . The company has made it clear that the man is not obligated to set up all three machines if all of them are down at the same time. This may or may not be the most efficient way to operate the Department, but

8. Also rejected in this case was the union's contention that the parties had intended to make three-man crews mandatory for reasons of safety, and the employer's argument that the crew size was determined by the power companies who used the services of the company in the instant case. The "safety factor" might help interpret an ambiguous contract, Mr. Loucks said. But this contract was clear on the face of it. And as to the reference to the company's customers, the arbitrator pointed out that the obligations of the employer to his own employees were still governed by the contract he signed.

9. 27 AAA 20.

this is a judgment which the company is free to make. The arbitrator finds that the workload of the one set-up man is not so unreasonable as to require the company to assign another man to the job.[10]

## Manning Changes

Negotiators of union contracts often face this dilemma: If they try to overcome an ambiguity in a contract so that it expresses more clearly a right which they believe they have in any event, and if that attempt fails, they run the risk that an arbitrator in the future will rely on this history of bargaining to rule that the right did not exist.[11]

10. The union had also relied upon an alleged practice, going back many years, of operating with two setup men. Mr. Berkowitz was not impressed by this argument, because the circumstances that required two setup men had altered. He wrote: "The only past practice worthy of designating as traditional and fixed was to have two setup men for the four machines, a situation which cannot be re-created."

11. For a well-expressed statement opposing the tendency to hold against a party an unsuccessful attempt to amend an agreement, see Ralph T. Seward, "Arbitration and the Functions of Management," *Industrial and Labor Relations Review,* January 1963: "One difficulty deserves special comment. What is the effect of an attempt to amend an agreement? Should an unsuccessful attempt to amend an agreement be held against the party that makes it? Should it mean that the substance of the proposed amendment cannot thereafter be held to be in the agreement by implication? Logically, of course, there are strong arguments for that point of view. Nevertheless, there are profound dangers in it. We are stuck with ambiguous language in labor contracts all over the country; contracts which were drafted under conditions which have since changed; contracts which no longer in their language represent the thinking of the parties; contracts which have been supplemented by so much in terms of practice, understandings, supplementary oral agreements, and all the rest of it, that their language, by itself, is almost irrelevant to the working framework of rights and obligations by which the parties live. As a result, because there are so many running disputes—endlessly running disputes—which arise out of these ambiguities, there is a vital need for a continuing effort by the parties to try to clarify the language. We may be reaching a point where either management or labor attempts to clarify its agreement almost at its peril. That is dangerous. It should be remembered that in large industry, at least, it is difficult, if not impossible, to amend detailed provisions of the agreement. In the basic contract negotiations, once the wage issues are settled (particularly if there has been a strike), the rush to get back into production is such that the detailed bargaining and consideration of contract language can rarely take place. That in itself is bad enough. If, in addition, we hold that every proposal toward amending con-

Precautions can, of course, be taken against this danger, as did management of *The Specialty Paper Company* (International Brotherhood of Bookbinders, AFL–CIO)[12] when it tried to get the union's concurrence in new manning procedures that would eliminate a full-time helper on certain machines.

The contract was quite clear on one point: Employees were assigned to departments, not to specific machines; the employer was specifically empowered to reassign workers wherever work needed to be done. It had been the practice since 1950, however, for a "brush dampening machine" to be run by an operator and a regular helper. During the most recent contract negotiations, the employer wrote the union that he wanted to reduce the number of helpers in the department and to change their title to "paperhandler." The union objected, and the subject was dropped. However, the company did state in writing that it intended to experiment with manning at a later date. There was some dispute as to the union's precise reply, but it seemed to be to the effect that whatever was done, the contract would have to be observed. Some time after the new contract was signed, management instructed the machine operator to work without a regular helper. He was told that assistance would be given when needed but not on a full-time basis.[13] This brought the matter before Carl A. Warns, Jr.

The union argued that if it had known the company had intended to put into effect the changes that had been rejected in negotiations, it would have insisted on a higher rate for the operator, to compensate for the extra effort and responsibility involved in working without a helper.[14] The company answered that it had always had the authority to change manning schedules, that it had not abandoned that right

---

tract language or clarifying it—offered to remove sources of dispute—is to be held against the offering party, efforts to clarify the language of agreements may be abandoned."

12. 13 AAA 21.

13. The operator testified that he was told he would have no assistance at all, but this conflict of fact is not relevant to the present discussion.

14. The union had also said that this was bargaining in "bad faith" and therefore a violation of the Taft-Hartley Act. Mr. Warns declined to express an opinion on that point because it was exclusively for the NLRB to determine whether the law had been violated. His authority, he said, was only to rule on whether the contract had been breached. For other cases in which a similar point was raised, see Chapter 1, note 28.

in negotiations, and that it had specifically made it clear that changes might occur in the future.

"Generally speaking," Mr. Warns wrote, "companies have the right to determine how many employees will perform a given job. Occasionally, but not often, the parties will specify in their contract the exact number and classification of employees assigned to a particular operation or machine." But the contract in this case, he said, was not one of the latter. "It follows that under the contract the company does have the right to reduce the number of employees on a particular job. Of course, the company cannot take this action or any other action if its proved purpose is to weaken the union or to discriminate against an individual employee. But the record is silent of any charge or proof that this was management's purpose in this case."

There remained only the "serious question" as to the effect of the exchange of correspondence with the union before the contract was signed. There can be no doubt, he wrote, that when a company "places matters before the union for approval or rejection and indicates by its actions that it considers such matters a part of the contract, rather serious practical shop and institutional problems may arise." But the saving fact, from management's point of view, was that the door had been left open for future manning changes.

### The Union's Recourse—New-rate Bargaining

What, then, was the union to do if it really believed that a new job, with a different work load, had been created by the removal of the helper? Mr. Warns said the union was not without recourse:

Whenever a company rearranges job duties in the interest of efficiency or adds to employees' responsibilities, it is well established that the employee through his union has the right to ask the company to bargain on a new rate which will properly reflect the increased responsibilities of the changed job. So if the company wishes to reduce the number of helpers and add additional duties to the operator and the remaining helpers, it is the right of the union when this is done to request a bargaining session on the rates of the employees affected. The union may do this at any time during the contract whenever the company makes decisions which measurably affect the employees' job duties, in a different way from that contemplated at the time the original rate was negotiated in the contract. In summary, management has the right to decide how many men they will employ on a given machine on an operation. There is nothing in this contract to vary the general rule. Since the company's actions during negotiations did not result in an understanding or agreement with the union, it follows that the company still retains the right to exercise in this case the traditional prerogatives of making essential manning determinations. The only qualification on the unilateral exercise of this right is that a proper rate be paid to the employees whose duties are changed. When these changes take place, the union is within its right in asking for bargaining sessions on possible increases due to increased responsibilities.

The same conclusion—that two men could be made to do the work of three, but that a new rate might have to be negotiated—was also reached at *Eppinger & Russell Company* (Industrial Union of Marine and Shipbuilding Workers, AFL–CIO).[15] Where the contract placed no limitation on the right of the company to combine jobs or reassign duties, wrote Paul W. Hardy, it was not wrongful to reduce a three-man crew to two and to assign the duties formerly performed by the third man to the other two. Mr. Hardy was convinced that the reduction in force was motivated in "good faith" and not executed "capriciously." He wrote: "Silence in the agreement leaves the company free to act in this area as long as it has some reasonable basis for its alteration of jobs or job content. The union's right to negotiate rates for changed jobs is not curtailed or restricted by any terms or silence of the agreement, for this is their duty, but this same agreement grants no right for them to negotiate on job content."

## Wage Adjustment Barred by Past Practice

At the *Kaul Clay Company* (United Stone and Allied Products Workers of America, AFL–CIO),[16] a shift in customer demand for products caused the company to transfer employees to larger machines, at which they expended more effort at no increase in piece rates. But a grievance demanding such an increase was rejected by Clair V. Duff, largely because "the basic bargaining pattern between the company and the union for more than twenty years" has been to make

15. 23 AAA 3.
16. 39 AAA 2.

no allowance for shifts to larger or smaller machines in response to customer demand. Speaking of this bargaining history, Mr. Duff wrote:

Changes in consumer demand, in the methods of operation of the kilns, and the location of the presses within the building, and other factors, resulted in no requests for adjustment of rates. Throughout all changes and all variations, the amount of compensation paid for the setting of a kiln never varied. The work load in any given week varied without causing a commensurate variation in pay. Some sizes of pipe yielded a good weekly return. Other sizes reduced earnings without reducing the amount of effort expended.

The only consolation the union was able to extract from this case was Mr. Duff's remark that "the very next variation in the demand for products may occasion an increase in earnings."

### Filling Idle Time

In many jobs, and especially in those that are geared to machine cycles, there is some idle time. The filling of such time with productive work is a constant challenge to managers, for it seems to be one way to reduce costs without asking employees to do more than they are paid for. Understandably, unions and employees do not always see this form of work-load change in that light.[17]

17. When employees are directed not simply to use idle time productively, but to work more intensively, a rate adjustment may be expected. It was perhaps with problems of this kind in mind that, for more than a decade, negotiators at *Randall Graphite Bearings, Incorporated* (International Union of Electrical, Radio and Machine Workers, AFL–CIO), 37 AAA 7, included in the agreements provisions stating: "Any employee required to operate two machines at the same time shall receive a twenty-five cents per hour premium during such operation." A dispute arose when management directed machine operators to perform shorter-cycle tasks with power tools while waiting for their machines to complete a cycle. The union thought that this circumstance brought the premium pay clause into effect. The company replied that the extra pay was due only when "two full-sized production tools were used simultaneously," and that there was no basis for the union's complaint that the foreman, filling every idle minute with a shorter-cycle task, was forcing employees to work more intensively. Calling attention to the words "machines" and "operation" in the quoted clause, A. B. Cummins said that the use of two machines did not necessarily mean that two operations were being performed. Furthermore, the

At the *United States Envelope Company* (Federal Labor Union No. 20681, AFL–CIO),[18] for instance, the management prerogative clause permitted the employer, among other things, "to decide . . . methods and schedules of production, including the means and processes of manufacturing, provided that the company will not use these prerogatives for the purpose of discrimination." Relying on this provision, management decided to rearrange the work assignments of eleven operators, three feeders, and four adjusters. The practice had been for an operator to be given temporary assignments in other departments when his machine was not operating, a circumstance that, according to management's figures, occurred about 20 percent of the time. This arrangement was apparently not satisfactory to management, for the operators were not quite as productive that way as they were in their regular departments. Consequently, revised procedures were established by which operators whose machines were down would feed the other machines. When all machines were running, the adjusters would do the feeding. In this way, it was possible to eliminate three feeders and run the department with fifteen employees.

The customary arguments for and against this change were heard by Robert L. Stutz. The union's principal contention was that no technological or operational change had occurred, but only a burdensome addition to the duties of the remaining employees. Moreover, as job classifications were incorporated in the agreement, job content could be changed only by mutual consent.

Management's answer to the assertion of an excessive work load was that operators were not supposed to be idle at any time. The only difference was that they would now be assigned to work exclusively in their own department, where they were needed, instead of in other departments. But as a preliminary issue, the company argued that the question was not arbitrable at all, because the union did not allege

---

company was not bound by past practice, which grew largely from the "carelessness" of supervisors who had approved premiums when not required by contract and who had treated the word "machines" as if it were synonymous with "operations." Although it is not uncommon for parties to "drift" into a practice which establishes special meanings for words, he continued, the arbitrator would have to be free of doubt to give such special meanings to words. The grievance was therefore denied.

18. 18 AAA 5.

discrimination as the motive for the change. Discrimination, it was pointed out, was the only forbidden motive expressed in the management rights clause.

Mr. Stutz upheld the union on the arbitrability question, but supported management on the merits of the dispute. The grievance was arbitrable, he said, because it turned on "the meaning and application of the agreement." More specifically, the grievance raised questions as to whether the change was within the scope of the management rights clause and whether the clause incorporating job classifications also barred "re-allocation of work" by implication.

Addressing himself to the merits, Mr. Stutz upheld management on the basis both of practical considerations and of his interpretation of the contract. "On the evidence offered," he wrote, "there appears to be nothing unreasonable in the action taken by the company in utilizing the operators' and the adjusters' time differently than in the past. An average of 2.2 operators is available at all times to assist the other operators. Since there are four adjusters who would be available to work on the 2.2 machines that are down, assuming change-over and minor repair (major repairs are done by other plant personnel), theoretically there would also be 1.8 adjusters available at any one time to assist the operators."

As to the argument that the contract contemplates the continuation of rates and jobs, Mr. Stutz wrote:

It seems to me rather that this section of the contract contemplates the continuation of the established rates as long as the jobs remain unchanged, and does not restrict the company in making necessary adjustments in job duties. If changes in job duties are made, however, it then becomes necessary for the company to bargain with the union over any rate change which may properly flow from the methods change, but the parties have made it clear that there is no rate question involved in this arbitration.

Finally, he wrote, the conclusion that the wage clause does not "freeze" jobs and job duties was also supported by another clause that made provision for employees whose jobs are "completely eliminated." Thus, as in many cases reported in this volume, it was possible to draw implied rights, as well as implied limitations, from apparently unrelated sections of the agreement.

## No Contractual Bar to Use of Idle Time

At first glance, it would seem that when a man who has been operating one machine is suddenly given a second to take charge of at the same time, his work load has increased. But this is not necessarily so; it all depends upon how the machines operate and what is expected of the employee. Monroe Berkowitz had occasion to make this point in a case of the *American Machine and Foundry Company* (United Automobile Workers, AFL–CIO).[19]

Before 1954 the company had only Potter and Johnson semiautomatic turret lathes in a certain department. In that year, however, it acquired a Mult-au-Matic turret lathe and assigned a worker to it. He was put in the top labor grade—one grade higher than the Potter and Johnson lathe operator. Subsequently, a second Mult-au-Matic machine was purchased, and a second lathe operator was assigned to it. When a third lathe of that kind was purchased, it was assigned to the two lathe operators. This led to the union's grievance. It was argued that as the "job write-ups" of turret lathe operators spoke of "machine" in the singular, only one lathe could be assigned to a man. If two were assigned, it called for a new classification, presumably with a higher rate. One of the company's arguments, in reply, was that the Mult-au-Matic was an automatic lathe; once set up and put into operation, it completed its cycle without further effort. On completing its cycle, it shut itself off and cut no more metal until prepared for the next cycle. Thus, the operation of two machines did not place any burden on the employee who attended them.

If the facts were as the union had alleged, Mr. Berkowitz said, the grievance might have to be upheld. But there were several other matters to consider that the union had not mentioned. One was that the "job write-up" of the Potter and Johnson operator also referred to "machine" in the singular, although those operators normally took charge of more than one lathe at a time. Although the waiver of a right by the union in the past would not necessarily be binding for the future, he observed, the facts did compel a conclusion that no "substantial change" in job classifications had occurred. Furthermore, even when two men were assigned to two Mult-au-Matic machines,

19. 3 AAA 2.

one of them performed the setups on both. In a sense, the other was his helper.

"As a practical matter," Mr. Berkowitz wrote, "the union may not have been disturbed by one man working on two machines, so long as there were only two men assigned to the two Mult-au-Matics. The protests arose only when the arithmetic of the situation was disturbed when the third machine came in unaccompanied by a third man. Under the contract, however, the union can force the company to re-examine the classification only if there has been some substantial change in it. In light of the finding that there has been no substantial change in either of these classifications, the conclusion must be that the union's grievance should be denied."

Where the increase in machine speed had the effect of using a machine tender's idle time, and where this increase did not impose "undue physical strain" on the employee, the company had the right to put that change into effect without negotiating a new hourly rate. This was the holding of William N. Loucks in *Lummis and Company* (Amalgamated Tobacco, Food and Allied Workers, AFL–CIO).[20]

The grievant in this case was an hourly rated employee whose job was to remove boxes of peanuts as they came from a machine and move them by hand truck to another location. A mechanical innovation made it possible for the machine to operate safely at higher speeds. As a result, the interval between loads of filled boxes which the grievant had to move was shortened. The union asked Mr. Loucks either to order the machine slowed down again or to direct a wage increase.

Mr. Loucks found this case "unusual" in that the union did not call attention to any contract clause that was allegedly violated. The union's attorney at the arbitration said the demand was justified "regardless of the contract." But pressed by the company's attorney, he finally asserted the recognition clause as the basis for the statement that a "unilateral" change in working conditions of the kind made was a violation.

The arbitrator ruled that it would be "indefensible" to hold that management could add to the work load under all circumstances without negotiating a new rate. But it would be "just as indefensible" to say that the company could not do so under any circumstances.

20. 35 AAA 12.

Whether the increase was justified would depend, he said, upon two criteria: "(1) How much of the increased work load was in fact merely a use of the employee's previously free time?; and (2) Is there reliable evidence creating a presumption that the handling of the additional boxes per hour causes undue physical strain upon the employee?"

In this case, he concluded, no violation had occurred because "stand-by or idle time" had been "absorbed" so that the employer could make use "of a larger percentage of the time he already has purchased at a negotiated price."

A remarkably similar situation existed at the *Cleaners Hanger Company* (International Association of Machinists, AFL–CIO),[21] including a similarly weak contractual basis for the grievance. Not surprisingly, the result was substantially the same as in the *Lummis* case. Maurice E. Nichols ruled that the company had the right to increase the speed of machines and add tasks to jobs without negotiating wage increases, where the purpose of the changes was "more efficient utilization of the machinery and operators," and where the work-load increase was not "unreasonable or unduly burdensome."

According to the union, wire-drawing machines that had generally operated in second gear were shifted to third-gear operation. This sped up production by about 30 per cent. Not only did the higher speed of the machines require more effort in managing the flow of the company's products, but more snarls and breaks occurred, which also added to the work load. The sole contractual basis for the grievance was a clause that required bargaining over wages and working conditions.

If the clause relied upon by the union were all that was involved, Mr. Nichols said, the grievants would have a good case.

But [the contract] gives to management the right "to manage and direct the employer's business in all its phases without interference, *except where specifically restricted by terms of this agreement.*" And no terms have been cited which contain those *"specific restrictions."* . . . It would be most unrealistic to conclude that [the clause relied upon by the union] was meant to freeze conditions exactly as they existed at the time the agreement was negotiated. Progress is important to the union just as it is to the company and progress requires change—change in methods

21. 47 AAA 9.

—change in employment—change in relationships. The language of the entire agreement between the parties is formulated to retain equity between the parties but not to preclude changes that are essential to progress.

## Using Machines to Capacity

The New York newspaper publishing industry produced two interesting cases involving the right of management to increase the speed of printing presses. Both grievances were initiated by the publishers[22] and both resulted in awards in favor of management.

The first case was that of the *Daily News* (New York Printing Pressmen's Union, AFL–CIO).[23] The union's position was that the contract lacked the customary management rights clause and that it contained manning tables and wage rates that were negotiated on the premise that presses would be run at 50,000 newspapers per hour. This argument was countered by the employer, who pointed out to the arbitrator, Peter M. Kelliher, that the union had sought unsuccessfully to obtain in the most recent contract a provision calling for an additional journeyman when speeds are increased.

Taking this fact, as well as others, into account, Mr. Kelliher upheld management.

Where hourly rates of pay are provided in contracts, it is contemplated that a change either by way of a decrease or increase in job content during the life of the agreement will not necessitate consideration of a new rate. While such a change does have meaning under an incentive or piece rate system, it has no application where hourly rates are provided. The general industrial relations understanding as evidenced by numerous court and arbitration decisions is that under an hourly rate pay system an employer has [a] right to expect a "fair day's work for a fair day's pay." Production and work loads may increase or decrease without consequent effect on hourly rates of pay.

Furthermore, he wrote, it would take "clear and precise language" to restrict managerial rights "to obtain full capacity production." On

22. For other examples of grievances pressed to arbitration by management, see *National Telefilm Associates* (International Brotherhood of Electrical Workers, AFL–CIO), 36 AAA 31, discussed in Chapter 4; and *Raybestos-Manhattan, Incorporated* (United Textile Workers of America), 29 AAA 1, in this chapter.
23. 26 AAA 18.

a matter as critically important as this, Mr. Kelliher concluded, the negotiators of the contract would not have relied upon "remote and generally unaccepted implications."

A special kind of a problem was presented in this case with the union's assertion that operation of equipment at the 60,000-per-hour rate increased "the hazards of the press room." Relying "solely on the evidence here presented," Mr. Kelliher rejected this contention. He was careful to add that his award applied only to operating conditions then in effect. He also recommended (but did not award) that increases in speeds be brought about gradually and that discussions be undertaken with the union to maintain safe and practical operating procedures.[24]

The second case occurred at the *New York Times* (New York Printing Pressmen's Union, AFL–CIO)[25] and was arbitrated by Peter Seitz.

24. For another case in which it was alleged that a work-load change created a safety hazard, see *Alco Products, Incorporated* (United Steelworkers of America, AFL–CIO), 7 AAA 3. The issue arose when management reduced locomotive engine crews by cutting the number of brakemen from two (and sometimes more) to one. The size of the crews in the past was determined in part by the physical layout of the plant: there were buildings, trackage, public street crossings, and a volume of material and traffic along the way which made it necessary, according to the company's safety manual, for a train crew to consist of an engineer, a conductor, and at least two brakemen. But with extensive demolition and improvement of the physical layout in 1958, management concluded that neither safety nor efficiency required more than one brakeman. As contractual authority for this change, the company cites the management prerogative clause which spoke of the right "to relieve employees from duty for lack of work or for other legitimate reason." The trouble with this position, Sidney Sugerman wrote, is that the company's own safety manual still calls for two brakemen. Moreover, it established procedures for changing regulations, procedures which were not followed in this case. "Indeed," he added, "the Manual still contains a disciplinary caveat against rule violations, however unthinkable its actual application to anyone running afoul of a rule solely by reason of acting or omitting to act within limitations set by the company itself . . . The company has to the extent of its contractual commitments and its own outstanding safety rules limited its otherwise exclusive managerial control of this area of decision. It may still have residual control in safety matters even under [the contract] but it has therein committed itself when changes are involved first to follow certain procedures which in this case have not been observed. Until these safety rules are properly changed so as to relieve the content of the job of brakeman of certain present safety duties, it cannot be said that there is a 'lack of work' or other legitimate reason for a lay-off."

25. 37 AAA 17.

It not only resulted in a dismissal of the union's grievance (that presses had been operated at speeds that constituted safety hazards), but an award upholding management's grievance[26] and granting "compensatory damages" to the company for losses resulting from the union's refusal to run the presses at the speed the employer directed.

Where the contract, although containing "detailed manning schedules," was silent as to speeds at which presses were to run, Mr. Seitz wrote, and where there was "no serious contention" that the parties had ever agreed to limit press speeds to 45,000 newspapers per hour, it was a "gross and inexcusable violation of the terms of the agreement" for a foreman (a member of the bargaining unit and the union) to refuse to comply with instructions to operate presses at 48,000 copies.[27]

One of the questions raised by the union was the inference to be drawn from the fact that the contract said a foreman would be the "unrestricted representative" of management. The contract could be construed to mean only that a foreman had "some latitude" in administering "broad publisher policy in the pressroom," Mr. Seitz said. It did not mean that he could alter management's instructions. This interpretation, he added, was consistent with past practice and the "realities" of newspaper publishing.

I do not, in this decision, undertake a full exposition of the range of meaning of "unrestricted representative." I only hold that determining the speed of presses has always been and continues to be a *managerial* decision, based upon a variety of engineering and business circumstances and factors; and that although the designated foreman is to be "unrestricted" in the manner in which he executes decisions as to the speeds of presses by giving orders to pressmen in charge, the basic decision is for the publisher to make.

Other union contentions, rejected by Mr. Seitz, were that there had been an "understanding" not to run the presses in excess of 45,000 newspapers per hour, and that a clause calling for continuation of

26. See note 22, this chapter.
27. Unlike foremen in manufacturing industry generally, foremen in newspaper publishing are named by management from among bargaining unit members. Under the contract, such a foreman is the "unrestricted representative" of management, but in the instant case, the foreman acted on instructions of the union president to stop the presses if any attempt was made by the company to run them in excess of 45,000 papers per hour.

the "status quo" pending "final action" on disputes gave the union the right to resist the increased speed. "The 'status quo' provision is an ancient one in the history of the relationship of the parties," he wrote.

Apparently, it is frequently invoked and, as frequently, the parties disagree as to its meaning and application. Although a definitive statement of its meaning and application seems to be sought here in order that future disputes might be avoided, I am loth to attempt such a statement and I am convinced that the decision in this case does not require it. I have no record before me which would enable me to envision the varieties of situations that could arise in the future; and in the absence of such a record, restraint is not only the better part of wisdom, but is equally imperative for an arbitrator. I do hold, however, that no "condition" holding speeds to 45,000 prevailed . . . which were required to be maintained pending final disposition of the dispute.

Moreover, he said, as presses had run faster than 45,000 in the past, "it is for the union, which invokes the 'status quo' provision, to demonstrate that the alleged condition existed." The evidence "fell short" of such a demonstration, he concluded.

There remained only the union's assertion that higher speeds were dangerous. Mr. Seitz found "no sound basis" for that statement. The presses were new, and they contained many safety features not in older models. In fact, they were rated for safe operation at 60,000 newspapers per hour. Furthermore, the arbitrator pointed out, the contract provided "Joint Conference Committee" procedure for resolving disputes without stoppages, and the union should have resorted to that machinery if it really believed an unsafe condition was created by the higher speed.

Not the least interesting feature of this case was the remedy. The publisher had shown that it had cost $1,838.90 to send pressmen home and move the printing plates to another location after the foreman had refused to let the machines be run at the proper speed. Mr. Seitz said there was nothing in the contract to prevent him from awarding that sum of money from the union treasury to the company, and he so awarded. At this point, the union put forward an ingenious argument: The company could have cut its losses and "mitigated damages" by countermanding its order and letting the presses run at 45,000. From that point of view, the monetary award would seem not to be justified.

Mr. Seitz disagreed with that approach. To have mitigated damages in that way, he said, would have resulted in the "erosion" of managerial rights. The company was therefore on "firm ground" when it decided it would rather close the plant than yield to the union's demands.[28]

## Decreasing Machine Speed and Adding Tasks

In most of the cases discussed above, management sought to increase machine speed. The case of the *Chicopee Manufacturing Company* (Textile Workers Union of America, AFL–CIO)[29] was different in that, for reasons of better quality control, management *decreased* the speed of carding machines. The work-load question arose when, to fill the estimated seventy-eight minutes per shift that were thus liberated, management required card tenders to sweep the aisles and perform other housekeeping chores in the vicinity of their machines. The union took the occasion to enter a number of complaints. It was said that working conditions in the card room were unpleasant to the point of being hazardous to health, that too much physical effort was required of employees, that the work load in this establishment was heavier than in comparable plants in the area, and that in any event the company's estimate of the time liberated by reduced machine speeds was inaccurate.

Addressing himself first to what he called a "subsidiary" problem, William W. Waite said that the change was a "routine" one, within the meaning of the contract, because it involved no technological innovation. The company therefore had the right to effect that change without the union's prior consent, although this did not deprive the union of the right to request discussion and arbitration of the work-load issue. As to the major issue, here again the company was upheld. "Admittedly," Mr. Waite wrote, the card room was "not the

28. Management had also asked for punitive damages, but this Mr. Seitz did not grant. Such damages, he said, are not part of the arbitrator's normal "arsenal of remedies." Moreover, punitive damages are unnecessary in this case as a deterrent. He concluded: "In the conduct of the officials of the union at this hearing, I observed no evidence of irresponsibility that would seem to justify the imposition of punitive penalties. The wrongful action of the past resulted from a misreading and misconstruction by its former President of the agreement as to its limits of permissible action in the protection of his constituents. Now that those limits have been more clearly drawn, I believe that no further deterrent penalty such as that asked by the publisher is called for."

29. 5 AAA 17.

pleasantest place to work." But none of the conditions the union complained of were different from what they had been for some time. Nor were the union's comparative work-load figures meaningful. "While all the comparisons submitted showed lower work loads than at Chicopee," he wrote, "it is altogether possible that numerous additional work elements offset this apparent discrepancy. In any case, [the arbitrator] had no opportunity to observe or study these other jobs and would not be justified in considering the bare figures submitted."

All of this brought Mr. Waite to "the central question" of whether the card tenders were actually performing more work under the new system. Again, the company was upheld. Neither the testimony nor his visit to the plant convinced the arbitrator that an excessive burden had been placed on the operators.

### Addition of Record-keeping Tasks

The resistance of employees to alterations in their customary tasks is evident in small, and even trifling, changes, as well as in important ones. This was demonstrated in a case of *American Bosch Arma Mississippi Corporation* (International Union of Electrical, Radio and Machine Workers, AFL–CIO),[30] arbitrated by Paul H. Sanders.

The company wanted hourly rated production workers to turn in to supervision certain forms on which they were to note the operation number, the part number, and the number of pieces produced. This was not required on a permanent basis; management said the information was needed only "from time to time as a temporary measure." According to testimony presented to Mr. Sanders, the work, when required, would take about five minutes per shift, and the results would be used by foremen in scheduling the next day's production. The grievance of the employees expressed considerable annoyance, partly because they believed previous work-load grievances they had won had already settled the issue in their favor. "We, the undersigned employees of Department 139," they had written, "object to the filling out of the time and production records that we are required to do. We request that these records be discontinued from our duty. We have already won several grievances on this which we cannot see any point in continuing the dispute."

Other relevant facts of the case were: (1) The contract included a

30. 16 AAA 4.

provision requiring the company to furnish the union with a new job description when jobs were changed; (2) it also contained a fairly standard management rights provision; (3) there was a list of job classifications and rates attached to the contract but without job descriptions; (4) management had a list of job descriptions which it had composed unilaterally; (5) there was no reference to record-keeping tasks in the description of the jobs in question; and (6) a paragraph was attached to the compilation of job descriptions, stating that they were "general in nature," intended only for identification of jobs, and not intended to limit jobs to the indicated duties.

"The arbitrator believes that the grievance in this case should be denied," wrote Mr. Sanders. "The addition of the reporting duties in this case may properly be regarded as an insignificant variation from previous duties and not such a substantial change as to amount to the revision of an existing job." And as for the past practice, consisting largely of grievances which had been granted, Mr. Sanders said the record was insufficient "to demonstrate a mutual intention to refrain from the addition of reporting duties to production employees."

The parties may vary or add to the written agreement by a clear-cut course of action indicating mutual agreement, but it is proper to impose on anyone asserting such variation a very heavy burden of proof. The references to past grievance dispositions did not satisfy that burden in this case. There may be a great many reasons why the company or the union may not wish to carry a particular grievance beyond a particular point. The arbitrator is not satisfied in this case that disposition of past grievances establishes mutual agreement in line with the position taken by the union in this particular grievance.[31]

## Fear of Rate-cutting

Very similar, in many ways, was the situation at the *DeLaval Steam Turbine Company* (United Steelworkers of America, AFL–CIO).[32]

31. For another case involving the right of the company to compel employees to keep production records, see *American Enka Corporation* (United Textile Workers of America, AFL–CIO), 45 AAA 2, arbitrated by H. Ellsworth Steele. The union's objection here was that a non-incentive job might be converted to an incentive pay basis if the union did not resist the keeping of these records. Mr. Steele said the work order was proper. The primary issue in this case is discussed later in this chapter.

32. 3 AAA 21.

In September 1958, the company established an incentive program for its maintenance department, but was lacking in data needed to establish a standard for certain jobs, among them crane operation. In order to get this information, management asked individual employees to write down on the back of work orders the elements of work actually encountered on their jobs. This applied not only to employees already on incentives, but to day workers as well. The latter were asked to note total elasped time spent on the job.

The union set forth five objections: (1) The task of writing belonged to non-bargaining unit clerical workers; (2) it was not necessary for maintenance employees to write out information that could have been transmitted orally; (3) employees might be subject to discipline for writing too little or for inadequate command of English; (4) information written down in an employee's own handwriting might later be used against him "if someone else did the job faster"; and (5) management did not allow sufficient extra time "for such things as crane delays."

Although some of the fears expressed in these five points seemed unjustified, Eli Rock said they had to be taken seriously because they were genuinely felt. Management had tried to reassure the employees that no harm would come from compliance, but the existence of the grievance was proof that the reassurance had not been altogether successful. He noted also that many companies have found difficulty in devising an incentive plan for maintenance employees, and that both parties wanted such a plan here to overcome the "disparity of earnings" between skilled maintenance men and less skilled production men, who, being on incentives, earn more.

At any rate, "understandable" as the attitude of the grievants was, Mr. Rock upheld the company.

In the light of the difficulty and uniqueness of the task, in the light of the various, detailed testimony at the hearing, the arbitrator is of the view that the company's general position that this is the only way in which an incentive system can be successfully operated among maintenance men must deserve credence. The argument of the union that the same objective could be achieved by having the employee report the necessary information orally to his foreman overlooks the fallibility of the average man's memory, a fallibility which, quite clearly, would hurt the men at least as much as the company. The argument that this work could be done by time study men would require time study men to accompany employees on some types of jobs permanently; and in any case, this is not a situation of a time study man setting up or *revising* standards, such as is normally done by time study men, but rather is one in which the employee reports facts so that *existing standards can be applied,* and the employees paid. The argument that a time clock be used would, even if feasible, apply to only a minority of the problem situations.

All of this is not to overlook that the requirement on the men here is still a unique one, that it is certainly not normally required of men on incentive, and that the reaction of some of the men to it is understandable. It must also be reiterated, however, that if an incentive plan for maintenance men is regarded as desirable from the point of view of both sides, there does not appear to be any other way of implementing it—or at least no other truly *workable* method was suggested to the arbitrator. Any basic objections which may be reflected regarding the whole idea itself, and the arbitrator by no means assumes that such objections *do* exist, should be reserved for contract negotiation time, the parties having apparently earlier reviewed and approved this plan in at least its general outlines.

Similarly, in the light of the above various facts, and in the light of the admitted willingness of the men to furnish the required information to the company orally, the arbitrator cannot reasonably view the requirement that the *same information* be informally written on the back of a simple work order as falling within the coverage of Article II (e) of the contract. There may be an understandable emotional difference between writing something down and reporting it orally; but in both instances, the essential task is *observing* what one does, and whether the result of the observation is reported orally or in writing must be regarded as secondary to the act of observation itself. At least, the arbitrator is constrained to this conclusion in *these* particular circumstances.

Finally, Mr. Rock said, insofar as there was substance to the fear of the crane operators that they might be disciplined unjustly for illegible entries, the remedy would lie in resort to the grievance procedure. Similarly, if these employees were given inadequate allowance for delay time, that problem could be dealt with "when a specific complaint" is filed. For all these reasons, he wrote, the grievance protesting the addition of record-keeping tasks had to be denied.

## Suspicion of Speedup

Employees who object to the addition of record-keeping tasks to their accustomed duties are often not so fearful of out-of-classification assignments as such as they are of time and motion studies or of production quotas, which, rightly or wrongly, they believe would lead to speedup or reduction of rates.[33] This belief was apparently the underlying reason for a grievance at the *E. R. Squibb Company* (Oil, Chemical and Atomic Workers, AFL–CIO),[34] arbitrated by James V. Altieri.

For some time, it had been the practice of maintenance mechanics to note on the back of work orders the identity of the employee performing the repair task and the time spent on the job. In February 1960, a new form was introduced and attached to each work order. Mechanics were instructed to note on this form, instead of on the reverse side of the work order, their clock number, the date, and the starting and stopping time for each job.

33. The fear of rate-cutting, while largely a heritage of the distant past, is not altogether baseless. See, for example, *Pratt, Read & Company, Incorporated* (United Furniture Workers of America, AFL–CIO), 29 AAA 2, arbitrated by Emanuel Stein. He held that where employees had been using a method of production different from one prescribed in a job evaluation plan, the employer, on learning of it, had the right to adopt the new method officially and re-study the job, setting new incentive rates which resulted in reduced earnings. The arbitrator rejected the union's contention that the new study was barred by a clause permitting production standards to be modified only when methods of production, among other factors, were changed. "That some changes in production methods did take place at some point may be inferred from the fact that, in 1960, the company recognized the original method could not be employed and adopted the new method." However, added Mr. Stein, "I am unable to reach the conclusion that the company had de facto adopted the new method so that a restudy of the job would be in effect barred" by the contract. Mr. Stein concluded: "Unless it can be demonstrated that the company had either expressly or by clear implication adopted some production method other than the one on which the production standard was based, I do not believe it can be barred from a re-study of the job consequent upon the adoption of the new method. . . . In so holding, I wish it to be clearly understood that I express no opinion as to the propriety of the new production standard adopted by the company pursuant to its restudy. This question was not submitted to me, and I do not pass upon it."

34. 25 AAA 11.

The union made it clear that they had no objection to the old record-keeping practices. But the new one, it said, was intended for use by job analysts, time study men, and cost accountants, under the direction of an outside management consulting firm. This made it improper to ask bargaining unit employees to have anything to do with it. A memorandum submitted by the union's attorney said: "The one significant fact that stands out in this case is that the data . . . are used specifically by the company for time-study purposes. There is not a shred of testimony to contradict the evidence that the . . . sheets, including the data put there by the maintenance mechanics, went to an industrial relations consultant of the company who, in turn, had jurisdiction over the time-study employees and analysts, all of whom are outside the bargaining unit. It is also uncontradicted that certain other time-study data was recorded on the very same sheets by time-study men and job analysts and that . . . all of the collected data was utilized for time-study and job analysis purposes."

The union also noted that the maintenance mechanic job description did not include any reference to record-keeping. It was conceded that not every detail of a job can be listed, but it was urged that "before a task or function can be recognized as part of the job when not specifically spelled out in the description, it must bear some relationship to the job or classification."

Resolving this controversy in favor of management, Mr. Altieri said that the purpose for which the new sheets were used was not relevant.

The arbitrator is unable to perceive the difference, essentially, between the duty included without objection in the functions of the mechanics for some years, namely, noting their elapsed time . . . [and] the requirement to note this type of information on the [new] sheet.

### Involuntary Transfer to Incentive Pay Basis

A most unusual case, in that the union protested *increased* pay, arose at *American Enka Corporation* (United Textile Workers of America, AFL–CIO).[35] What the union feared in this case was that jobs would be converted from an hourly rated basis to an incentive rate of pay, in violation of a clause stating that no employee would be

35. 45 AAA 2.

compelled to work at an incentive job against his will, nor would he be obliged to remain on an operation if it was converted to incentives.[36] The problem arose because car loaders, who were hourly rated employees, worked at a sufficient pace to earn the incentive rate, and they found the extra pay (ranging from fourteen cents to six dollars) in their weekly pay envelope. The union's grievance read:

The union requests the company stop trying to force the incentive system on these car loaders . . . or anyone else, and stop breaking the agreement between the union and the company.[37]

A secondary but related issue in this case was whether the company had the right to compel the car loaders to keep the production records on the basis of which the incentive payments were made.[38]

H. Ellsworth Steele said that the order to keep records by itself was not wrongful, nor was it wrong for the company to have made time studies of the car-loading job. But the record-keeping and the time study, together with the fact that employees were given incentive pay, had the effect of establishing an incentive job. "It would be difficult to draft a clause placing greater stress on the worker's right to make the decision whether or not to work on incentive," he wrote.

To make a time study of a job does not *alone* place it on incentive. The requiring of workers to make out records of their production does not *alone, or in conjunction* with a time study, place a job on incentive. When a job has been time studied, records kept of output and workers paid accordingly, however, that job, in my judgment, has been "converted to incentives" or "changed to incentives."

Whether or not a worker produces at a pace above a 60-point hour is of major economic significance to the worker and to the company seeking

36. The relevant contract language read: "The company shall have the right, in assigning employees to jobs on which incentive rates are available, to assign thereto employees who are able and willing to meet the production requirements of the job. . . . The individual shall not be obliged to remain on operations hereafter converted to incentives against his will. Change to incentives shall be voluntary."

37. It is perhaps worth noting that the union's grievance did not ask that the extra earnings be returned to the company, and although this part of the grievance was upheld, no recoupment of money was directed by the arbitrator.

38. For other cases in which keeping of production records was at issue, although under different circumstances, see notes 30, 31, 32, and 34, this chapter.

efficient and profitable operations. The worker's pace may have an important bearing on the company's long run ability to offer him employment. Nevertheless, this case must be determined under the contract as it now reads, as both parties have stressed in the hearing. The worker's pace determines the economic effectiveness of an incentive application, but does not "convert" a job to incentive.

The award therefore read: "The company is directed to cease using an incentive system to determine the pay of workers on the Car Loading and other jobs in which incentive rates have been made available unless each worker involved clearly indicates that it is his (or her) will to be paid on an incentive basis. This award does not direct the company to cease requiring workers to make out production records."

### Increasing Output on Incentive Jobs

In the *American Chain and Cable* case, discussed earlier in this chapter, Lloyd H. Bailer suggested that the incentive worker who holds back production is, "in a sense," only "penalizing himself." The issue before him involved an hourly rated job, and it was not necessary for his purposes in that case to go into a more lengthy discussion of the work-load and production problems of employees whose pay is measured directly by output. But those problems do exist.[39] In some industries—brick and clay, for instance—the practice has developed

39. At *The High Standard Manufacturing Company* (International Association of Machinists, AFL–CIO), 48 AAA 4, an unusual case arose because employees were working *faster* than the company wanted them to. This case came before Louis Yagoda. The reason for the extra speed, of course, was that the employees were paid piece rates; the more they produced, the more they earned. It so happened, however, that the employees achieved the added earnings by tampering with the machine to increase the cycles of operation beyond a point management thought was safe or good for the equipment. This had actually been a problem in the plant for at least five years. Finally, the grievant, a shop steward, who was "probably more intensely addicted to breaking the machine cycle and more consistently successful at it than his fellow employees," was caught with more work produced than his machine should have been able to do in the time it was running. The result was a four-week disciplinary suspension, which Mr. Yagoda reduced to two weeks because of the "long tolerance of the practice by management and its persistence among a number of employees," and also because the penalty may have been unduly heavy, the employer hoping that punishment of a union steward would have the desired deterrent effect.

of certain employees leaving work when the day's "task" is done, although some time may be left in the normal workday. Attempts to change this practice, or to keep it from extending to classifications where it had not been practiced, lead to one kind of work-load grievances. Furthermore, in many other industries, incentive-rated employees sometimes "peg" production at a prearranged level while staying at their machines to the end of the shift. The object here may be to prevent earnings from reaching a point where, they fear, the piece rate might be endangered. And finally, even incentive-rated employees may have duties added to their tasks that management believes to be too minor to justify retiming of the job and that the employees believe entitle them to an increased rate. Such changes, too, lead to work-load grievances.

## Removal of Employee with Lowest Incentive Earnings

One object of an incentive system is to encourage employees to produce as many units as possible within a given period of time and thereby to reduce overhead and machine-amortization costs per unit. From this point of view, the slow producer is not fulfilling expectations. Can an employer remove from an incentive job a worker who, while producing enough to earn some bonus, is nevertheless the slowest of the lot? This question came before Robert L. Stutz at the *Grinnell Corporation* (United Steelworkers of America, AFL–CIO).[40]

The contract stated that employees producing at 75 per cent of the incentive pace were to receive base rates. That was the point at which those who worked faster would receive incentive pay. It happened that a certain employee was able to earn 18 per cent above base rates, but that was less than other employees in his classification were able to earn. Believing that 100 per cent of standard was not only possible, but enforceable, management demoted this employee to a non-incentive job.

Mr. Stutz returned the grievant to his incentive job, with the following bit of instruction on the meaning of "average" and other statistical terms:

Standard time values represent the time necessary for the *average* experienced operator to perform the operation working at a normal incentive pace. The fact that the standard represents the time necessary for the

40. 47 AAA 2.

average experienced operator presupposes that a below-average operator will not be able to meet the standard and an above-average operator will be able to exceed the standard. It should not be necessary to remark here that in any average cross-section of employees there will be variations in ability to produce any given product. This is also true of any group of experienced operators. The standards under this contract presumably are set with this fact in mind and it is only to be expected that, without artificially pegged production levels, production performance under the plan will follow the usual frequency distribution curve. However, as time goes by, that curve gets skewed to the right as low producers are eliminated—by one method or another—and high producers stay on the job.

The company's action was incorrect, he said, because it did not simply let the frequency distribution curve be skewed to the right by natural attrition of the work force; instead, it forced skewness by demotion of the grievant. He concluded: "If the company's view were upheld, the lowest producer would perform at a minimum of 100 per cent and the average would therefore be pushed even higher. Eliminating [the grievant's] performance . . . would result in raising the average from 117 percent to 120 percent. There is no contractual basis for the company's position."

A variation of the problem discussed in the *Grinnell* case was that of the employee who, although on an incentive job, did not manage to earn more than base rates. Did the fact that the contract provided for such rates (as well as for more pay to those who worked faster) mean that the employer could do nothing about the minimal producer? This question arose at the *John Wood Company* (United Electrical, Radio and Machine Workers, AFL–CIO),[41] when the union protested discipline of a marginal worker. According to the union, discipline was warranted only where the failure to earn more than base rates was deliberate. Horace A. Ruckel wrote: "There is no question about the right of an employer to discipline employees for substandard performance provided that its exercise is not unreasonable or arbitrary, or restricted by other provisions of the collective bargaining agreement."

The purpose of the incentive system is to induce employees to work faster by making available to them a premium wage in return for the extra effort. . . . As I read it, [the contract] means only that employees *when*

41. 20 AAA 17.

*working* on an incentive job are to be paid not less than their day rate if they do not make standard. It is not a guarantee that they shall always be assigned to incentive work. . . . Nor, as I view it, is it a guarantee against discipline.

## *"Pegging" Production*

That work-load problems do not disappear when employees are paid on an incentive basis was also demonstrated at the *United States Ceramic Tile Company* (United Glass and Ceramic Workers of North America, AFL–CIO).[42] On January 20, 1961, after making time studies, management announced that operators would be expected to produce 1,200 pieces per day. For the next six weeks, three employees, who had generally produced about 950 per day, were spoken to frequently about their failure to meet the standard. One employee did improve his output. The other two, who did not, were given thirty-day suspensions. Whether the discipline was proper need not concern us here, although it did occupy the attention of the parties and the arbitrator, Robert G. McIntosh. In arguing the case, however, the union put forward the view that by paying incentive, bonus or piece rates, the company had, in fact, established a "task" system, which precluded the promulgation of new standards of production. To this, Mr. McIntosh responded:

This controversy raises the age old question of what may an employer do to insist on a reasonable day's work for a reasonable day's pay. There can be no controversy that under the rules applicable to labor-management relations, the basic one is that management has all rights except those which it has bargained away. In going over this contract between the parties and carefully reading it and making any inferences therefrom, it cannot be said that the company, in this instance, has anywhere relinquished its prerogative of determining what is a fair production standard. If, however, the union finds or feels that any work load, and certainly a production requirement could be fairly said to be such, is too great or unfair, the parties have agreed that this might be arbitrated through the grievance procedure before an expert in such things.

We are not concerned in this controversy with the fairness or unfairness of the standards set. We must therefore assume, until challenged in some

42. 39 AAA 19.

other and appropriate way, that they are reasonable and fair. Our concern here is whether the company had any right to establish such standards. Since the contract does not restrain management from fixing such standards of production so far as the basic agreement between the parties is concerned, the inquiry as to the right of the company to fix production standards must be answered in the affirmative. . . .

As to the incentive, bonus and piece work portions of that agreement, there can be no question that what was done here does not come within the accepted meanings of those types of managerial operation. The union has claimed that standards fixed herein actually established a task system in that if the employee did not meet it, he was disciplined. The arbitrator has made a study of the concept of task in employee-employer relations and it seems to be the accepted idea that a task is the setting of a fixed production for a day which the employee may finish in any time during the eight hour period. If he finished in two hours, he is privileged to cease from working and may go home, or if he takes a longer time, at any time short of the eight hour period if he finishes he may go home and still receive the full day's pay.[43]

### Incentive Jobs Become Task Jobs in Practice

A different fact pattern was presented at *Raybestos-Manhattan, Incorporated* (United Textile Workers of America, AFL–CIO),[44] and this difference led Wayne E. Howard to conclude that a piece rate system had been converted into a *"de facto"* task system.

For more than fifteen years, it had been the practice of incentive-rated employees in the Hot Press Department to stop work one-quarter to one-half hour before the end of the shift, notwithstanding contractual language to the contrary. They did not, however, leave the plant until the end of the working day. Seeking to put an end to this practice, the company filed a grievance,[45] asking for full enforcement of the contract and for the right to discipline employees refusing to discontinue the old practice. Mr. Howard denied the grievance. By

43. For a similar decision, see the award of Harry J. Dworkin in *Kaul Clay Company* (United Stone and Allied Products Workers of America, AFL–CIO), 38 AAA 15.

44. 29 AAA 1.

45. For examples of grievances pressed to arbitration by the employer, see note 22, this chapter.

their practice, he said, the parties had "created an exception to the undiluted application" of the contract insofar as the Hot Press Department was concerned.

The crucial question in any such determination . . . lies not in what the parties may term the job in their agreement nor in what company or union witnesses may have termed it in their testimony, but rather in how they have operated the job in practice. For over fifteen years the employees in the Hot Press Department have been consistently behaving as though the work in question was task work. . . . The long-established, uniform, consistent, and unequivocal practice by which the Hot Pressers met an informal "bogey" or production standard, thereupon stopping the operation of the F-23 Department presses prior to the conclusion of their shift, has become so inextricably a part of the job assignment and working conditions of that job as to have created an exception to the provisions of [the hours-of-work provision] and to have made a *de facto* task job rather than a piece-rate job in the operation of presses in the F-23 Department. For these reasons the Hot Pressers are entitled to carry out these practices until the parties by negotiation change them.

The employer in this case had had no difficulty in finding awards by other arbitrators holding, as in the two cases above, that piece workers must work a full day if management so requires. Mr. Howard found no conflict between their views and his own. In the cases cited to him, he pointed out, there was not as clear, consistent, or "uniformly applied" a practice as there was in this case. The arbitrator made it a point to emphasize that he was neither approving nor disapproving of the early-quitting practice. "The right to the current work arrangement stems from the parties' own agreement, deduced from their conduct over the years, and not from a conclusion based on equitable entitlement." If the situation was really as intolerable as the employer said it was, he suggested, the remedy was to be found at the bargaining table.

### Extension of Early-quitting Practice

Under a contract that *did* recognize the right of task or piece workers to go home before the end of the contractual eight-hour day, did piece workers who had not formerly left early have the right to begin doing so? This question arose under most interesting circumstances at the *Oak Hill Fibrebrick Company* (United Stone and Allied Products

Workers, AFL–CIO).[46] The practice was recognized by the following two sections of Article VII of the contract:

Section 1. The regular work days shall consist of a maximum of eight (8) consecutive hours of work, exclusive of lunch time, during any twenty-four (24) hour period, and the regular work week shall consist of forty (40) hours. For the purpose of computing weekly overtime, the regular work week shall commence at 12:01 A.M. Monday.

Section 2. Task and Piece Workers, upon completion of their tasks, shall be credited, for the purpose of weekly overtime, with eight (8) hours. If the employees continue to work beyond their tasks they shall be paid at straight time for the balance of the eight (8) hours. Employees, who, after completing their task, go home and are called back subsequent to their starting time to do additional work on a later shift of the same day, shall be paid time and one-half for the work performed on the later shift. This premium pay shall be considered daily overtime.

The privilege of leaving early, had not, however, been enjoyed by all employees. Evidence was in part conflicting, but the practice seemed well established in the industry and in this company for in-centive employees, but not for hourly paid workers, to leave early. A. B. Cummins, who arbitrated the case, said it was "not too essential" to obtain "exact data" on this point, because the object of the union's grievance was to extend the privilege of early quitting to classifications of employees that had not had that privilege in the past.

Mr. Cummins' first conclusion was that the early-quitting practice was "basically optional" and "subject to the needs of work schedules." It came about because the flow of work and work schedules did not "fit together." Furthermore, the clause relied upon by the union, which recognized that some employees would leave early and made provision for computation of overtime pay, did not say which classifications would enjoy the privilege. "The fact that the provision recognizes the existence of a variety of practices in incentive workers going home early or working a full eight hours may not be taken to create a right in an incentive employee to decide upon his own length of work day," he wrote. In short, Mr. Cummins ruled that the eight-hour day must remain the "term of reference for management planning," and that he could not extend the early-quitting practice to employees as a matter of right.

46. 11 AAA 10.

# 8

## ATTRITION AND AUTOMATION

*". . . to produce more with the same amount of human effort is a sound economic and social objective."*
—From the 1950 contract between General Motors and the United Automobile Workers

There is a qualitative difference between lack-of-work layoffs and the elimination of jobs due to technological innovations. When the demand for the company's product falls it is not difficult for workers to understand that some of them must be laid off for a time. And the almost universal system of layoff by seniority satisfies their sense of justice and logic. Although the separation from the active payroll of the company may prove to be permanent for some, it is possible to believe, at least at the beginning, that all will be recalled before their seniority is terminated.

But the situation is otherwise when an employee is replaced by a machine. There is a disturbing finality about that kind of job loss, and the necessity for it is not always apparent. That improved technology has always created more jobs than it has destroyed is, of course, true. But this gives us no assurance for the future. And even if it did, the worker who loses his job by automation can hardly be blamed if he finds little comfort in assurances that what has happened to him will benefit the economy as a whole. Similarly, it may be true, as some have

204

shown, that automation upgrades as many jobs as it downgrades.[1] But this, too, is a fact of greater interest to the social scientist than to the worker, for it is the *job* that is upgraded, not necessarily the employee who held it.

## Technological Changes

It is not always easy to tell why a union will accept with apparent equanimity the appearance of new equipment, only to protest several years later, when a change occurs that is far less drastic. This is a

1. The establishment of new jobs at a higher level of skill creates opportunities for employees but does not necessarily foreclose grievances. This was illustrated at *Sylvania Electric Products, Incorporated* (International Union of Electrical, Radio and Machine Workers, AFL–CIO), 14 AAA 6. When the plant in which this grievance arose was acquired, in 1944, it was used mostly for the manufacture of radio and television equipment. Gradually, however, production shifted to radar and other military electronic equipment. The next important change occurred in 1954, when all radio and TV work was transferred to another plant. Only complex electronic equipment was manufactured from that point on. The effect of this on the work force was to increase the relative importance of highly skilled employees. The dispute in this case involved the right of the company to establish the new job of "performance analyser," in the face of the union's insistence that the duties were nothing but a combination of two existing jobs—"performance tester, electronics" and "analyser, electronics." A collateral issue was raised in the union's objection to the company's decision that only those who possessed a Federal Communications Commission license could hold the new job and that a written test would be administered to help determine whether applicants had the requisite ability. As to the first question, Clair V. Duff dismissed the union's contention that no new job was involved at all because the performance analyser and the employees in the two older classifications used the same basic tools. That would be like saying, he commented, that a piano tuner and a concert pianist were alike because both worked on the same instrument. Furthermore, the fact that the company was paying the performance analyser a higher rate than either of the other two classifications was compelling proof of the good-faith economic motive. He wrote: "We did not discover any economic motive or other business reason why the company would pay *additional* money to the Performance Analysers, unless management intended to assign more skillful duties to, and to place greater responsibilities upon, men in this classification, because all other working conditions are the same. The Performance Analysers work shoulder to shoulder with the Testers and Troubleshooters. The physical demands upon them are identical. In addition, the two jobs (Tester and Troubleshooter) which the union alleges have been combined, continue to exist with *no reduction in the number of employees*

question that frankly mystified David P. Miller at the *National Dairy Products Corporation* (Retail, Wholesale and Department Store Union, AFL–CIO).[2] Perhaps the union acquiesced earlier because the employer was expanding his facilities and no loss of employment was involved in the elimination of a certain operation. But that did not explain the grievance completely; for the final change, which brought on the union's protest, also involved no layoff of any bargaining unit employee.

The company operated a dairy, receiving milk from farmers who arranged for delivery, either in their own tank trucks or in vehicles owned by independent haulers. To guarantee sanitary conditions, it was the practice until November 1957 for bargaining unit employees to prepare cleaning solutions and to scrub the tanks manually after every delivery. There was never any question about anyone but employees of the dairy doing that work, because the humidity in the tank cars was high, and it was dangerous for the haulers to scrub the tanks and then drive out into the cooler air.

Late in 1957 the dairy moved to a new plant, which was equipped with semiautomatic machines for cleaning tanks. Bargaining unit employees still prepared the solutions, but it was now the independent haulers who coupled intake and outlet hoses, and pushed the buttons to start and stop the flow of cleaning solvents. So far, there was no objection on the part of the dairy's employees. In April 1961, however, the plant was remodeled to increase its capacity, and completely auto-

---

*assigned thereto.* Clearly, the company has not created this new job as a subterfuge to have testing work performed less expensively or to eliminate employees in the other occupations, the duties of which and compensation for which have continued unchanged. . . . The job of Performance Analyser is a *new occupation*—not a re-arrangement of the duties of other jobs."

See also *Schaeffer Brewing Company* (International Brotherhood of Firemen and Oilers, AFL–CIO), 51 AAA 7, where the installation of new automated equipment caused a semiskilled maintenance job to be the object of competition between two unions on the premises. Israel Ben Scheiber was the arbitrator. Formerly, a member of one of the unions had oiled the equipment during lunch and coffee breaks, and a maintenance mechanic, who belonged to another union and unit, did the more comprehensive lubrication. When the new equipment was installed, both unions claimed full jurisdiction over all maintenance. Mr. Scheiber endorsed the company's solution, which was to divide the work between the two unions, in the same proportion as it had done in the past.

2. 40 AAA 20.

matic washing equipment was installed. The chief difference was that the washing cycles were now accomplished much as in a domestic washing machine, without resetting controls and pushing buttons separately for each rinse. It was a slight change, and although there was again no loss in employment, this time a grievance was filed.

"If the modernization affected anyone it affected the haulers," observed Mr. Miller. "For the real effect was that it simplified and reduced the tasks they performed." He added that if the company should go back to the manual scrubbing system, bargaining unit employees would have to be permitted to do the work. But those employees never had worked on semiautomatic or completely automated equipment, so it could not be said that their jobs were affected by the most recent change.

Mr. Miller said that three facts were influential in his decision: (1) there was no industry-wide practice supporting the union's claim for tank-cleaning work; (2) there was no contractual relationship between the employer and the haulers, the contractual relationship being between the employer and the farmers; and (3) the volume of bargaining unit work for employees of the dairy had increased "despite automation and simplification of the bulk tank washing system."

## Elimination of Job Following Automation

Faced with a substantial loss of jobs following installation of automatic equipment, the union at the *Long Beach Oil Development Company* (Oil, Chemical and Atomic Workers, AFL–CIO)[3] sought to rely on every provision of the agreement that was remotely relevant. This included the seniority clause, a maintenance-of-crews provision, the wage and classification schedule, safety regulations, and duration-of-the-agreement and the wage reopening clauses. But none of this prevailed. Lawrence R. Guild ruled that notwithstanding these provisions, management "in no way exceeded its prerogatives" when it reclassified downward and transferred nine of thirteen machine operators who were no longer needed in their accustomed jobs. Beginning about 1953, but more intensively since 1958, the company began installing automatic control and reporting equipment at its water injection wells. It was thought that this automation project would make it unnecessary

3. 49 AAA 11.

for any employees to be physically present. But partly because of the union's resistance, four operators were permitted to remain in their classification, one to be on duty at all times, so that human action could be taken if anything should go wrong with the automatic controls. The other nine operators became the grievants in this case.

"I find no support in the wording of the agreement for the union argument that jobs are 'frozen' until and unless some renegotiation occurs," Mr. Guild observed. "[The contract] provides that the company may establish new work classifications, but that the rate of pay for such may be, at union request, subject to collective bargaining. Presumably, any problem of working conditions would be handled under [grievance procedure]. There is no basis in the wording or implication of [the duration-of-the-contract and reopening provision] for asserting that the company has relinquished its continuous function of managing."

Taking up the union's references to contract provisions one by one, Mr. Guild said it was not possible to accept an interpretation of the seniority provision "which would literally prevent any reduction of force unless negotiated with the union." Nor did the maintenance-of-crews provision, which dealt with replacement of absent employees, apply. Finally, the union's reliance on the wage classification section of the contract was not persuasive because that section states only that work "peculiar" to a job will be done by the men regularly assigned to that job "when such work is available." In short, "several operators continue to do operator's work, and I cannot agree that work 'peculiar' to this classification is being performed by other groups."[4]

## Delayed Impact of Automation

In negotiating a contract in February 1958, management of the *Corn Products Refining Company* (Oil, Chemical and Atomic Workers,

4. The union had also argued that the equipment required constant attendance for reasons of safety. Mr. Guild found no basis for that contention. In any event, he said, if an equipment failure should occur, a hazard might exist only if employees were physically present. "If there is increased risk of property damage, which there may or may not be, the decision to assume such risk rests with the company," he wrote.

AFL–CIO)[5] agreed to a provision that gave preference for other jobs in the plant to employees with three or more years of seniority whose jobs disappear because of "technological improvements or automation." Not all employees who met the seniority requirement became eligible for this benefit. The coverage was limited to those "who presently work on manual types of operations" and are "subsequently displaced" from their departments "due to" the indicated technological developments.

Because technological improvements may be gradual, while a contract has a fixed starting date, it was perhaps inevitable that a dispute should have arisen as to whether employees who were displaced *after* the execution of the contract, but because of technological improvements which were made *before* the contract was signed, were eligible for preferred placement in other jobs. This issue came before Peter M. Kelliher.

One grievant was a boiler room attendant who, even before the signing of the contract, had to be transferred to another maintenance job because of the reduced need for steam and the installation of new boilers with "push button" controls. The layoff, however, occurred after the effective date of the contract. "The controlling condition is whether the employee was presently on a manual type operation from which he was displaced subsequent to the adoption of the contract," the arbitrator reasoned. "The evidence does indicate that but for the three new boilers with their push button controls and greatly increased capacity, the old boiler with its largely manual type of operation would continue to function during the summer months to meet the need for steam. . . . The essence of the problem confronting the parties at the time they adopted [the automation provision] was the displacement of employees. The parties were aware that these types of changes had occurred before February 16, 1958, and would continue to occur after that date. The contract contains no limitation to changes occurring after the effective date of the contract."

In short, Mr. Kelliher concluded that what had happened to the boiler attendant was a reaction to automation, albeit a delayed one. The grievant therefore had the right to assert his more than three years of seniority to claim a job elsewhere in the plant.

5. 10 AAA 5.

## Reaping the Benefits of Improved Technology

The introduction of new and more efficient machinery inevitably raises two questions: What effect does the new equipment have on the work load of the operators? And who is to reap the benefits of improved technology? Both questions were raised in a case of the *Wickes Corporation* (United Steelworkers of America, AFL–CIO).[6] Leon Herman ruled that a contract requiring that rates set for new or changed jobs "bear a fair relationship to other jobs in the plant" did not require a higher rate for a brake operator assigned to an improved hydraulic press brake. Testimony offered at the arbitration hearing, and his own observation of the job, led him to the conclusion that "the similarities and disparities between the old and new machines are pretty much in balance, and that the work and responsibilities on the new machine, viewed overall, are substantially equal to the work and responsibilities on the old machine."

The union had also argued that the savings resulting from installation of the improved machine should accrue "to the benefit of the brake operator." It was a rather simple argument, but one which does appeal to the employee who sees his work suddenly become more productive. Mr. Herman's reply: "The answer to this argument is that any savings in production costs in which labor is entitled to share must be secured through negotiation, not arbitration, and must improve the lot of the work force as a whole, rather than any one individual member of the group. Nothing in the company-union agreement authorizes a distribution of company profits to the employees, or to any employee, through the medium of labor arbitration. Such matter must be left to the usual form of bargaining between the company and the union, and cannot be delegated to an arbitrator without the clearest statement of authority. This has not been done, nor does it appear to have been intended by either party under the terms of their agreement."[7]

The same kind of a problem arose at the *Armco Steel Company* (United Steelworkers of America, AFL–CIO).[8] The parties had agreed

6. 12 AAA 4.
7. For other cases in which wage increases were requested on the basis of the greater efficiency of new equipment, see Chapter 7.
8. 30 AAA 15.

that incentive rates could be revised when jobs were altered, and that adjustments would also take place when work was performed "over and above a fair day's work."[9] The question was whether incentive rates needed to be adjusted owing to the use of new jet burners at certain furnaces that, according to the union, increased output by one-third to one-half and resulted in increased use of the idle time of crane operators.

A. B. Cummins disagreed with the view that earnings should have increased in direct proportion to the increase in open hearth activity. The union's argument, he said, implies that the "original work and process delay pattern" was "frozen," and that every increased use of idle time must be paid for additionally. "Now and then an agreement will contain a provision that permits such a result," he wrote, "but the present one does not." Furthermore, if the union's grievance were granted, it would have the effect of creating inequities with respect to other jobs on which time was fully utilized.

The arbitrator did not deny that such an invasion of idle time might occur, resulting in a serious inequity with respect to other jobs, as to justify a new rate. But his observation of the disputed jobs, and his own computations, did not support the contention that rates were then out of line.

## Technological Displacement Allowance

Provisions for lump-sum severance pay to employees whose jobs are discontinued because of technological improvements or automation

9. This agreement was expressed in the following two paragraphs:

"9.62    The company shall change existing incentives or, if necessary, shall establish new incentive plans to replace existing plans, when they require revision or replacement because of new or changed conditions resulting from mechanical improvements made by the company in the interest of improved methods or products, or from changes in equipment, manufacturing processes or methods, materials processed, or quality or manufacturing standards.

"9.63    It shall be the intention of the company to establish such new and changed incentives to provide equitable compensation for work performed over and above a fair day's work for which the hourly wage rates have been established in Subsection 9.1 of this Section. It is understood by the company and the union that the rate of current production in various producing departments may be above or below the production standard that would be expected in the performance of a fair day's work."

are a means not only of "buying back" the jobs of employees but of winning the cooperation of the work force in the program as a whole. However carefully such provisions are drafted, however, some possibility of misunderstanding remains. At the *Celanese Corporation of America* (Textile Workers Union of America, AFL–CIO),[10] for instance, the technological displacement provision seemed to state exactly what was meant ("changes in plant or equipment," "changes in process operations"), and what was not meant, by the terms.[11] It was particularly careful to state that technological change "shall not be confused with furloughs brought about in a normal manner because production of any kind or variety or any product by any department or section of the plant is not required by the employer at the time for the purpose of sale, use or inventory." Still, a circumstance arose that to the union, but not to the company, called for technological allowance pay.

The circumstance was simply that the company had decided to move a department from one plant to another, in another labor market area, so that its product—extruded film—could compete more ef-

10. 35 AAA 22.

11. The contract read: "The employer will pay technological displacement allowances to employees displaced by technological changes and for whom no other jobs are open, upon the following terms and conditions: Any employee shall be considered displaced by technological change when his particular job is permanently abolished. because of: 1. Changes in plant or equipment, or 2. Changes in process operations. Displacement by technological changes shall not mean or include any jobs temporarily discontinued because of trade conditions such as lack of demand for any of the products the employer may have been at any time manufacturing. That is, abolition or discontinuance of a job due to technological change shall not be confused with furloughs brought about in a normal manner because production of any kind or variety or any product by any department or section of the plant is not required by the employer at the time for the purpose of sale, use or inventory.

"Should displacements be made because of change in plant or equipment or process operations in any department or section, a worker so displaced shall be given five (5) days to decide whether to avail himself of the benefits provided for in the Article and lose his seniority (plant and departmental) or to be assigned to the job held by the man with the least plant seniority on the lowest rated job in the plant. All displacements shall be made in accordance with seniority. In case of discontinuance of job by reason of technological changes as defined above, the employer agrees to give such employee, who has two or more years of continuous service, separation allowance equivalent to one week's average pay for each full year's service."

fectively. Arbitrator Sidney A. Wolff said it was not necessary for him to determine whether the transfer of the department was a "technological change" within the strict sense of the term, because the parties had given that term their own meaning when they made it synonymous with "changes in plant or equipment." The company and the union had each cited incidents in the past intended to show that its interpretation had been followed. As between the two accounts of past practice, Mr. Wolff found the union's more persuasive.

Whatever doubt there may be as to the meaning intended to be given by these parties to the contractual definition of a technological change is completely dispelled when the past practice is revealed with regard to Celanese and the Textile Workers Union. This practice clarifies beyond question that it has been the consistent practice of Celanese, under contract at its other plants with the Textile Workers Union, and having a clause similar to Article XVI, to recognize as a technological change the closing down of a particular department with a permanent abolition of jobs and the transfer of its operations to another plant, in circumstances similar to those here involved. This practice may properly be resorted to in order to ascertain how the parties themselves intended Article XVI to be applied. Surely, in the absence of a provision to the contrary, the manner in which the provisions of Article XVI have been applied by the same parties at other divisions is persuasive in concluding that they intended the same words to be applied in the same way at Belvidere, should the occasion arise.

Consequently, it is my conclusion that, in the absence of the "spoken word" or other writing indicating a contrary intent, when the parties wrote Article XVI into their contract, implied, if not expressed, was the understanding that the clause would be interpreted in the same manner as it had been interpreted over the years at other Celanese plants with the same clause in their contracts with the Textile Workers Union. Thus, the practices—"the industrial common Law"—developed at the Celanese plants under its contracts with the Textile Workers Union, must be deemed as much a part of the Labor Contract as though therein specifically set forth (*Steelworkers* v. *Warrior & Gulf,* United States Supreme Court, June 20, 1960).[12]

The identical clause was the subject of a dispute at another division of *Celanese Corporation of America* (Textile Workers Union of

12. See discussion of the *Warrior & Gulf* case in Chapter 1.

America, AFL–CIO).[13] This time, the problem was whether a technological displacement allowance was due employees who were retired or transferred to other jobs coincidentally with technological changes. William N. Loucks said the company was correct in its assertion that such pay had to be given only when workers lose employment *solely* because of one or more changes enumerated in the technological displacement clause.[14]

The grievance in the case had a history going back as far as the early 1950s. At that time, more than a hundred "cheese twisting machines" were shut down because of a falling-off of the demand for the product. When employees who were laid off approached the point in time at which their seniority would be terminated, the union sought to invoke the technological displacement allowance (TDA) provision in their behalf. But management rejected this attempt, pointing out that the conditions precedent for that benefit had not occurred. The jobs would run again, it was said, when there was renewed demand for the product.

But in 1960, the issue took a new form when management scrapped twenty of those old machines. Coincidentally, one employee died, two retired, one took an admittedly voluntary transfer, and the fifth took a transfer which the company said was voluntary but which the union said was forced as an alternative to layoff. These five were not replaced, and the union said that TDA benefits were due.

Mr. Loucks' understanding of the TDA clause was that the benefit was due when five conditions were met:

1. The employee's job must be discontinued because of changes in plant or equipment.

2. The employee's job must be discontinued because of changes in process operations.

3. Either of the above changes must cause the particular job to be permanently abolished.

4. A temporary discontinuance of the job because of "trade conditions" must not be involved.

5. The employee must in fact have lost his employment as a result of one or more of the "changes."

13. 36 AAA 28.
14. For the text of this clause, see note 9, this chapter.

Mr. Loucks said he would resolve the dispute on narrow grounds. If he found in any one of the five critical points a disqualifying circumstance, he would not rule on whether the other conditions had been met. His conclusion was that the five employees in whose behalf the union had grieved did not meet the requirements of his fifth point. As none of the five grievants had been replaced, their jobs did in fact disappear, he wrote. But that was not sufficient to invoke TDA benefits, because the incidents of their separation from those jobs "would have occurred whether or not the machines had been scrapped." If any loss of jobs had occurred, it was only on the part of "someone who would have been used as a replacement," and such a person, even if identifiable, would not be eligible for TDA for other reasons.

Mr. Loucks had been shown two prior awards, by Louis L. Jaffe, turning on the same clause, which these parties had apparently been using in their contracts virtually without change since the late 1940s. Mr. Jaffe's decision was adverse to the union,[15] and the union had not sought in subsequent negotiations to change the language to overcome the effect of Mr. Jaffe's ruling. This was an additional reason for Mr. Loucks' decision in favor of management. He wrote:

These two citations must clearly interpret Section 16 of the agreement as including the requirement referred to above as the "fifth criterion" for a valid contractual claim to a TDA, i.e., some employee must in fact have lost his employment as a result of one or more "changes." Despite the fact that this criterion was explicitly spelled out by an arbitrator as an inherent part of Section 16 as that stood in the contracts on the dates of the two Jaffe arbitration awards, the parties have made no substantive change in Section 16 on this matter. If the Jaffe interpretation was *not* the mutual intent of the parties in their previous agreements in effect at the time of the Jaffe awards, the parties were free to change these provisions so as to indicate that their mutual intent was not that which Arbitrator Jaffe found. Since the Jaffe awards were against the union claims, it presumably would have been the union which would have sought such change in the course of subsequent negotiations. However, there is no evidence before this arbitrator that any such change was requested by the union. In the light of these facts, the arbitrator must

15. Mr. Jaffe had written: "It is not the permanence of the removal of the *machines* which is important, but rather the permanence of the removal of the *employees* involved."

accept the Jaffe interpretation of Section 16 as having become a controlling interpretation of Section 16 for purposes of the instant case.

### Job Discontinuance

Throughout this volume, examples have been cited of jobs becoming obsolete long before remedial action was taken. Management often finds it convenient to tolerate a certain amount of inefficiency, making the drastic change after the incumbents retire or otherwise leave the jobs. The same approach to personnel policies was revealed at the *National Gypsum Company* (Oil, Chemical and Atomic Workers, AFL–CIO),[16] except that the incident that triggered management's decision to discontinue several jobs was not the voluntary departure of employees, but the breakdown of equipment.

Many years ago the company had shipped virtually all of its products by rail. Freight car switching operations on the premises were then performed by the railroad. Beginning about 1940, however, a gradual increase in the proportion of truck shipments took place. At the same time management felt the need to improve the handling of the small amount of rail shipments that remained. A switch engine and other equipment were therefore purchased, and a three-man crew was engaged to switch and spot cars. The trend in favor of over-the-road shipments continued for about two decades. Although the company's switching crew occasionally had to work overtime to fill rush orders, the average number of cars spotted per day fell regularly. Finally, in March 1959, when the switch engine broke down, the company declared the jobs of its three-man crew "discontinued," and reinstalled the practice of letting the railroad perform that free service.

Invoking their seniority, the three displaced employees bumped into other jobs, so that none was laid off, although there was some loss of hourly earnings. The union's grievance was that what had happened was not a legitimate job discontinuance within the meaning of the contract, but subcontracting of bargaining unit work.

Clearly, characteristics of both situations were present here. On the one hand, the need for spotting and switching cars had not completely disappeared; the evidence showed that there was need for about one and one-half hours of this work daily. On the other hand, at least to

16. 12 AAA 11.

management, this hardly seemed sufficient to maintain a full-time three-man crew. The union's proposed solution to the dilemma was for management to invoke the clause permitting it to assign out-of-classification work on a temporary basis to employees who did not have enough work of their own to do.

But none of this was enough to overcome the company's case, in John H. Piercey's judgment. He said that the change in job requirements was so substantial as to amount to the "virtual cessation of the job," clearly authorizing "the procedure of job discontinuance under the contract." Moreover, the temporary transfer clause the union had cited did not *require* the company to combine jobs, it only *permitted* it. The choice was management's, and the grievance was therefore denied.

## Reassignment of Remaining Duties after Job Discontinuance

In the *National Gypsum* case, the small amount of car switching that remained was given to an outside company, the railroad. But the more usual remedy is to let other employees in the classification of the discontinued job absorb the remaining tasks. At the *Jenney Manufacturing Company* (Oil, Chemical and Atomic Workers, AFL–CIO),[17] however, a special problem presented itself because the employee whose job was discontinued was the sole survivor in his classification.

Some months before the layoff, the company had hired a consulting firm to advise on increasing the efficiency of its wholesale distribution of gasoline and motor oil to service stations. The study resulted in recommendations that the company reduce its fleet of vehicles, increase storage facilities at the service stations, improve its preventative maintenance program, and make other changes. When this was done, it became necessary to lay off one of its four mechanics and its only mechanic's helper. A small amount of helper work remained. Management transferred these duties to other classifications and prepared to meet the union's grievance.

As did the union in the *National Gypsum* case, the union here urged that the remaining helper work be done by a helper whose idle time would be filled by out-of-classification assignments. Such assignments

17. 43 AAA 9.

were permitted under the following clause, upon which the union relied:

CLASSIFICATION AND ASSIGNMENT CHANGES. Normally employees will be assigned to work in their own classifications. When necessary the company may assign employees to work in other classifications provided that when working in [a] higher paid classification the employee shall receive such higher rate for the duration of his assignment and when working in a lower classification, the employee shall continue to receive his regular rate. Any claim for higher pay under this section shall be made within five (5) days of employee's receipt of pay check.

The company's answer was that the cited clause was intended to protect the rates of employees during temporary transfer and was never meant to apply to permanent discontinuance of jobs. Moreover, there always were overlapping assignments; the transferred duties could not be said to have been exclusively those of the mechanic's helper.

To begin with, Donald J. White emphasized that the reduction in force was "legitimate" in that it did not result from subcontracting, which would not have been lawful under the contract. He also pointed out that the grievance was narrow in scope; the union was saying only that the company had to keep the sole occupant in a classification as long as there was "*any*" work of that kind to do, no matter how little.

With this introduction, Mr. White proceeded to his analysis of the quoted clause:

This arbitrator doubts seriously that the parties negotiated that provision with the type of situation in mind which is involved here, for the clause seems to me more or less the same as clauses commonly found in agreements to deal with the problem of temporary out-of-classification assignments. But whether the surmise is correct or not, it must be observed that without any qualifying language whatever except with relation to the rate of pay to be given the employee, [this clause] says the company may, when necessary, assign employees to work in other classifications. The presence of the language "when necessary" may be presumed to impose at the most an obligation on the company to proceed in good faith, and surely it would be proceeding in good faith to assign people out of classification when the effect would be to utilize the work force efficiently. Under the circumstances, the employee's interests would be protected because he would have to get the highest rate applicable on the basis of the work assigned.

In other words, he agreed in general with management's line of argument. The conclusion he reached was not affected, he said, by the statement of the contract that employees would "normally" be assigned to work in their own classifications. He observed that the language immediately following that phrase granted broad powers to management to direct out-of-classification assignments. Moreover, as the employer had pointed out, the disputed work was transferred to employees who had performed similar work in the past as "secondary" duties.

In this case, the union had argued that classifications had to be retained for the life of the contract because they had been negotiated. This is the issue, it will be recalled, that was discussed by Brecht, Horlacher, Mittenthal, and others.[18] Mr. White seemed to take his stand with those who were not inclined to agree that broad implications could be drawn from the wage schedule alone.

It is clear that the parties negotiated a wage scale for known or identified classes of work. . . . But this is quite different from negotiated classifications where the clear purpose is to construct set categories of work such that the work in a given category might be assigned only to an employee in that category. Such an arrangement would go far beyond the negotiation of a wage scale and therefore would have to be evidenced by specific contract language to that effect.

## Technological Displacement and Unfilled Vacancies

When technological changes cause a job no longer to be "a production necessity," ruled Aaron Horvitz in *American Radiator and Standard Sanitary Corporation* (International Union of Electrical, Radio and Machine Workers, AFL–CIO),[19] the union's consent was not required before a job could be discontinued. The union had argued that a clause barring changes in wage rates or job classifications implied that jobs would continue, but Mr. Horvitz reminded it that a rate schedule and a clause protecting classifications were not the same thing.[20] The union's testimony about the understanding of the parties

18. See Chapter 6.
19. 18 AAA 9.
20. The effect of negotiated rates on management's right to change job content was discussed more fully in Chapter 6.

with respect to rates was relevant only "when, as and if [the job] is being performed," he wrote. And if the employer should decide to reactivate the discontinued job, he would be bound to pay the agreed-upon rates. But that was the extent of the obligations the arbitrator would impose on the company, in view of the facts of the case.[21]

A job discontinuance problem also arose at the *American Chain and Cable Company* (United Steelworkers of America, AFL–CIO),[22] where management decided to leave unfilled the maintenance helper jobs that had been vacated by the death of one employee and the retirement of another. Unlike several cases discussed in this chapter, in which the union urged temporary out-of-classification work assignments as an alternative to letting a job disappear, the union here found contractual authority for its grievance in the job-bidding provision. It was argued that the failure to post the vacated job for bidding reduced the promotional opportunities which were presumably promised by implication in the contract. Furthermore, the union said, a consequence of not filling the vacancies was that employees in skilled classifications were "degraded" by being compelled to perform the duties of helpers, and that the journeyman-helper ratio was upset.

None of this was persuasive to William Dall. He observed that the contract gave management the right "to manage the business and plants and to direct the work forces." This was more directly relevant to the situation at hand than the job-bidding provision upon which the union depended. Moreover, he said, there was nothing in the contract to prevent skilled workers from doing some unskilled work. "If there is a certain amount of ridicule attached to these periods of lower level duties," the arbitrator wrote, "there is at least the reward of full compensation." As to the union's final point that unfilled vacancies disturbed the normal ratio of helpers to journeymen, Mr. Dall wrote: "Whatever the union's contention, the company can change this ratio as it wishes in order to maintain efficiency in the way the company decides. The jobs [of the deceased and retired employees] were maintained for long service employees and not necessarily because of the need for full-time helpers."

21. Mr. Horvitz said this decision did not diminish the right of any employee to press to arbitration a grievance in which it might be alleged that the elimination of the job in question here imposed an excessive load on other employees.

22. 25 AAA 20.

A promotion can be cause for rejoicing, not only for the employee immediately upgraded, but also for those who hope to move into the vacancies subsequently created. But when a company decides to promote a man out of the bargaining unit and then leaves his job unfilled, the response is anything but joyous. Something of the sort happened at *WBEN, Incorporated* (National Association of Broadcast Employees and Technicians, AFL–CIO).[23] For about fifteen years, an employee was classified as a "radio and television engineering supervisor," a bargaining unit position despite the exalted title. From about 1948 on, especially with the advent of television and the increase in the station's staff, this employee began doing less and less manual work and correspondingly more supervisory work. Eventually, he was in charge of seven other employees and was making effective decisions in purchasing equipment, a task that brought him into close contact with managerial and executive personnel.

Some time in 1960, when the broadcasting company moved into new quarters, management began grooming this engineering supervisor for the managerial position that would become vacant after the retirement of an executive. The retirement took place on schedule, and the promotion out of the bargaining unit quickly followed. Now, from his new vantage point as a manager, he continued to supervise the same seven employees who were under his jurisdiction before. At the same time, he performed other work which he had not done in the past. What bothered the union, however, was not that its former member was now a member of supervision, but that the company chose to leave the vacancy in the bargaining unit unfilled. In short, the union had lost control of a job.

The question before James J. Healy was whether a vacancy had really been created by the promotion. If the work the engineering supervisor formerly did was properly transferred out of the unit, there was no vacancy left to be filled. On the other hand, if supervision of the seven employees was really bargaining unit work, a bargaining unit employee would have to do it.

Mr. Healy said that where the nature of the job had changed to such an extent that the employee was performing supervisory duties half the time, the employer had the right to transfer him and his duties out of the unit. Furthermore, contractual procedures for filling vacancies,

23. 39 AAA 8.

relied upon by the union, were not controlling, because they did not *require* vacancies to be filled. In other words, they did not diminish management's rights to determine the size of the work force.

The union claim that a vacancy exists which the company is obligated to fill has validity *only* if it is found that the transfer of duties was violative of the agreement. Under the terms of the agreement it is evident that the company has the right to determine the size of the working force. It may increase or decrease the number of jobholders, subject only to the procedural requirements stated in the contract. The arbitrator is also of the opinion that [the promotion clause], as the company points out, is primarily a prescription of the criteria to be used when a vacancy occurs which has to be filled.

But the union did salvage a slight moral victory from this case. The union was correct, Mr. Healy wrote, in its assertion that if the company were permitted to transfer work out of the union's jurisdiction "arbitrarily," it would make a "mockery" of the agreement.[24] But those were not the circumstances of this case. The company had established "strong justification," the arbitrator said, for the "amalgamation of duties," representing "about a 50-50 combination of what had been bargaining unit work and management work." This change was drastic enough to justify treating the job "as a bona fide management job."

### Non-technological Job Elimination

At the *Roxbury Carpet Company* (Textile Workers Union of America, AFL–CIO),[25] the union took the position that the elimination of jobs resulting from the introduction of new machinery was one thing, but elimination of jobs due to non-technological changes in the flow of work was something else. Unfortunately for the grievants, both

24. Management conceded that it did not have unlimited power to transfer work out of the bargaining unit. Mr. Healy wrote: "In its brief, the company acknowledged that it did not have the right to engage capriciously in this type of action; it recognized further that its decision would have to undergo close scrutiny to be certain there was an adequate regard for the institutional and individual rights under the agreement. In effect, each case of this type must be handled on a separate basis."
25. 20 AAA 6.

were held by John A. Hogan to be equally within the rights conferred upon management by the contract.

Facing the problem of increasing complaints by customers that carpets were not being delivered on time, management engaged a firm of outside consultants, who recommended a new "prescheduling" system, intended to eliminate bottlenecks as carpets moved from one department to the next. According to the company, the installation of this system did not involve speedup. Time intervals for the performance of particular tasks were based upon past experience. The saving was to result only from elimination of waiting time. In fact, however, ten jobs were eliminated through prescheduling, some of the duties involved being transferred to remaining jobs.

The work assignment clause of the contract was quite broad:

The employer shall have the right to change or introduce machines, processes and method of manufacture for the purpose of insuring the efficient operation of the mill and utilizing the employee's working time most productively and without adversely affecting the workers' physical or mental condition or causing undue fatigue.

But broad as it was, the union did not believe that it covered situations where no new machines or chemical and mechanical processes were involved. Prescheduling as such was all right, union spokesmen said at the arbitration hearing, because that had to do with the activities of supervisors. But the change in job assignments of bargaining unit employees was forbidden.

Calling close attention to every word in the quoted clause, the company argued that the phrase "method of manufacture" covered the situation exactly. If it did not, the phrase would be redundant and meaningless. Mr. Hogan agreed with management that a prescheduling production control system was a sufficient change to invoke the quoted clause. The term "method of manufacture" must be construed in the light of the "purpose and intent" of the clause, he said.

It seems to be clear that manufacturing is concerned with getting out production and that all methods and processes used to get out that production are methods and processes of manufacture. The manufacturing process is not limited to machine process or chemical process . . . A change in the layout of machines or the layout of work is a change in the method of getting out the work and, under normal interpretation, is a change in the method of manufacturing . . . The new system of laying out the work (if it was to be meaningful as an attempt to utilize the employee's working time most efficiently) required that work assignments and job content be rearranged, and this resulted in eliminating some jobs. The contract does not freeze job content or guarantee employment. Therefore, unless the evidence shows that the changes adversely affected the workers' physical or mental condition, or caused undue fatigue, the conclusion must be that the change conformed to the purpose of the clause.

The only remaining point to be disposed of was whether an undue burden of work was placed on any employee. Mr. Hogan was shown no evidence of it, and he thought it worth mentioning that although there had been some discussion between the parties about excessive work loads, no grievances were filed on that issue.

## Protection Against Future Job Loss

In an atmosphere where unemployment is an ever-present fear, if not an immediate prospect, management and labor are usually equally interested in giving preference to present employees for new, and perhaps more secure, jobs that may open up. The only difficulty is that employees do not always have enough facts about future prospects for a risk-free decision as to whether to transfer to new jobs. Even for management, presumably possessed of more knowledge, the element of gamble is not completely absent.

An illustration of this problem was seen in the case of the *Great Atlantic and Pacific Tea Company* (International Brotherhood of Teamsters, Independent).[26] The 1957 contract included a clause stating that if the company opened a new warehouse within the geographical jurisdiction of the union, present employees would be given an opportunity to transfer "conditional on immediate acceptance," before new workers were hired. Management subsequently did open a new warehouse, to which about 200 of 516 employees polled chose to transfer. More than 100 new employees were thereupon hired to staff the new installation, and additional hiring took place in subsequent months. The same union was certified as bargaining representative at the new warehouse, and a contract was concluded.

26. 8 AAA 4.

Early in the next year, the company began laying off employees at the old location. This led to a grievance in which the union complained that employees at the old location should have been given preference over eight employees hired at the new warehouse subsequent to the initial staffing operation. It was apparently the union's feeling that management had not disclosed plans for the future that were necessary for the employees in the old warehouse to make a meaningful decision as to whether to transfer; and the purpose of the grievance was not only to extend the period of time within which those facing layoff could transfer, but to obtain information for future decisions.

Sidney A. Wolff decided one aspect of the case in favor of the company, and another in favor of the union. Management was "entirely justified," he wrote, in assuming that the employees at the old warehouse who did not apply for transfer were not interested in doing so, and that it would only have been a "futile gesture" to ask them again.

In this regard I cannot ignore the fact it was some weeks later that the question was raised by the . . . employees and then only after the company began its lay off. The failure to raise the issue sooner coupled with their earlier refusal to accept the transfers . . . must be deemed a waiver. . . . True, as has been noted, [the grievants] were not concerned with their transfer rights earlier since they were not being laid off but they may not sit idly by, permit the company to take on the new people and acquiesce in what is now claimed to be a violation of the contract and then, finding themselves subject to layoff . . . seek to have an arbitrator upset the employment of a group of men whose status and employment rights have already become fixed under the provisions of the . . . collective bargaining agreement made with the same union [at the new warehouse].

But the union was upheld in the argument that the contract at the new location did not put an end to the preferential hiring provision at the old warehouse. The grievants therefore had a right to first call for transfer to the new locations to fill jobs that might become available.

The company is now on notice that [the grievants] are no longer waiving their transfer rights . . . with respect to jobs not yet in existence. It is therefore my award that as jobs hereafter open up [at the new warehouse] the company shall, in accordance with the provisions of [the contract] first offer the jobs to the . . . personnel [at the old warehouse], then, if not accepted promptly, the company is free to obtain its personnel elsewhere. Since posting . . . may not reach the attention of the laid off employees, the mailing of copies of the posted notice to them at their last known address . . . shall constitute a sufficient offer, and in making this ruling, I do so with the consent of the parties so as to avoid controversy in the future. . . .

On the question of giving employees information about future operations, Mr. Wolff upheld the company again. In offering future jobs, he wrote, "the company is not obligated under the present agreement to furnish the employees with facts pertaining to the company's future operations so that they could be in a better position to weigh the pros and cons before accepting or rejecting. Article XIV lays down no such requirement and I may not impose any such requirement upon the company, as the union would have me do, for the agreement itself denies me the 'power to add to' its provisions."

### Bumping of Unit Employees by Non-unit Personnel

In many ways, the job losses that distress bargaining unit members most are those that result from the return to the unit of supervisors and other non-unit personnel. Almost by definition, these returning employees have considerable ability and seniority; if they have the right to assert seniority in the bargaining unit at all, they usually are in a position to claim the more desirable jobs. Employees are, of course, accustomed to bumping each other when there are fewer jobs than employees. But to have to compete with a foreman for a rank-and-file job somehow seems unfair, even when it is sanctioned by the agreement.[27]

27. An unusual contract interpretation problem was raised at the *Westinghouse Electric Corporation* (Federation of Westinghouse Independent Salaried Unions), 39 AAA 7, where the union thought that a clause stating that foremen "may be" returned to the bargaining unit under certain conditions meant that, even in the presence of those conditions, the union had a veto power over such return. Sidney L. Cahn ruled for the company. The fact that the language of previous contracts contained the words "shall be returned" did not alter his conclusion. In the first place, he said, the contract as a whole showed that when the parties intended to give the union a controlling voice in a matter, they did so in explicit language. Furthermore, there was no evidence that the union negotiators had called attention to the significance of the words they were proposing when "may" was substituted for "shall." Mr. Cahn said the "sole

Almost invariably, foremen who have never been in the bargaining unit have no seniority standing.[28] If they are removed as foremen and transferred to bargaining unit work, they have the status of new employees. But with those who were promoted from the ranks, the situation may be different. Under some contracts, they may retain seniority already accrued, but not add to it during the time they are outside the unit. In others, full accrual may be permitted. Collective bargaining agreements also occasionally limit the circumstances under which a supervisor may assert seniority for return to the unit. Thus, for instance, he may be permitted to return to his old classification only if it does not involve displacement of a worker presently employed.

## *Retention* vs. *Accrual of Seniority*

Arbitrator William E. Simkin resolved a typical dispute at *Joseph T. Ryerson and Son, Incorporated* (United Steelworkers of America, AFL–CIO).[29] The issue was the seniority status of a foreman who had once been in the bargaining unit. Demoting him to the ranks, the company credited him not only with the seniority he acquired in the bargaining unit, but also with seniority for the time spent outside the unit. The union believed he had lost his seniority when he left the

---

doubt" about the validity of the company's position as to the intention of the negotiators was created by union testimony about "an alleged conversation" between the chief negotiator for the company and three union officials. However, even if the union's version of the informal conversation (disputed by the company) were accepted, what was said was "at best ambiguous" and can not override "the clear and unambiguous pattern illustrated by the series of written proposals advanced by the parties."

28. See, for example, *The Cared Corporation* (United Steelworkers of America, AFL–CIO), 8 AAA 6. The contract granted accumulated service credit to "employees in the bargaining unit who are promoted to the position of supervisor" and who thereafter are returned to the bargaining unit. The company thought this provision also justified crediting a downgraded supervisor who had never been in the bargaining unit with seniority for the time he had spent as a supervisory employee. Lewis M. Gill disagreed. "Whatever may be said of the merits of granting accumulated service credit to ex-supervisors who did not originate in the bargaining unit," he wrote, "it is clear that this contract did not provide for it.

29. 22 AAA 17.

unit; on coming back to a bargaining unit job, he was a new employee, without seniority.

Mr. Simkin noted that the contract did not deal with the question specifically. But there was one clause that listed a number of circumstances under which seniority would be terminated. Accepting a promotion to foreman was not one of the circumstances. From this he drew two conclusions:

1. The ex-foreman was properly credited with the seniority he had once acquired in the unit. His past service was "money in the bank" as far as seniority was concerned. Consequently, his return to the unit was not as a "new employee."

2. On the other hand, it was an error for the company to credit the ex-foreman with seniority for time spent outside the unit:

In the absence of a contract clause or a clear understanding as respects supervisors, seniority for job rights purposes is a concept that is related realistically only to bargaining unit work. Supervisors normally have no formal job rights seniority on supervisory positions while they are supervisors. If prior bargaining unit service is not lost under this contract when a man becomes a supervisor because it is not terminated by any contract provision, it is just as difficult to find a contract provision that provides for accumulation.

The employer had relied on a clause defining seniority as "length of continuous service in the warehouse," but Mr. Simkin said the company was overlooking the real meaning of "continuous service" in that context. "It would be reading a great deal into this [language]," he said, "to conclude that the words 'continuous service' mean continuous service as an employee or as a supervisor or as a clerk." Management had also referred to another phrase in the contract which, without mentioning the bargaining unit, spoke of terminal dates of employment. This was "admittedly in the company's favor," the arbitrator wrote; but it could still not be controlling, because it was clear that "the parties have never grappled with this issue directly in negotiations." Instead, the question of seniority status of foremen was "swept under the rug," leaving the unclear language of the contract unchanged.

The same question arose at the *Mississippi Lime Company of*

*Missouri* (United Glass and Ceramic Workers, AFL–CIO).[30] The contract read:

It is agreed that an employee who is promoted to an administrative, clerical or supervisory position, shall in case he is returned to his former job, retain his seniority and privileges in the line-up he left, provided he takes a withdrawal card from the union.

As the union read the sentence, seniority was "frozen" when a man was promoted to a supervisory capacity. It thawed again and resumed accrual when he once more became a member of the unit. The use of the word "retain" in the clause absolutely barred any possibility of accumulation by a foreman. To this the company answered that a man cannot realistically "retain" his seniority unless he maintains the "relative status" he had when he left the unit. This required accumulation.

Robben T. Fleming found both answers possible in a reading of the contract clause itself. "We have not learned to use words so precisely that they can have only one possible meaning." As there was doubt in his mind as to what the negotiators had meant when they drafted the agreement, he turned to the past practice of the parties. Here he found support for the company position. The quoted clause had been in effect for four years, during two contracts. "Under both there had been a uniform practice of according accumulated seniority to supervisors."

While disposing of the grievance before him largely on the basis of past practice, Mr. Fleming expressed five general principles that, he said, usually apply in cases of this kind.

1. Seniority is a valuable right with a long history in American trade unionism and it ought not to be lightly discarded.

2. Seniority is clearly a creature of the contract and the parties may give it whatever form they desire. Moreover, seniority rights, once given, do not vest and may be changed from time to time as new contracts are negotiated.

3. Where the contract says nothing about seniority for supervisors, but lists the usual ways in which seniority may be broken, an individual does not lose the seniority rights acquired up to that time simply because he becomes a supervisor. He does not, however, continue to accumulate

30. 1 AAA 16.

seniority thereafter because he is no longer covered by the contract and the contract says nothing about seniority for supervisors. He can keep what seniority he acquired as a production worker because the contract does not state that he loses it by becoming a supervisor.

4. A production worker who is promoted to supervision retains the seniority acquired prior to promotion, but he may not exercise it while in the supervisory ranks because he is not covered by the contract. If the company returns him to the production force he may then exercise the rights which were frozen when he was promoted.

5. Where the contract is not silent but specifically grants seniority rights to supervisors, the question becomes one of contract interpretation.

## Past Seniority Protected in New Contract

The premise that "seniority is . . . a creature of the contract," in the words of Mr. Fleming, quoted above, and that parties may measure seniority in any way they wish, was also illustrated at the *American Radiator and Standard Sanitary Corporation* (International Molders and Foundry Workers, AFL–CIO).[31] The arbitrator was Robert G. McIntosh. Under contracts negotiated in 1955 and 1956, an employee was credited with "full seniority," despite his supervisory position outside the bargaining unit. In 1957, however, the agreement was modified, so that a foreman returning to the bargaining unit would have accrued seniority only in the classification or department into which he was demoted.

In 1959 a foreman was demoted, making it necessary to compute his accrued seniority, and raising the critical question of whether the 1957 modification had erased the seniority he had accrued under the 1955 and 1956 contracts. Mr. McIntosh did not question the right of parties to wipe out previously accrued seniority by newly negotiated rules, but he ruled that in this case they did not do so. His conclusion was based on a clause in the 1957 contract, stating that "the provisions and conditions set out in this Agreement shall supersede the provisions and conditions as set forth in any previous Master Agreement, but shall not be retroactive beyond its effective date."

"Thus it is obvious," Mr. McIntosh wrote, "that both parties agreed that whatever rights, privileges or advantages an employee obtained

31. 7 AAA 24.

under a specific contract should not be taken away from him by a subsequent contract or an interpretation of such subsequent contract." Therefore, he concluded, the foreman, having once been credited with service in a certain department, could not be stripped of that seniority retroactively.

## Effect of Seniority Termination Clause

The contract at *Mohasco Industries, Incorporated* (Textile Workers Union of America, AFL–CIO)[32] seemed very clear on the seniority status of employees who transfer to supervisory jobs; they were to retain the seniority they had, but not accumulate more while outside the unit. But the contract did not say anything about the seniority status of employees who transfer to non-supervisory jobs outside the unit. This gap led to a dispute which was resolved by Lloyd H. Bailer in a manner that upheld neither the union's nor the company's theory of the case.

In April 1957 a frame spinner with about fourteen years' seniority in the bargaining unit was about to be laid off for lack of work because her job was discontinued. It happened, however, that there was a vacancy as a yarn weigher, a job that was non-supervisory but outside the bargaining unit. The job was offered to the frame spinner as an alternative to layoff, and the offer was accepted. She held this job for three years, and was again laid off because the yarn-weighing job was discontinued. The layoff continued until November 1960. At that time, on the assumption that this employee still had the fourteen years of seniority she had accumulated between 1943 and 1957, management recalled her to a bargaining unit job.

At this a grievance was filed. "You can give her a job in the bargaining unit as a newly hired employee," the union said in effect, "but you cannot credit her with previously accrued seniority. That seniority was lost when she agreed to take a job outside the bargaining unit in 1957." The union added that if the negotiators of the contract had intended to let non-supervisory, non-unit personnel retain seniority, they would have so stated, just as they did in the case of supervisory employees. Management's answer was that the omission of reference to non-unit personnel, other than supervisors, was not significant, and

32. 46 AAA 1.

that the principle of limited protection that was applied to foremen should logically be extended to other similarly situated employees.

Reading the contract in its entirety, Mr. Bailer found a solution in the seniority clause, a provision which neither party had relied upon. Under that clause, seniority could be terminated under any of four circumstances: when an employee quits; when she is discharged for just cause; when she fails to report from layoff within a specified number of days after her recall; and when she remains on layoff without being recalled for up to thirty-six months, depending upon her length of service. The controlling facts in this case, he said, were threefold: First, the former frame spinner had taken a non-bargaining unit job because she faced a *layoff*. Secondly, her length of service protected seniority during layoff for three years. And finally, this seniority would not have been lost during those thirty-six months if she had gone to work for another company while awaiting recall. It seemed to Mr. Bailer that an employee who took a non-unit job with her own employer while waiting for her regular work to become available should not be treated less favorably.

Unfortunately for this employee, however, the attempt to return her to the bargaining unit with her fourteen years of seniority intact occurred more than three years after she had left the unit. That compelled a decision in the union's favor, although for reasons different from those the union had urged.

### How to "Retain Accumulated Seniority"

In the *Mohasco Industries* case, the contract permitted employees promoted to supervisory positions to "retain," but not "accumulate," seniority. But what would a contract mean if it said that foremen transferred back to the bargaining unit "shall retain accumulated seniority"? This ambiguity was put before Mark L. Kahn at the *General Refractories Company* (United Brick and Clay Workers, AFL–CIO).[33] On the answer to this question depended the job tenure of an employee—the grievant in this case—who had never left the unit.

The clause in which that phrase appeared established two different procedures for invoking seniority: A supervisor who wanted to return to the bargaining unit within ninety days of his promotion could re-

33. 34 AAA 19.

claim his old job immediately, but one who stayed away longer would first have to take the "lowest ranking job" within the unit and later move up to a higher classification when the opportunity presented itself. In either case, however—and this was the point Mr. Kahn said the union overlooked—the supervisor brought with him full seniority credit, including time spent outside the bargaining unit.

"The union appears to agree with the company that employees temporarily promoted to supervisory positions are entitled to return to the unit with the same seniority they would have had if they had never left the unit," Mr. Kahn observed. "In my view, there is no contractual basis for inferring any distinction in seniority status between temporary and longer promotions: in both situations, the employees 'shall retain accumulated seniority,' and if the temporarily promoted employee has accumulated seniority while a supervisor so has the employee who served as a supervisor in excess of ninety days."[34]

## Bidding for Bargaining Unit Jobs

In the cases discussed immediately above, the issue was how to compute the seniority of returning non-unit employees. Another category of dispute over non-unit personnel is not how much seniority they have, but how they may assert it. This was the problem in the case of *Maier's Bakery* (Bakery and Confectionery Workers, AFL–CIO),[35] where L. G. Lichliter ruled that a supervisor may not bid for unit jobs while outside the unit. To claim a unit job, he must first get back into the unit, which may mean taking whatever is available at the time and then waiting for an opportunity to move up.

This ruling came about after a vacancy in the cake mixer classifica-

34. The union had also argued that an oral understanding had been reached during negotiations that the relevant clause would be applied as the union urged in this case. Mr. Kahn would not credit that argument, particularly since the disputed clause appeared in contracts between the union and other companies in the industry and was applied in the manner urged by the employer. Even if something "ambiguous" had been said during negotiations by a management spokesman, the arbitrator ruled, it would not be sufficient to overcome past practice in the industry. For that practice to be reversed, the union would have had to "pursue the matter further in negotiation."
35. 1 AAA 17.

tion was posted for bidding on the company bulletin board, in accordance with the contract. One of the foremen thereupon notified management that he was resigning his supervisory position in order to get that job. Two other employees, not in supervisory capacities, also entered bids. As the foreman had more seniority, he was awarded the job, whereupon the union filed a grievance. Both sides agreed that the issue turned on interpretation of this clause:

ARTICLE V. An employee employed in a supervisory capacity by the Employer and, therefore, ineligible for Union membership, upon ceasing to hold such supervisory position shall be entitled to membership in the bargaining unit and upon becoming a member of the bargaining unit shall have seniority based upon his original date of employment by the Employer regardless of prior Union affiliations.

The union's position, briefly, was that the foreman's bid could not be honored until after his application for membership in the union was received. This occurred after the closing date for determination of the successful bidder. Management answered that the resignation from the supervisory position occurred before the closing date for bids and that nothing else mattered.

The arbitrator upheld the grievance, but on grounds different from those asserted by the union.

In the first place, the article nowhere deals with the question as to who is eligible to bid on a posted job, nor can we find any mention of that subject elsewhere in the contract. All that this article does is to provide that *"upon becoming a member* of the bargaining unit" a former supervisory employee's seniority shall include those years of service he has previously spent with the company outside the unit. It does not say *how* a supervisory employee can become a member of the unit, and certainly a resignation from the position of foreman, with nothing more, could not of itself have put [the foreman] among the classification of jobs which comprise the bargaining unit. It goes without saying that to be eligible to bid on a posted job in the absence of any governing contractual language, the bidder must at that time be a member of the unit.

The argument of the union that union membership is a requirement of bidding is equally erroneous. If an employee, holding a job with the company which is within the unit, seeks to bid on a posted job, he has every right to do so even though not a union member, provided he applies for membership within thirty days, as required by Article I.

In view of the foregoing, we must conclude that under the contract, (1) Only employees who are part of the collective bargaining unit may bid for posted jobs, (2) Resignation as foreman did not, of itself, constitute [the foreman] a member of the unit, and (3) Awarding the job of mixer to [the foreman] was erroneous.

It would appear, therefore, that in order to compete with bargaining unit employees for the posted job, the foreman would have had to resign his supervisory job unconditionally, taking any job open within the bargaining unit. From that vantage point, he could then bid to become a cake mixer. Whether this could be accomplished within the few days during which bids were open, however, was not clear from the facts of the case as revealed in the arbitrator's written opinion.

## Making Room for a Returning Foreman

Two cases of the *New Jersey Zinc Company* (United Steelworkers of America, AFL–CIO), decided about a month apart, point up variations of the same problem. The first,[36] arbitrated by George Savage King, involved no important conflicts of fact. The issue was simply whether, under a contract permitting employees who transfer outside the union to accumulate non-unit seniority against the time they might have to return, a returning employee could claim only a vacant job, or a job in the lowest classification (as the union believed), or could bump a junior (as the employer argued).

Finding the contract clause "ambiguous," Mr. King looked to "the whole agreement" for clues as to what the negotiators had intended. This led him to the conclusion that the company was correct. The arbitrator found it relevant that the union had proposed a clause during contract negotiations which would terminate an employee's seniority when he moved to a non-unit job. The employer rejected that proposal, and the matter was dropped. Another relevant fact was that the contract contained provisions for dealing with employees who, after accepting a promotion within the unit, chose to go back to their own jobs or were found unsuitable for the upgrading. Mr. King observed that the parties had experienced "no difficulty" in stating the conditions under which such employees could displace others, and the

36. 41 AAA 18.

conditions under which they could take only vacant jobs or jobs in the "lowest classification," awaiting the next opportunity to move back where they had come from. It followed, he said, that if the parties had intended similarly to restrict the returning non-unit employee, they would have done so in equally clear language. Therefore, he concluded, "the company exercised its right to assign the returning employee to the job which his experience and seniority entitled him to" even though it meant the displacement of a junior.

The second case[37] was arbitrated by Charles O. Gregory. Contract provisions were, of course, the same, but the facts were somewhat more complicated. At the time a foreman was returned to the bargaining unit, some job transfers of bargaining unit employees were put into effect. As the company explained it, the foreman was displacing a junior employee, as he had the right to do, and successive bumps and job transfers followed. But in the union's view, a new job had been created, and the vacancy should have been posted for bidding by seniority.

Mr. Gregory said that "at first glance" there did appear to be a conflict between the provisions cited, for both the foreman-seniority provision and the job-bidding clause seemed applicable. But, he added, on closer examination, the conflict disappeared. If, as the union argued, the foreman was placed in a newly created job, the company was only doing what one provision of the agreement specifically said it could do. If, on the other hand, the foreman was placed in an existing job which was not vacant, but which was simultaneously vacated by the transfer of another employee, that, too, was proper under the agreement. Under the circumstances, Mr. Gregory wrote, it was not necessary for him to determine how the vacancy came about.[38]

### Foreman Limited to His Old Classification

In a case at the *American Radiator and Standard Sanitary Corporation* (United Automobile Workers, AFL–CIO)[39] the right of a fore-

---

37. 42 AAA 20.

38. Mr. Gregory acknowledged that the union might "take issue" with the way an employee was transferred to create a vacancy, but its grievance in this case "was not filed with such a course in mind."

39. 33 AAA 13.

man to return to the unit was not questioned, but the position he could occupy was in dispute. The difficulty was that, under the contract, a returning foreman was permitted to be placed in the classification he had occupied before his promotion. But the classification which the foreman had occupied no longer existed in the bargaining unit.[40] Under the circumstances, management believed it was equitable to place the returning foreman in a job that was comparable, or of equal status, with the one he had held. This, the company said, would be Assembler A—the highest classification in the Assembly Department.[41] The union's contention was that the man should have been placed in the Assembler C classification (the job he was originally hired in), so that the higher job would be available to a bargaining unit member through the bidding system.

Lloyd H. Bailer first defined the area of agreement and of disagreement:

The parties are in agreement that, at management's option, an employee who has been promoted out of the bargaining unit may be returned to the unit with accrued seniority (including service credit for time spent in non-bargaining unit employment with the company) and that he may be placed in a classification which he formerly occupied in the unit. The union agrees that in returning to his former classification such an employee may be allowed to displace a less senior employee, if necessary, in that classification. The difference between the parties arises out of the fact that upon returning [the foreman] to the bargaining unit, the company placed him in a classification which he had never held before, although [he] had previously worked as a bargaining unit employee in the same department and at a similar level of skill.

Examining the job-posting-and-bidding provision, which formed the basis of the union's case, Mr. Bailer found this "sequence of steps" to be followed in filling vacancies: (1) from the night shift on the same job, subject to another provision of the agreement; (2) from

40. The demoted foreman had been hired as an Assembler C, and subsequently was promoted to assistant to the foreman, then a bargaining unit position. Later, at the company's request, that position was removed from the bargaining unit. The foreman was still later promoted to assistant foreman, and then to a full foreman. When his reduction to the ranks took place, the job from which he had been promoted out of the unit was non-existent.

41. There had been no Assembler A at the time the foreman held the position of assistant to the foreman in the Assembly Department.

within the occupational group concerned; and (3) from qualified applicants outside that occupational group.

The arbitrator thought it important to observe that this procedure is not invoked when the job of a laid-off employee becomes available. In that event, the worker on the layoff list can assert his prior claim to the work. "In effect," he said, "the parties have accorded to employees returning from non-unit employment to a unit classification they formerly occupied a similar exemption" from the section providing for the filling of vacancies by the three-step sequence. But "there is no evidence that it has ever been the mutual intent of the parties to grant the same exemption with respect to assigning a 're-turning' employee to a classification he has not occupied before."

In view of the foregoing analysis of the evidence, it is concluded that upon being returned to the bargaining unit [the foreman] was entitled to exercise his accrued seniority only in the Assembler C classification, where he had previously worked. It further is concluded that when an Assembler A position became available on December 6, 1960, the most senior Assembler A man who had been downgraded on layoff . . . was entitled to be placed in this position.

# 9

## GENERAL CONCLUSIONS

When to the sessions of sweet silent thought
I summon up remembrance of things past,
I sigh the lack of many a thing I sought,
And with old woes new wail my dear time's waste.
. . . . . . . . . . . . . . . .
Then can I grieve at grievances foregone,
And heavily from woe to woe tell o'er
The sad account of fore-bemoaned moan,
Which I new pay as if not paid before.

—WILLIAM SHAKESPEARE

The several hundred grievance arbitration cases in this volume reflect the difference in outlook between management, with its technological radicalism, and the union, with its job-conscious conservatism. By and large, this is the conflict with which we have been concerned in this volume.

To say that this conflict exists as an aspect of collective bargaining is not to say that, but for the presence of the union, management would be free to resolve all manpower utilization problems purely on its own terms. As we have indicated in the introductory chapter, the common law rights of the employer extend no further than his economic power to enforce them. The fact is that in an unorganized establishment, as in a unionized one, employees restrict production to conceal loose rates, they rebel at out-of-classification assignments, and

239

they slow up when they think they may be working themselves out of jobs. Many work-restricting practices are expressly against company rules, but foremen know when to look the other way, for the labor market situation does not always favor the employer. Moreover, when there is not enough work to go around, seniors expect to be favored over juniors, even if the latter have greater ability. In this respect, too, the unorganized shop in a generally industrialized area is not greatly different from an organized plant. In short, even in the absence of a union, managerial rights are not without their implied limitations.

Nevertheless, the presence of a union does make a difference. Where employees bargain collectively, the more or less informal work restrictions are codified and given legitimate status. No longer can they be terminated at the will of the employer when the balance of power shifts in his favor. But by the same token, the privileges that employees might take for themselves are also limited by the code. In other words, manpower utilization becomes under collective bargaining a matter of contract, bargainable in exchange for other considerations. Not the least of the changes wrought by collective bargaining is that the union now has easy access to machinery for challenging managerial decisions that affect either the job security of employees or its own institutional security.

It is probably just as well that President Truman's 1945 Labor-Management Conference[1] broke up without reaching an understanding on the proper limits of collective bargaining. As the participants were too far apart for real agreement, a mediated formula would have been necessarily general and, therefore, of no real use as a guide to companies and unions. Moreover, a joint statement of principle would have transferred the futile discussion to the local bargaining level, where still another debate over "principles" that turn out to be expediencies is not particularly needed.

The course of events following 1945 was much more constructive. Negotiators of contracts did what they could to draw a line between areas of managerial freedom and areas of joint control: Some matters were left entirely within the scope of the employer's authority; others were subject to management action, after notice to the union; and still other matters were to be acted upon only on mutual agreement. These lines of demarcation were not always clear and sharp, nor were

1. See Chapter 1, note 5.

they always wisely drawn. That is one reason why the labor-management community has evolved its system of grievance arbitration. But at least the parties could proceed on the basis of rules compiled by themselves for their own needs. The extent to which they fashioned a viable system is revealed in the kinds of grievances that have arisen and the manner in which they were resolved.

One observation to be drawn from these grievances is that labor-management relations have never developed into a partnership of equals. There is rather a division of roles that permits management to function as the initiator of action in the work place and reserves to the union the right of appeal. The fear that unions would eventually wrest control of basic work decisions has not been justified. Indeed, unions feel most comfortable in their appellate roles; they could probably not be enticed into situations where they would have to share management's day-to-day decisions and take the consequent responsibility. To be sure, if a production line is discontinued, the union may have something to say about the order of layoffs, and an arbitrator may award back pay to an employee wrongfully sent home. But the economic decision to produce fewer products will not be affected. (This assumes, of course, as has been the case in every instance discussed in this book, that discrimination against employees or an attempt to destroy the union was not the motive.) Similarly, when an employer decides that work is to be done another way, it may raise the possibility of a hundred different grievances—rates, work loads, out-of-classification assignments, etc.—but his right to be obeyed will not be questioned. A rarely encountered exception to this rule would be a work order involving a health or safety hazard.

The experience of the parties with the sometimes explosive question of subcontracting is especially revealing. As we have seen, most contracts are silent on the matter, either because the negotiators see no problems ahead, or perhaps because they see more problems than they can cope with during the relatively short time at their disposal. In any event, although the silence does not denote an absolutely free hand, it does bespeak rather broad rights. Seldom are unions upheld in their protests against contracting out under contracts that do not expressly limit the employer's right to do so. And in the few exceptional cases, a monetary remedy is usually denied. By and large, unions are able to extract only the comfort of dicta, in which arbitrators point out that despite the silence of the contracts, management is subject to implied covenants of good faith. It is not without significance that although arbitrators caution against bad faith with almost monotonous regularity, that fault was not found by arbitrators in any of the cases discussed in this volume.

Where collective bargaining agreements do contain restrictions on contracting out, unions are of course on firmer ground. But even here, most grievances are denied. For one thing, contractual restrictions tend to be mild; an obligation to give the union advance notice of subcontracting, or a promise not to subcontract work that an employee on the layoff list could do, is not difficult for an employer to comply with. Furthermore, the question of good faith and economic necessity plays a great role—and here again the facts generally favor management. Cases have been cited in Chapter 3 in which employers misconstrued the collective bargaining agreements and committed errors in judgment. But not once was it shown that management was trying to "undercut" the union or escape contractual obligations to its employees.

As one moves from subcontracting to such questions as changing job content, out-of-classification work assignments, and performance of bargaining unit work by non-unit personnel, the contractual restrictions become much stronger. Not surprisingly, unions win such cases more often than they do subcontracting grievances. In work assignment cases, which turn more on contract interpretation than on equitable considerations, the employer's defense of good faith has much less persuasive value. Convinced that management had honestly believed it was acting properly under the contract, an arbitrator may decline the union's request for monetary damages, but this will not alter his decision that the contract has been breached.

If there is any area in which arbitrators can be said to be "strict constructionists," it is in interpreting contract clauses that touch on seniority rights, the integrity of the bargaining unit, or the protection of job and classification lines. Commonly, in such cases, the employer is able to show what he regarded as economic necessity for overlooking contractual restraint. And as a rule, there is no doubt that economic advantage was involved, if not actual necessity. But this is not usually accepted as sufficient reason to disregard contractual obligations. In one case, for instance, management showed that a protested transfer of work out of the unit was made to restore logic and order to work relationships. The arbitrator could see the logic, but the contract language was clear; if the negotiators chose to establish an illogical pattern, he said, it was not for him to change it. Similarly, it was shown in several cases that work performed by bargaining unit employees could be done more efficiently by non-unit employees. But where the agreement clearly identified those tasks as bargaining unit work, and where management had not been given contractual authority to reassign it, arbitrators had no choice but to uphold the grievances.

Many of these decisions seem unduly harsh until one realizes that the arbitrator is a judicial officer with a very limited role. Unlike arbitration of wages or new contract terms—a fairly rare occurrence —grievance arbitration is limited to interpretation and application of the contract as written and applied by the parties. This does not leave room for an arbitrator to impose on the relationship of the parties his own concept of how they should deal with one another. If the arbitrator knows the parties well and is reasonably certain they will not take it amiss, he may include in his written opinion some unasked-for advice. But this is usually regarded as risky. In any event, advice on matters not within the scope of the arbitrator's authority need not be accepted.

This limitation on the grievance arbitrator's authority is not necessarily a weakness. Clauses which, in their application, lead to harsh consequences for one party or another were negotiated in exchange for other provisions of the agreement. An agreement that only millwrights will do machine repair work, for instance, may have been the *quid pro quo* for the union's agreement that employees could be disciplined for refusing reasonable overtime assignments. Even if the application of that contract meant that work on the night shift had to be halted while a day shift millwright was brought in, at premium call-in pay, for a few minutes of work, who is to say that the employer was still not getting the better part of the total bargain? And could an arbitrator permit exceptions, where the contract provided for none, without also looking into the bargaining history and perhaps reconsidering other sections of the agreement?

The grievance arbitrator's limited authority disappoints the union on occasion, as well as the employer. This is particularly true where the issue in dispute involves matters very important to the union, but where the losses, if any, were negligible. As the arbitrator can award monetary relief only to compensate for losses, but can not impose a penalty, unions often believe a finding by an arbitrator that a foreman has performed ten minutes of forbidden work, for instance, does not constitute a deterrent to repeated *de minimis* violations. One can occasionally observe in the arbitrator's written opinion accompanying the award the same sense of frustration, but there is little he can do except award the union's remedy which, however costly it might seem in terms of the work done (four hours' call-in pay for the ten minutes of work), is still disproportionate to the union's sense of loss.

In most cases, the limitation on the arbitrator's authority is not a fatal defect. It may result in an award which displeases one of the parties, but it does not prevent a final resolution of the dispute. On the other hand, there are occasions when the restricted authority of the *ad hoc* grievance arbitrator seems to result in an inadequate award. Disputes over fundamental changes in the composition of the work force due to automation are examples. In a sense, an automation dispute is like neither a new contract problem nor a grievance problem, although it has characteristics of both. The difficulty that arises in these technological cases is that the arbitrator, restricted by the contract, often finds insufficient guidance within its terms. To try to discover the probable intent of the negotiators, where the latter probably had not thought of the problem at all, is at best a futile exercise. Yet, that is what arbitrators are compelled to do when the evidence shows that the parties have simply "swept under the rug" a difficult problem, trusting to luck that no issue would arise.

But issues do arise. A departmental seniority provision may be quite adequate for ordinary reduction-in-force situations. But when a plant is automated one department at a time, and where no provision has been made for plant-wide bumping or retraining, there is little the arbitrator can do to prevent hardships the parties surely could not have intended. These new problems can be attacked both in arbitration and in collective bargaining. It may be advisable, when parties submit automation disputes to an arbitrator, to enlarge the scope of his authority, permitting him to go beyond the limits of a contract that did not envision such comprehensive changes. The new authority need not be unlimited; parties can still establish criteria for the arbitrator to follow. Something of the sort is now being done in many wage arbitration cases. Parties who would not want an arbitrator to set wage rates in general, purely on the basis of his own sense of equity, nevertheless permit him to decide how much of an increase (or decrease) is warranted by changes in productivity, in the cost of living, in the labor market area, or in competitive plants since wage rates were last set.

Undoubtedly, however, the best solution to the problem of awards fashioned with inadequate tools lies in collective bargaining. The practice of leaving gaps in the contract was more supportable when collective bargaining was new, and when contracts were negotiated after acrimonious organizing campaigns. Today, hundreds of thousands of contracts are renegotiated routinely at their expiration. The parties should therefore be able to take the time for leisurely consideration of more difficult issues. "Crisis bargaining" has its uses as a form of public relations, when a party believes it is necessary to enlist support in case of a strike. But it does not create an atmosphere for constructive solutions. In steel manufacturing, in meat packing, and in other industries, companies and unions have already established joint committees for long-range planning on such matters as the synchronization of the rate of technological displacement with the rate of attrition. Some of these joint committees have enlisted the aid of impartial arbitrators as permanent advisers. Others call upon neutrals for help only when the need arises. There is no doubt that in most mature labor-management relationships, the parties will be able, without the help of mediators or arbitrators, to provide in their contracts against foreseeable contingencies. If disputes should arise in the future —as they perhaps inevitably will—the requirement that an award stay within the framework of the contract will be a workable one. In the long run, if parties are to be well served by a system of arbitration that leaves initiative in their hands, that initiative will have to be exercised.

It would be unfortunate if the hundreds of grievances discussed here gave the impression that management faces harassment at every turn. As a matter of fact, there has been noteworthy accommodation of viewpoints between labor and management as a result of several decades of collective bargaining. A change in the attitude of unions to incentive plans is one example. There was a time when, in labor's vocabulary, the phrase was synonymous with exploitation or speedup. Today, if there is a strike over an incentive plan, more likely than not the union is seeking to obtain one, or to improve an existing plan. There is also a high degree of acceptance by labor of the need for technological change, even though employees often suffer immediate loss. As the cases involving changed and discontinued jobs indicate, grievances arise almost exclusively out of situations where work is rearranged *without* the introduction of new machinery.

Nor is it true, as folklore would have it, that management is single-mindedly concerned only with profits, regardless of human consequences. Even if employers were so inclined, the Great Depression has left the country with little tolerance for unemployment. But the fact is that management shows a remarkable degree of sensitivity to broader implications of its technological innovations. It is significant that the practice of paying "red circle" rates to employees whose jobs were downgraded by job re-evaluations did not develop under union pressure. Similarly, the inclination to wait until incumbents retire or quit voluntarily before their jobs are discontinued—a practice we have seen illustrated in many of the cases in this volume—also results from an understanding of the need to balance technological and human values.

It would be pointless to hope for a perfect reconciliation of labor and management viewpoints. True, job security depends, in the final analysis, on the ability of American industry to provide profitable jobs. From this point of view, companies and unions have identical interests. But each side has its own emphasis, its own special preoccupations. And each has its own institutional role to play. Employers are expected to be more alert than employees to the need for economy of operations. Unions, on the other hand, think first of protecting job rights. If each side is also aware of the other's problems in a secondary way, the clash of viewpoints can be kept short of the point of impasse. But it is doubtful whether any beneficial result would follow if either partner in labor-management relations became so "understanding" of the other as to neglect the contribution which it uniquely makes to the economy. Fortunately, under the American system of industrial relations, and in our pluralistic society, no such abdication of function is likely to occur.

# ARBITRATORS

# TABLE OF CASES

249

# SUBJECT INDEX

258